Frommer's

PORTABLE
Savannah

2nd Edition

by Darwin Porter & Danforth Prince

Here's what critics say about Frommer's:

"Amazingly easy to use. Very portable, very complete."

—*Booklist*

"Detailed, accurate, and easy-to-read information for all price ranges."

—*Glamour Magazine*

Wiley Publishing, Inc.

Published by:

WILEY PUBLISHING, INC.
111 River St.
Hoboken, NJ 07030-5774

ISBN-13: 978-0-7645-7528-0

ISBN-10: 0-7645-7528-7

Editor: Tim Ryan
Production Editor: Ian Skinnari
Photo Editor: Richard Fox
Cartographer: Roberta Stockwell
Production by Wiley Indianapolis Composition Services

For information on our other products and services or to obtain technical
support, please contact our Customer Care Department within the U.S. at
800/762-2974, outside the U.S. at 317/572-3993 or fax 317/572-4002.

Wiley also publishes its books in a variety of electronic formats. Some con-
tent that appears in print may not be available in electronic formats.

Manufactured in the United States of America

5   4   3   2   1

Contents

1 The Savannah Experience   1

   1 Frommer's Favorite Savannah Experiences 2

   2 Best Hotel Bets 4

   3 Best Restaurant Bets 6

2 Savannah's History & Culture   9

   1 History of a City 9

   2 Savannah's Architecture & Art 17

   3 The Art of Dining, Savannah Style 21

3 Planning Your Trip to Savannah   25

   1 Visitor Information 25

   2 When to Go 25

     Savannah Calendar of Events 26

   3 Money 27

     What Things Cost in Savannah 28

   4 The Active Vacation Planner 28

   5 Specialized Travel Resources 30

   6 Getting There 32

     Fast Facts: Georgia 33

4 Getting to Know Savannah   34

   1 Orientation 34

     Neighborhoods in Brief 35

   2 Getting Around 38

     Fast Facts: Savannah 38

5 Where to Stay in Savannah   40

   1 Along the Riverfront 40

     Family-Friendly Hotels 45

   2 Nearby Hotels & Inns 57

6   Where to Dine in Savannah   60

   1   Along or Near the Riverfront 60
   2   In the Historic District 65
           Family-Friendly Restaurants 70
   3   In & Around the City Market 71
   4   In the Victorian District 74
   5   On the South Side 74

7   Exploring Savannah   76

           Sightseeing Suggestions 76
   1   Historic Homes 78
   2   The Best Museums 80
   3   Historic Churches & Synagogues 81
           Gateway to Historic Savannah 83
   4   The Forts: Civil War Memories 84
   5   Spooky Cemeteries 85
           Martinis in the Cemetery 86
   6   Black History Sights 86
   7   Literary Landmarks 89
   8   Especially for Kids 90
   9   Organized Tours 90
           A Visit to the Old Customs House 91
  10   Sports & Outdoor Activities 92
           Exploring the Savannah National Wildlife Refuge 93

8   Savannah Strolls   96

           *Walking Tour 1: Midnight in the Garden
           of Good & Evil* 96
           Walking Tour 2: Historic Savannah 103

9   Shopping   107

   1   Shopping A to Z 107

Savannah After Dark 113

1 The Performing Arts 113
2 Live Music Clubs 114
3 Bar Hoppin' & Pub Crawling 115
4 Gay & Lesbian Bars 118
5 Dinner Cruises 119

 Day Trips & Overnights from Savannah 120

1 Tybee Island 120
   Strolling Around Isle of Hope 124
2 Hilton Head 125
3 Daufuskie Island 154
4 Beaufort 157
5 St. Simons Island 164
6 Sea Island 172

Index 174

   General Index 174
   Accommodations Index 178
   Restaurant Index 179

List of Maps

Greater Savannah   36

Where to Stay in
   Savannah   41

Where to Dine in
   Savannah   61

Savannah Attractions   79

Walking Tour: Midnight
   in the Garden of Good
   and Evil   97

Walking Tour: Historic
   Savannah   105

Tybee Island   121

Hilton Head   134

Beaufort   159

ABOUT THE AUTHORS

A team of veteran travel writers, **Darwin Porter** and **Danforth Prince** have produced numerous titles for Frommer's, including best-selling guides to Italy, France, the Caribbean, England, and Germany. Porter, a former bureau chief of the *Miami Herald,* is also a Hollywood biographer. His most recent releases are *The Secret Life of Humphrey Bogart* and *Katharine the Great,* the latter a close-up of the private life of the late Katharine Hepburn. Prince was formerly employed by the Paris bureau of the *New York Times,* and is today president of Blood Moon Productions and other media-related firms.

AN INVITATION TO THE READER

In researching this book, we discovered many wonderful places—hotels, restaurants, shops, and more. We're sure you'll find others. Please tell us about them, so we can share the information with your fellow travelers in upcoming editions. If you were disappointed with a recommendation, we'd love to know that, too. Please write to:

Frommer's Portable Savannah, 2nd Edition
Wiley Publishing, Inc. • 111 River St. • Hoboken, NJ 07030-5774

AN ADDITIONAL NOTE

Please be advised that travel information is subject to change at any time—and this is especially true of prices. We therefore suggest that you write or call ahead for confirmation when making your travel plans. The authors, editors, and publisher cannot be held responsible for the experiences of readers while traveling. Your safety is important to us, however, so we encourage you to stay alert and be aware of your surroundings. Keep a close eye on cameras, purses, and wallets, all favorite targets of thieves and pickpockets.

FROMMER'S STAR RATINGS, ICONS & ABBREVIATIONS

Every hotel, restaurant, and attraction listing in this guide has been ranked for quality, value, service, amenities, and special features using a **star-rating system.** In country, state, and regional guides, we also rate towns and regions to help you narrow down your choices and budget your time accordingly. Hotels and restaurants are rated on a scale of zero (recommended) to three stars (exceptional). Attractions, shopping, nightlife, towns, and regions are rated according to the following scale: zero stars (recommended), one star (highly recommended), two stars (very highly recommended), and three stars (must-see).

In addition to the star-rating system, we also use **seven feature icons** that point you to the great deals, in-the-know advice, and unique experiences that separate travelers from tourists. Throughout the book, look for:

Finds	Special finds—those places only insiders know about
Fun Fact	Fun facts—details that make travelers more informed and their trips more fun
Kids	Best bets for kids and advice for the whole family
Moments	Special moments—those experiences that memories are made of
Overrated	Places or experiences not worth your time or money
Tips	Insider tips—great ways to save time and money
Value	Great values—where to get the best deals

The following **abbreviations** are used for credit cards:

AE	American Express	DISC	Discover	V	Visa
DC	Diners Club	MC	MasterCard		

FROMMERS.COM

Now that you have the guidebook to a great trip, visit our website at **www.frommers.com** for travel information on more than 3,000 destinations. With features updated regularly, we give you instant access to the most current trip-planning information available. At Frommers.com, you'll also find the best prices on airfares, accommodations, and car rentals—and you can even book travel online through our travel booking partners. At Frommers.com, you'll also find the following:

- Online updates to our most popular guidebooks
- Vacation sweepstakes and contest giveaways
- Newsletter highlighting the hottest travel trends
- Online travel message boards with featured travel discussions

The Savannah Experience

If you have time to visit only one city in the Southeast, make it Savannah. It's that special.

The movie *Forrest Gump* may have put the city squarely on the tourist map, but nothing changed the face of Savannah more than the 1994 publication of John Berendt's *Midnight in the Garden of Good and Evil.* The impact has been unprecedented, bringing in millions in revenue as thousands flock to see the sights from the bestseller and the 1997 movie directed by Clint Eastwood. In fact, Savannah tourism has nearly doubled since publication of what's known locally as The Book. Even after all this time, many locals still earn their living off The Book's fallout, hawking postcards, walking tours, T-shirts, and in some cases their own careers, as in the case of the Lady Chablis, the drag queen in The Book who played herself in the film.

"What's special about Savannah?" we asked an old-timer. "Why, here we even have water fountains for dogs," he said.

The free spirit, the passion, and even the decadence of Savannah resemble those of Key West or New Orleans rather than the Bible Belt down-home "Red State" interior of Georgia. In that sense, it's as different from the rest of the state as New York City is from upstate New York.

Savannah—pronounce it with a drawl—conjures up all the clichéd images of the Deep South: live oaks dripping with Spanish moss, stately antebellum mansions, mint juleps sipped on the veranda, magnolia trees, peaceful marshes, horse-drawn carriages, ships sailing up the river (though no longer laden with cotton), and even General Sherman, no one's favorite military hero here.

Today, the economy and much of the city's day-to-day life still revolve around port activity. For the visitor, however, the big draw is Old Savannah, a beautifully restored and maintained historic area. For this we can thank seven Savannah women who, after watching mansion after mansion demolished in the name of progress, managed in 1954 to raise funds to buy the dilapidated Isaiah Davenport House—hours before it was slated for demolition. The women banded together as the Historic Savannah Foundation, and then went to work buying up architecturally valuable buildings and reselling them to private owners who promised to restore them. As a result, more than 800 of Old Savannah's 1,100 historic buildings have been restored and painted in their original colors—pinks and reds and blues and greens. This "living museum" is now the largest urban National Historic Landmark District in the country—some 2½ square miles, including 21 1-acre squares that survive from Gen. James Oglethorpe's dream of a gracious city.

1 Frommer's Favorite Savannah Experiences

- **Experiencing a 19th-Century Ambience**   Like Charleston, Savannah is one of the top two cities in the Deep South where you can experience what elegant life was in the 19th century by checking into a B&B in a restored historic building. If you're a man sitting in one of these Victorian parlors, surrounded by wall paintings of bygone belles, you'll feel a little bit like Rhett Butler come to call on Scarlett. Typical of these is the Eliza Thompson House, built around 1847 in Savannah's antebellum heyday.

- **Wandering the Isle of Hope**   Spanish conquistador Hernando de Soto came here 4 centuries ago looking for gold. The island later became a place of refuge for Royalists escaping the guillotine of the French Revolution. Today, the Isle of Hope, 10 miles south of Savannah, is an evocative and nostalgic reminder of Savannah's yesteryears. You can go for a stroll in a setting of oaks lining the bluff, plenty of Spanish moss, and Georgia pine, dogwood, magnolia, azalea, and ferns.

- **Having a Picnic Among Plantation Ruins**   There is no more evocative site in the Savannah area for a picnic than Wormsloe State Historic Site at 7601 Skidaway Rd., 10 miles southeast of town. A picnic here can be combined with an exploration of the Isle of Hope. Now ruins, these grounds were once part of a 900-acre estate that belonged to Noble Jones, an 18th-century Colonial who came to Savannah with James Oglethorpe in 1733. Nature trails are cut through the property, and there are picnic tables. The property is reached along a beautiful oak-lined drive that makes you think you're on the road to Tara.

- **Pursuing Grits, Game & Gumbo**   In the state of Georgia, only the much larger city of Atlanta equals Savannah in the number of

Impressions

Savannah is America's Mona Lisa. *Gaze your fill, look all you will. (For once it's quite polite to stare.) You may never fathom the secret of her smile, but like those who love and live with her, you will know the endless rich rewards of trying.*

—Writer Anita Raskin

fine restaurants. Since the mid–18th century, Savannah and the Low Country have been known for their abundance and variety of food, and lavish eating and drinking have long been loyal customs. The surrounding area was (and is) rich in game and fish, including marsh hen, quail, crab, and even deer. To these hunters' trophies were added the bounty of local gardens, including those old favorites—collard greens, beets, turnips, peas, okra, and corn on the cob. That corn was ground into grits as well, and the okra was used to thicken gumbos, for which every Savannahian seems to have a favorite recipe.

- **Finding Your Own** *Forrest Gump* **Bench**   Arm yourself with a box of chocolates and set out to find your own historic Savannah square like Tom Hanks did in the film *Forrest Gump,* where he began to spin out his adventures. Find the square of your choice, perhaps Chippewa Square (where Forrest actually sat), sit down, enjoy those chocolates, and watch the world go by. Savannah revolves around its historic squares, and it's said that if you sit on a bench long enough, everybody in Savannah will eventually pass by.
- **Enjoying a Martini in Bonaventure Cemetery**   In The Book, Mary Harty invited John Berendt, the author of *Midnight in the Garden of Good and Evil,* for martinis in this moss-draped cemetery. It has since become a tradition to partake of this quaint custom. On the former grounds of an oak-shaded plantation, you can enjoy your libation in the midst of the long departed. Of course, the proper way to drink a martini, as in The Book, is in a silver goblet. Your seat? None other than the bench-gravestone of poet Conrad Aiken.
- **Taking a Pub Crawl Along the Riverfront**   Savannah has the best, friendliest, and most atmospheric pubs in Georgia, none more alluring than those along its historic waterfront. On St. Patrick's Day, people drive down from South Carolina or up from Florida to go pubbing. But on any night you can

stroll along the cobblestones searching for your favorite hang-out. Often you get staged entertainment. If not, count on the locals to supply amusement. It's all in good fun, people having a hot time in an atmospheric setting of old warehouses that represents one of the Deep South's best recycling programs.

- **Hitting the *Midnight in the Garden of Good and Evil* Trail** It was The Book, by John Berendt, that put Savannah on the tourist charters, and it seems only appropriate to take our walking tour to see where the adventures in The Book unfolded. On the tour you can explore such sites as the Mer-cer House, where the shooting of the blond hustler, Danny Hansford, took place. From there you can take in other major sites in The Book, including the house of Serena Dawes, that so-called "soul of pampered self-absorption."

- **Spending a Day at the Beach on Tybee Island** East of the city, Tybee Island, in addition to its golden sands, is a place to have fun. Sun worshippers, joggers, surf-casters, kite-flyers, swimmers, and mere sightseers come to escape the oppressive heat of a Savannah summer. Join the pelicans, gulls, and shore-birds in the dunes for beach dynamics. You'll be following the footsteps of Blackbeard, who often took refuge here. It is believed that many of the pirate's treasures are still buried at Tybee. To cap off a perfect day, head for Fort Screven, a Civil War fort. Then climb to the top of the lighthouse for a panoramic view of coastal Georgia.

- **Camping It Up at Club One** From Clint Eastwood to Demi Moore, from Meg Ryan to Bruce Willis, every visiting movie star or celebrity heads to this rollicking joint. 'Tis true that some Savannahians refer to it as a gay club, and there are those who would never darken its door. But the club attracts a wide spectrum of humanity because it's known for having the best entertainment in Savannah. Sometimes even the fabled Lady Chablis, empress of Savannah, appears here. This drag queen gained prominence in John Berendt's book, *Midnight in the Garden of Good and Evil,* and played herself in the film (Diana Ross wanted to). The dancing here is the hottest in Savannah.

2 Best Hotel Bets

- **Best River Street Rejuvenation** The cotton warehouses along the Savannah River have been turned into hotels, shops, and restaurants, none restored better than the **River Street Inn**

(© **800/253-4229** or 912/234-6400). A flourishing storage warehouse for cotton until the boll weevil came, it dates from 1817, when it was constructed of ballast stones brought over from England. Today, it is the epitome of comfort and charm with memorable views of the Savannah River.

- **Best B&B in the Historic District** Savannah's classic inn of charm and grace, **Ballastone Inn** (© **800/822-4553** or 912/236-1484), an 1838 building, has been given the glamour treatment. You're housed in a 19th-century-style interior, but with far greater comforts than the antebellum wealthy of Savannah used to experience. Polished hardwoods, elaborate draperies, and well-polished antiques set the stage for a grand B&B experience.

- **Best Victorian Charm** In the vanguard of posh Savannah B&Bs, **The Gastonian** (© **800/322-6603** or 912/232-2869) incorporates two Italianate Regency buildings constructed in 1868, 3 years after the Civil War. Beautifully restored, it has been turned into a boutique hotel of Victorian charm. Queen Victoria herself, were she to miraculously return, would feel right "comfy" here in this cozy enclave. The AAA has awarded the Gastonian four diamonds, the highest rating possible.

- **Best Deals on Suites** The aptly named **Clubhouse Inn & Suites** (© **800/258-2466** or 912/356-1234) offers roomy and attractively furnished suites that begin at $89, each ideal for a family. With its upgraded decor and furnishings, you get first-class comfort. Many of the suites open onto private balconies. Rates include a generous buffet breakfast.

- **Best Rescue of a Decaying Building** Dating from 1873, the **Hamilton-Turner Inn** (© **888/448-8849** or 912/233-1833) has been much restored after falling into decay. Today, the four-story French Empire house is one of the most upscale B&Bs in Savannah. The building earned notoriety in John Berendt's *Midnight in the Garden of Good and Evil,* but those high-rolling party days are over. It's now a serene oasis.

- **Best & Most Opulent B&B** Built in 1892, **Kehoe House** (© **800/820-1020** or 912/232-1020) is no longer a funeral parlor but an inn of such grace that it ranks among the finest in Georgia. Its fabrics, furniture, and comfort make it an adult retreat of flawless taste. Tom Hanks stayed here during the filming of *Forrest Gump.*

- **Best for Grand Hotel Style Living**   Built in 1890 as the city's grandest hotel, today's **Hilton Savannah DeSoto** (✆ 800/426-8483 or 912/232-9000) is a monument to the grand life. Completely renovated in the 1990s, it is once again an address of lavish comfort with a certain charm, especially for such a commercial hotel. The public rooms, such as the 18th-century drawing room, reflect a Colonial theme.

- **Best for Old South Nostalgia**   Small in scale, the **Olde Georgian Inn** (✆ 800/835-6831 or 912/236-2911) is a charmer occupying a clapboard-sided Victorian house from 1890. It's filled with real Southern comfort and a sense of Victorian style, with a mixture of 19th- and early-20th-century furnishings. Each unit comes with a fireplace.

- **Best Moderately Priced Hotel**   The most appealing of the city's middle-bracket but large-scale hotels, the **Hampton Inn Historic District** (✆ 800/426-7866 or 912/232-9700) opened in 1997, rising seven redbrick stories. Although modern, it pays homage to Savannah's past, including its big-windowed lobby designed to evoke an 18th-century city salon.

- **Best Value**   Adjacent to Chatham Square, **Bed & Breakfast Inn** (✆ 888/238-0518 or 912/238-0518) lies in one of the oldest and most historic parts of Savannah. Its guest rooms are exceedingly comfortable and some of the most affordable for those wishing to stay in the historic core. Furnishings are a combination of antiques and tasteful reproductions.

3 Best Restaurant Bets

- **Best Restaurant**   In the Victorian District, **Elizabeth on 37th** (✆ 912/236-5547), with its modern Southern cuisine, is not only the most glamorous and upscale restaurant in Savannah, it serves the most refined cuisine. In a palatial neoclassical villa from the turn of the 20th century, you can carve some indelible culinary memories here, the menu reinforced by an impressive wine list.

- **Best Southern Cuisine**   The **Lady & Sons** (✆ 912/233-2600) is the domain of Paula Deen, who, along with her sons and $200, launched this temple of gastronomy. She's Savannah's most well-known cookbook writer, sharing the secrets of her kitchen. We always drop in for her chicken potpie topped with puff pastry. It doesn't get much better than this.

- **Best International Cuisine** Praised by magazines along the East Coast, even *Playboy,* **45 South** (© **912/233-1881**) serves a gourmet Southern cuisine but roams the world for its culinary inspiration. Even your own mama can't make better chicken breast with truffled pâté or sliced breast of pheasant with foie gras. A maximum of restraint, a minimum of fat, and supreme artistry in orchestrating flavors characterize the cuisine.

- **Best Low Country Cuisine** Stylish and casual, **Sapphire Grill** (© **912/443-9962**) is an upscale bistro. The "coastal cuisine" of Christopher Nason wins raves among food critics. It's based on seafood harvested from nearby waters. Wait until you sample the James Island littleneck clams tossed in foie gras butter. The able service and impressive wine list contribute to the allure.

- **Best for Seafood** Many restaurants in Savannah serve good seafood, or else they're soon out of business. But **The Olde Pink House Restaurant** (© **912/232-4286**) seems to put more flavor into its offerings than its competitors do. You don't get just fried fish here, but the likes of black grouper stuffed with blue crab and drenched in a Vidalia onion sauce, or else crispy scored flounder with a tangy apricot sauce. That the setting is both elegant and romantic makes the Pink House even more appealing.

- **Best for Prime Rib** Chain restaurants rarely make Frommer's "best of" lists. There is one exception in Savannah: **The Chart House** (© **912/234-6686**). Its prime rib is slow-roasted and served au jus. The specially supplied beef is corn fed, aged, and hand-cut. Beef-eaters are in heaven here. The chefs prepare a mean lobster as well.

- **Best Cajun/Creole Cuisine** Overlooking the Savannah River, **Huey's** (© **912/234-7385**) has a kitchen that would hold its own in New Orleans. If you like all those good things like jambalaya, andouille sausage, crayfish étouffée, and oyster po'boys, welcome home. Even homesick Louisiana visitors show up here "for a feasting."

- **Best for Barbecue** The good people of Savannah don't survive on oyster po'boys or catfish suppers all week. At least once a week they like barbecue. For that tasty treat, many of them show up at **Wall's** (© **912/232-9754**). This is an affordable, casual, family-style restaurant, where the barbecue is something to write home about. The sauce and the slow cooking are part of the secret—that and the hickory wood used. Of course, no Southern chef reveals all his secrets for barbecue!

- **Best for Breakfast**   Everybody, or so it seems, shows up at **Clary's Café** (℃ **912/233-0402**). A Savannah tradition since 1903, the cafe today has an aura of the 1950s. You expect James Dean to show up on a motorcycle wearing blue jeans and a leather jacket. The cafe was featured in the film *Midnight in the Garden of Good and Evil.* Among the dozens of breakfast offerings, we go for the chef's special: Hoppel Poppel (scrambled eggs with chunks of kosher salami, potatoes, onions, and green peppers).

- **Best Down-Home Favorite**   For "belly-busting food," **Mrs. Wilkes' Dining Room** (℃ **912/232-5997**) is a Savannah tradition. Visitors and locals have been standing in line here since the 1940s for real down-home Southern fare. Mrs. Wilkes' time-tested recipes get a workout every day, feeding generations of the local citizenry on barbecued chicken, red rice and sausage, corn on the cob, squash and yams, and any dish with okra. And what would a meal be without Mrs. Wilkes' corn bread and collards?

- **Best Fusion Cuisine**   The most eclectic bistro in town, **Bistro Savannah** (℃ **912/233-6266**) serves a mixture of Southern with Fusion cuisine, inspired by a culinary geography that ranges from the bayou country of Louisiana to Thailand. Not only do they make the best seafood bouillabaisse in town, they serve such temptations as crisp pecan chicken with a blackberry bourbon sauce.

- **Best Japanese Restaurant**   The first Japanese restaurant to open in Savannah, **Musashi** (℃ **912/352-2128**) remains, even today, the best place in town for an Asian meal. Chefs here specialize in a *teppanyaki* cooking style and are artists in slashing up delicate pieces of shrimp, seafood, chicken, and steak. Musashi also serves Savannah's best value lunch.

2

Savannah's History & Culture

In this chapter, we'll take you from the city's founding in Colonial days, through its many stages of growth, decline, and rebirth, with special attention paid to the art and architecture that make this Southern city unique. We'll also learn about the city and its people through a tour of the Low Country cuisine.

Savannah's history has been the subject of countless novels, most of them centered on its rich antebellum heyday. When General Sherman made it the final goal of his infamous "March to the Sea," Savannah earned a dubious distinction in the annals of American history.

From battles with American Indians, British troops, Yankees, Spaniards and, ultimately, civil rights advocates, the role of Savannah has been unique in the South, although it most closely parallels the history of its neighbor, Charleston.

Before Savannah became General Sherman's "Christmas gift" to Abraham Lincoln, how did it all begin?

1 History of a City

COLONIAL DAYS

It was in 1733 that British Gen. James Edward Oglethorpe (1696–1785) landed on the historic bluff above the Savannah River to found what was to become the 13th colony in America. The land was wilderness, but the British wanted to build a buffer zone between their colony in South Carolina and the "Spanish menace" to the south in Florida.

Still in his 30s when he sailed into Savannah, Oglethorpe had already served in the military for 21 years, been a member of Parliament for 11 years, and served on a committee that uncovered widespread abuse of prisoners in England's jails. He had also spent 5 months in jail for killing a man in a brawl. After one of Oglethorpe's friends died in debtor's prison, Oglethorpe vowed to prevent similar deaths by establishing a debtor's colony (his own stay in the slammer must have motivated him as well). On June 9, 1732,

King George II granted a charter to Oglethorpe and 20 others (the "Trustees") for the creation of a new colony to be called Georgia, after the king.

Many hundreds in London applied to sail west, but only 114 men and women were chosen, as well as a doctor and pastor. There would be freedom of worship in this new land on America's southeast coast, providing a settler wasn't a slave, a Roman Catholic, or a lawyer.

Seven months after being granted the charter, the colonists sailed from the port at Gravesend, England, aboard an overcrowded vessel called the *Anne*. They were heading west on a rough, wave-tossed voyage into an uncertain future. The crew and passengers were close to starvation when they landed at Savannah. It was good for them that the Native Americans were friendly, because the Indians could easily have overpowered the weakened crew.

Like Columbus in the Bahamas, Oglethorpe and his colonists did not discover an unoccupied Savannah, but encountered an already inhabited land of Native Americans. The Low Country area of Georgia, or so it is believed, had actually been inhabited by nomadic Indian tribes since the end of the Ice Age when vegetation returned to the land and animals roamed its plains.

The Yamacraws, a small tribe, had fled the Spanish conquistadors in Florida and had moved north to settle in Georgia. It was this group of Indians that were on hand to greet Oglethorpe. Instead of attacking, the Yamacraws were hospitable to these invaders who would change their continent forever. The Indians not only lived in peace with Oglethorpe's colonists, but they would, in time, help them fight off invasions by both the Spaniards and other hostile tribes in the future.

While in London, Oglethorpe had fantasized about the new city he wanted to found in the Americas. For this dream city, he wanted rectilinear streets that would cross at right angles. The core of town would be filled with squares which would be earmarked as "green lungs" or public parks so settlers could "breathe the fresh air."

Savannah was laid out in "wards" around these central squares. He also established a 10-acre Trustees' Garden modeled after the Chelsea Botanical Garden in London. He set aside space for markets and public areas.

The garden was doomed to failure because the wrong plants were put into the ground. The mulberry trees died, denying a home to silkworms, and the vines planted in the vineyards didn't bear grapes.

Oglethorpe viewed himself as the spiritual leader of the colony, and indeed he was called "Father Oglethorpe" by the colonists. His new city had been founded only 6 months before a new set of colonists arrived from Europe, many escaping religious persecution. The ban on Catholics was rescinded. Not just Catholics, but Jews and Protestants also arrived, many coming from Iberia, especially Portugal.

By the mid-18th century, colonists in Georgia began to import slaves. They'd seen how their wealthy neighbors to the north in South Carolina were prospering in an economy fueled by slave labor. In a few short years, one out of every three persons in the colony was a slave, working the rich plantations that enveloped Savannah to its west.

Politically, the colonists in Georgia turned back further expansion by the Spanish coming north from Florida. Originally, the Spanish had wanted to make Georgia a colony. Oglethorpe, helped at the time by his Native American friends, thwarted their plans.

The founding father stayed in Savannah until 1743, finally giving up his dream and sailing back to London. The throne felt that Oglethorpe had failed as an administrator, and he was replaced by William Stephens, who was sent to govern in his place. The Trustees originally named by the king held onto their charter until 1752 before finally abandoning it. A political movement at the time wanted to turn their Low Country area into another royal colony like that enjoyed by South Carolina, centered at prosperous Charleston.

By 1754, a royal colony was established. Savannah became one of the leading ports of the Southeast, although it never overtook its major rival, Charleston. That prosperity of Low Country plantations became especially marked when the French and Indian War of 1763 came to an end. Britain won Florida, which ended Spain's attempts to forge colonies along the east coast of America.

Goods intended for the "back" or "up" country of Georgia arrived in Savannah.

The slaves began to build plantations for the growing of cotton, and these Colonial buildings soon came to dominate the landscape in the Low Country enveloping Savannah.

THE AMERICAN REVOLUTION

At least a decade before the American Revolution, the residents of Savannah were beginning to defy their English rulers. British property was being destroyed, and so-called "Liberty Boys" often fought openly with Loyalists. The much-hated Stamp Act of 1765 didn't go over with the colonists, who objected to the tax on every printed item.

Savannah even staged its own version of the Boston Tea Party.

The raucous Peter Tondee's Tavern at Whitaker and Broughton streets became the center of a growing rebellion in Georgia led by the Liberty Boys. The name came from their compatriots in Charleston, who had adopted it from "Boston's Sons of Liberty." In defiance of royal authority, they flew a flag, featuring a rattlesnake with 13 rattles. Each of these rattles symbolized a different American colony.

These grog-swilling colonists defiantly wore homemade Liberty stocking caps and went so far as to erect a so-called "Liberty Pole" in front of Tondee's Tavern. This historic tavern also figured in Georgia history after the Declaration of Independence was drafted in Philadelphia and was first read in Georgia in front of it. It was also at Tondee's Tavern that the Liberty Boys first heard the news of the battles of Lexington and Concord. The die was cast: America's war of freedom had begun, even though there were many Loyalists still residing in Georgia.

By June 28, 1776, the battlegrounds had come to South Carolina and Georgia as well. The first major victory for the American freedom fighters came on June 28, 1776, when Gen. William Moultrie defeated an invading fleet of 50 British warships. Although outnumbered and lacking adequate ammunition, the revolutionaries battled the British from a fort hastily assembled on Sullivan's Island.

This early victory was followed by disaster. Before Christmas of 1778, the city of Savannah fell to British troops, with Charleston falling in the spring 2 years later. In their victory, British troops sought vengeance. They executed many patriots and robbed and pillaged from the richest homes in the area.

In October 1781, word reached Savannah that the British "sword of surrender" had been presented to the American forces at Yorktown. "Mad" Anthony Wayne and his troops arrived to reclaim the city in 1782. The British were defeated, and many die-hard Loyalists in Georgia returned to Mother England, never to be seen again.

After the Revolution, Savannah was made the capital city of Georgia, a position it would lose in 1786 to Augusta, which in time would lose out to Atlanta.

COTTON IS KING

In the years following the Revolution, commerce in Savannah boomed. The demand grew for Sea Island cotton. On the Low Country plantations, cotton was king, and Savannah was the port from which to ship it north or abroad.

In 1793, Eli Whitney invented the cotton gin on a plantation near Savannah. A former schoolteacher from the North, Whitney invented the gin with the aid of a widow, Catherine ("Caty") Greene who ran the plantation and had been married to Nathanael Greene of Revolutionary War fame. The cotton gin allowed seeds to be removed with far greater speed and efficiency than by existing methods. Low Country cotton plantations would flourish for at least the next 6 decades.

All Savannah turned out to welcome Pres. George Washington on his visit in 1791. A parade and a ball were held in his honor.

Both Europe and America focused on Savannah in 1819 when the S.S. *Savannah* became the first steam-powered vessel to cross the Atlantic. The vessel departed Savannah on May 22 of that year, arriving at the port of Liverpool a record 29 days later. Triumphantly, the ship went on to Glasgow, Stockholm, and even St. Petersburg in Russia. But in 1821, the vessel was caught in gale winds and capsized off the shores of Long Island.

Disaster stuck Savannah in 1796 and 1820, when two major fires left about half the city in ruins. The famous Savannah city market was burned in both instances. As if the fire of 1820 didn't devastate Savannah enough, a yellow fever epidemic broke out. It is estimated that about one-tenth of the city's population died. Yellow fever was to strike again and again for the rest of the 19th century.

Antebellum Savannah was at the peak of its prosperity, fueled by cotton and slavery. But ominous clouds were on the horizon as tensions between the North and South grew steadily worse.

THE CIVIL WAR ERA

There was rejoicing on the streets of Savannah as its neighbor, South Carolina, seceded from the Union on December 20, 1860. The election of Pres. Abraham Lincoln, who was despised in Savannah, had demoralized the city. In 1861, Georgia followed South Carolina in separating itself from the Union, and when Confederate troops fired on Fort Sumter that same year, war was declared. Calling it "the War of Northern Aggression," Savannahians hoped for an easy, quick victory.

Within a few months, federal troops occupied much of the coastal lowlands of the Carolinas and Georgia, leaving only the port cities of Wilmington, Charleston, and Savannah in Confederate hands, albeit blockaded by the Union Navy.

On April 11, 1862, Union cannons fired on Fort Pulaski, 15 miles east of Savannah. They overcame the masonry fortification, but Savannah was months from occupation. In just 30 hours, Union forces had captured Pulaski, signaling the end of masonry fortifications.

With its port blockaded by the Union, Savannah suffered greatly during the war. The city endured bravely, both men and women aiding the war effort. Goods were hard to come by, as Savannah had always looked to the sea for its livelihood.

Except for a few skirmishes and the bombardment of Charleston in 1863, the Carolinas and Georgia escaped heavy fighting until May 1864, when Union Gen. Ulysses S. Grant told Gen. William Tecumseh Sherman to "get into the interior of the enemy's country as far as you can, inflicting all the damage you can against their war resources." Thus began Sherman's famous "March to the Sea," the world's first modern example of total war waged against a civilian population. Savannah was the final target.

Sherman fought his way south from Chattanooga, Tennessee, to Atlanta, a key railroad junction, which the Confederates evacuated on September 1, 1864. Leaving Atlanta burning, he departed for the sea on October 17, cutting a 60-mile path of destruction across central and eastern Georgia. "We have devoured the land, and our animals eat up the wheat and corn fields close," Sherman reported. "All the people retire before us, and desolation is behind. To realize what war is, one should follow our tracks."

Despite his orders, looting and pillaging were rampant, but there were few attacks on civilians and none against women.

Sherman arrived at Savannah on December 10, in time to make the port city a Christmas present to Lincoln. (Fortunately, he did not burn the city.) In January 1865, he turned northward into South Carolina. He torched 80 square blocks of Columbia in February. Confederate Gen. Joseph E. Johnston made several attempts to slow Sherman's advance. One such attempt was the Battle of Rivers Bridge, between Allendale and Erhardt, South Carolina, in February; the last was the Battle of Bentonville, near Durham in central North Carolina, in March. On April 26, 2 weeks after Gen. Robert E. Lee surrendered to Grant at Appomattox Courthouse in Virginia, Johnston met Sherman at Durham and handed over his sword. The war in the Carolinas and Georgia was over.

SCALAWAGS, CARPETBAGGERS & JIM CROW

The Civil War survivors straggled home to face Reconstruction. At first, Confederate war veterans dominated the state legislatures in Georgia. They enacted so-called Black Code laws, which gave some rights to the newly freed slaves but denied them the vote. This and other actions infuriated the Republicans who controlled the U.S. Congress and wanted to see the South punished for its rebellion. In 1867, Congress passed the Reconstruction Act, which gave blacks the right to vote and divided the South into five districts, each under a military governor who had near-dictatorial powers. Approximately 20,000 federal troops were sent to the South to enforce the act.

Recalcitrant white officials were removed from state office, and with their new vote, the ex-slaves helped elect Republican legislatures in all three states. Many blacks won seats for themselves. Despite doing some good work, these legislatures were corrupt. They also enacted high taxes to pay for rebuilding and social programs, further alienating the struggling white population.

White Georgians also complained bitterly about "scalawags" (local whites who joined the Republican party) and "carpetbaggers" (Northerners who came South carrying all their possessions in bags made of carpet). The animosity led to the formation of two secret white organizations—the Knights of the White Camelia and the Knights of the Ku Klux Klan—that undertook by terrorism to keep blacks from voting or exercising their other new rights. The former slaves were also disappointed with the Republicans when it became obvious that they wouldn't receive the promised "40 acres and a mule." Those who did vote began to cast them for their former masters. Factions also developed within the local scalawags and the Northern carpetbaggers.

During Reconstruction, blacks from plantations from throughout Georgia flooded into Savannah, living in poverty. For the planters, though, cotton returned as king and would reign supreme until the coming of the boll weevil.

All this set the stage for whites to regain control of Georgia in 1871. By 1877, Pres. Rutherford B. Hayes, a Republican, withdrew federal troops from the South. Reconstruction was over.

During the next 20 years, white governments enacted the Jim Crow laws, which imposed poll taxes, literacy tests, and other requirements intended to prevent blacks from voting. Whites flocked to the Democratic Party, which restricted its primaries—tantamount to elections throughout the South—to white voters. Blacks who did try to vote faced having the Ku Klux Klan burn crosses on their lawns, or even being lynched. Indeed, "strange fruit" hung from many Southern trees during this period.

Racial segregation became a legal fact of life, from the public drinking fountains to the public schools. The U.S. Supreme Court ratified the scheme in its 1896 *Plessy v. Ferguson* decision, declaring "separate but equal" public schools to be constitutional. Black schools in the South were hardly equal, but they surely were separate.

Throughout the 19th century, Savannah remained rigidly segregated. In 1878, the first public school for blacks was opened. That was followed in 1891 by the first public college for blacks. Educational segregation remained in place until well into the 20th century.

Savannah was sucked up in the Spanish-American War of 1898, when it was a port of embarkation for troops headed for Havana.

SAVANNAH IN THE 20TH CENTURY

As Savannah entered a new century, it was economically powerful, its ships fanning out to take Georgia exports such as lumber around the world. Savannah's men marched off to World War I.

Upon their return, economic devastation set in. The boll weevil attacked the cotton fields in the Low Country plantations around Savannah. King Cotton was dethroned. If that weren't enough, America entered a grave Depression during the Hoover era.

The Democrats remained supreme in Savannah, and racial segregation was a way of life. The city's economy was helped when the Eighth Air Force was founded outside Savannah, restoring some vigor to a sagging economy.

But Savannah was literally falling apart. Its historic buildings were being torn down or left to rot. In 1955, a group of determined ladies saved the historic Davenport House from the wrecking ball, and Savannah began to take preservation seriously.

Though caught up in the civil rights movements of the 1960s, Savannah was not a battleground for the movement the way some Southern cities were.

In May 1981, antiques dealer Jim Williams shot his lover/assistant, a hustler named Danny Hansford, 21. As a result, through a complicated legal process, Williams became the first person in Georgia to be tried four times for murder before he was finally acquitted.

The case could have slipped into history as another gay murder. However, the writer John Berendt drifted into town one day, became intrigued by the story, and eventually wrote his megabestseller, *Midnight in the Garden of Good and Evil.*

His original agent turned down the story as too bizarre and "too regional." Buyers of books felt otherwise and, in time, Clint Eastwood even directed it as a movie.

To the amazement of Savannah, the Berendt book put the city on the tourist map, as millions began to visit. Through the interest created by what is locally called The Book, Savannah became a tourist attraction to compete with Charleston to the north.

2 Savannah's Architecture & Art

For art and architecture, Savannah is outclassed by Charleston to the north. But Savannah is not without its own accomplishments.

The greatest collection of evocative architecture lies in the historic district, around which you can walk at your leisure, discovering the old buildings, churches, and squares. Some structures are from the Colonial era; others perhaps inspired by the Adam brothers or built in the Regency style. There are tons of ironwork and antique buildings in brick or clapboard. Even modest town houses from the 18th century are restored and have become coveted addresses and homes of charm.

Because many of its residents lacked money in the final decades of the 19th century and the beginning of the 20th, antique structures were allowed to stand, whereas many American cities destroyed their heritage and replaced them with modern buildings. By the time Savannahians got around to tearing down their antique structures, a forceful preservation movement was launched—and just in time.

What you won't see, as you travel through the Low Country around Savannah, is a lot of plantations where cotton was king. Much of these have *"Gone With the Wind."*

THE FIRST CITY

In 1733, at the founding of Savannah, James Oglethorpe faced a daunting challenge. He not only had to secure homes for Trustees and colonists, but he also had to construct forts around the new town of Savannah to fend off possible Indian raids, even though the local Native Americans were friendly.

Since they weren't well built and since they were later torn down to make way for grander structures, none of the founding fathers' little wooden homes remain today. But that town plan as envisioned by Oglethorpe back in London still remains. He wanted an orderly grid composed of 24 squares. In case of rebellion he also wanted "mustering points" where troops could gather to squelch the problem.

Nine years after the colonists arrived in port, they had enough money and building materials to construct their first church, which quickly became the most elaborate structure in town. Called "The Orphan House," this landmark building no longer stands. The church took its name from the Bethesda Orphanage founded by the evangelist, George Whitefield, in 1738. Along with Oglethorpe, Whitefield believed that rum drinking caused a yellow fever–like disease but that beer drinking was acceptable. This philosophy was expounded to the congregation of Georgia's first church.

After the Revolutionary War, the port of Savannah began to grow rich on profits it made shipping sago powder, beef, pork, animal skins, tar, turpentine, and other exports. Money generated from this thriving trade with Europe, especially London, was poured into architecture. Grander homes began to sprout on the squares of Savannah. Still, none of these early structures equaled the glory of the rival city of Charleston. While visiting the family of Gen. Nathaniel Green, Eli Whitney invented the cotton gin in 1793, bringing even greater prosperity to the area, which led to even grander building.

Only one structure remains from this post-Revolutionary era. Built by James Habersham, Jr., in a Georgian style, it is covered in pink stucco. Underneath the stucco is a solid brick foundation. Today it is a well-recommended restaurant and bar, known as The Olde Pink House Restaurant (p. 67), open to the general public at 23 Abercorn St.

The reason so little architecture from the post-Revolutionary era survived is that a disastrous fire struck in 1796, burning block after block of the city, evocative of the burning of Atlanta during the Civil War to come.

In 1820, another devastating fire swept over Savannah, destroying architectural gems that had been erected by builders from both Charleston and the North. The fire arrived just at the time a yellow fever broke out. Thousands of slaves died in the fever, temporarily slowing down building efforts because they were used for the hard labor on the construction projects. Work on rebuilding Savannah was further slowed down when cholera broke out in 1834.

But through it all, Savannahians survived and prospered and continued to pour money into elaborate structures, many of which remain today, especially those constructed of brick. The Federalist style was very prevalent, as it was along the east coast of America. Some builders, perhaps those with Loyalist hearts, preferred the Georgian style. Locals continued to spend money on churches, notably the Independent Presbyterian Church of Savannah, whose architectural beauty competed with that of some of the finest churches of Charleston.

THE REGENCY STYLE SWEEPS SAVANNAH

The cotton planters with their newfound money invited William Jay from London to come to Savannah in 1817. He introduced the Regency style, which became all the rage in Savannah.

Some of his structures still stand today. His greatest achievement was the Owens-Thomas House, the best example of English Regency architecture in the United States. Inspired by classical buildings, the flourishing style was named for King George IV, who ruled as prince regent from 1811 to 1820. The house overlooks Oglethorpe Square and was standing in 1825 to welcome the marquis de Lafayette when he was the guest of honor in Savannah. The French war hero addressed a crowd of Savannahians from the cast-iron veranda on the south facade of the building. The historic house is today called the Owens-Thomas House and is a landmark. The building was constructed in the main from "tabby," which is a concrete mixture of oyster shells, sand, and lime. The Grecian-inspired veranda on the southern facade was the first major use of cast iron in Savannah. As an architectural device, cast iron later swept the city.

Jay also designed the Telfair Mansion in a neoclassical Regency style. It was constructed in 1818 for Alexander Telfair, the scion of Edward Telfair, a former Georgia governor and Revolutionary War hero. When the mansion was bequeathed to the city for use as a museum, it was formally opened in 1886. Many notables attended; most of the crowd's interest focused on Jefferson Davis, the former president of the Confederacy.

The Irish-born architect Charles B. Cluskey (1808–1871) arrived in Savannah in 1838 and stayed for almost a decade, becoming known for his antebellum architecture influenced by the Greek Revival style. The elite of Savannah, prospering from neighboring plantations, hired him to design their town houses, including the Champion-McAlpin-Fowlkes house in 1844. He served as city surveyor of Savannah from 1845 to 1847, when he went to Washington with plans to renovate the White House and Capitol (few of his ideas were carried out, however).

Another antebellum architect, John Norris (1804–1876), flourished in Savannah between 1846 and 1860. His most famous landmark is the Savannah Custom House, which was constructed between 1848 and 1852 in the Greek Revival style, with its mammoth portico. In the same general style, he also designed many more notable structures throughout the city, including the Andrew Low House in 1849.

A competitor of his was John B. Hogg, who hailed from South Carolina. His most notable structure is the Trinity United Methodist Church at 225 W. President St. The church was built of stucco over gray brick, the famous "Savannah grays" form of architecture. The building became known in Georgia as the "Mother Church of Methodism."

As Georgia, along with South Carolina, moved closer to the horror of the Civil War, Savannah architecture stood at the peak of its beauty and charm. A visitor from London claimed, "Savannah puts on a hell of a good show. It's not London but not bad for a colony."

WAR, RECONSTRUCTION & PRESERVATION

Unlike Atlanta, Savannah was not burned to the ground, with no Scarlett O'Hara fleeing into the night to escape the flames. Even in 1864, after all the wartime deprivation suffered by the long blockade of its port, Savannah was a worthy "gift" when Sherman presented it as a Christmas present to Lincoln.

The Civil War brought poverty to most Savannahians, and the decades of Reconstruction meant the end of opulence. Oglethorpe's original town plan had stretched from 6 to 24 city squares. Architects of renown avoided building in Savannah, going to richer cities.

The famous "Savannah grays" (bricks) ceased production in the 1880s. Many buildings fell into ruin or decay. Modern structures outside the historic core were haphazardly constructed, although the Victorian era produced some notable structures to grace the cityscape.

Just when it appeared that Savannah was going to rot away in the hot Georgia sun, the preservation movement of the 1950s came at the 11th hour. Historic Savannah was saved and restored during the latter part of the 20th century and awaits your discovery in the 21st century.

THE ART OF SAVANNAH

In antebellum days, portraiture was the most common form of art in the Colonial era. Any moderately well-off family commissioned rather idealized portraits of its family members, at least the gentleman and lady of the house. Most of the portraits were either in oil on canvas or in watercolor. In some rare instances, the portraits were done on ivory.

The subjects of the portraits are attired in their "Sunday go-to-meeting" garb. If a setting was used as a backdrop, it was romanticized—an elegant drapery, a Grecian column, a distant view of the ocean.

With the coming of the deprivations caused by the Civil War and the lean poverty years of the Reconstruction era, Savannah was more in survivalist mode than in the mood for painting.

Slowly, Savannahians began to find time for art again, although the decades produced no known national painters.

As time went on, a number of self-taught artists emerged in Savannah and the Low Country. Many of them were black, working in a folk art medium. Sometimes they painted on unpainted clapboard from some abandoned barn or other structure. The Telfair Museum is the exhibition center for these self-taught artists, exhibiting Low Country art in various temporary exhibitions.

Among the other artists who have distinguished themselves in modern times was Leonora Quarterman (1911–79), who became one of the best-known watercolorists in the South. Her silkscreen prints of Savannah and of Georgia coastal scenes are highly prized by collectors today.

Christopher Murphy (1902–73) was a native of the city who became known for his drawings that captured both the cityscape of Savannah and the coastal landscape of the Low Country coastline. His originals and reproductions still come on the market from time to time and are as sought after as those of Ms. Quarterman.

3 The Art of Dining, Savannah Style

Savannah is the capital of the Georgia Low Country and the coastal sea islands, site of many former rice and cotton plantations.

In recent years, Savannah chefs have moved far beyond the "grits-and-greens" type of cookery, creating fresh combinations from traditional ingredients. For example, instead of black-eyed peas cooked in bacon fat, you might get black-eyed-pea salsa. Instead of fried shrimp, you might get, for example, smoked shrimp and melon gazpacho. Instead of Southern fried chicken, you might get stuffed breast of chicken with a crabmeat and artichoke dressing.

COLONIAL CUISINE

Oglethorpe's Colonials found a Low Country made up of marshes and saltwater creeks. They turned to these for a harvest of shrimp and oysters. For meat, the forests were full of game such as rabbits. The Low Country also yielded marsh hens, doves, pigeons, and quail. Deer were hunted at night by torchlight. By 1800, visitors reported seeing the old City Market (since burned down) overflowing with corn, peas, okra, field greens, beets, squash, turnips, sweet potatoes, beans, and even eggplant. The bean of choice was the black-eyed pea, which was African in origin. Combined with rice, it became Hoppin' John. Many Savannahians still eat hoppin' John on New Year's Day. Tradition has it that it will bring them luck in the coming year.

The Colonials roasted their meat over fires on spits. Rare meat was considered not only the best tasting but the healthiest. In time, however, beginning in the 1800s, the iron kitchen range was introduced. Cooks started cooking their meats well-done, and even today many Savannahians will eat their meat only well-done.

From the Native Americans Oglethorpe encountered when he landed, the Colonials learned how to make corn bread, which they called hoecake, pone, or "dodgers." The seasoning in this first early American version of corn bread? Bear grease. For many Savannahians during the blockade of the Civil War, corn bread and some milk were all they had to sustain life.

In the Savannah tradition, meat was preferred if it had "steak of lean and a streak of fat." Some early settlers liked boiled fat—no lean.

When slavery became a factor in the colony, many Africans introduced recipes remembered from their distant homelands. Dishes became hotter and spicier, especially with the use of red pepper.

Sometimes vendors, such as the shrimp man, came around from door to door (back door, that is), hawking his fresh shrimp carried in a basket on his head.

FAVORITE SAVANNAH FOODS

The Southern love for pork was and is economical. Hogs were easier to raise than cattle. Hogs more or less took care of themselves, foraging for their food. Cows take longer to raise. A succulent hog can add to its body weight 150 times in just 1 year of life. Savannahians found that all parts of the hog, even the head, could be consumed.

From the hog they smoked hams, made sausages, dried cracklings for corn bread, and saved the fat for lard, which they used in virtually

---

Impressions

The land belongs to the women, and the corn that grows upon it; but meat must be got by the men, because it is they only that hunt. This makes marriage necessary, that the women may furnish corn and the men meat.

—James Oglethorpe on Savannah's Native Americans (1733)

Impressions

Oh, lady, if yo' want to tas'e somethin' sweet,
Jes' take a li'l onion an' a li'l piece o' met
An' mix 'em wid yo' tender, pure, raw s'rimp.

—Traditional vendor call

every dish, most often to season greens and other vegetables. Salt pork preserved the meat during long cold winters and came in most handily during the long siege caused by the Civil War.

Barbecued pork remains the favorite meat dish of Savannah, followed by Southern fried chicken, of which every chef has a special recipe. Beef lags a distant third. Even today, many Savannahians, except those with more sophisticated palates, do not eat lamb.

The tomato, which is now integral to most Southern meals, from fried green tomatoes to soups, was thought to be poisonous before the Civil War. Some Savannahians believed that it had the power to act as a love potion—hence they called it the "love apple." After the Civil War, the tomato came into favor and started to appear in okra-laced gumbos, in soups, in catsup and, miracle of miracles, to be eaten raw by the most daring of diners.

Although botanically a fruit, the Supreme Court in 1893 declared the tomato to be a vegetable. At the same time, eggplants, peppers, avocados, peas, beans, cucumbers, and squash, though botanical fruits, were also ruled vegetables. All of these found favor with the diners of Savannah. A true Savannahian will only eat a fresh tomato between late May and early August.

Lima beans, sometimes cooked with okra, became the best-known bean for consumption in Savannah. Named for their place of origin, Lima, Peru, the bean became known as "butter beans" in Savannah.

Savannahians also love sweet potatoes, and they are fashioned in countless dishes, with sweet potato pancakes a favorite, especially at Sunday brunches.

Southerners also take to greens, especially collards, which are served almost invariably cooked in pork stock, with corn bread used to mop up the "pot liquor."

Grits appear frequently, most often at breakfast. Savannahians have learned to spice them up in several versions, including cheese grits.

Impressions

She spread a table for us, brilliant with white linen, and china, and silver, and entertained us with tea and bread and butter, potatoes at my desire, eggs, and other good things. No, it would not have been more possible for a meal spread by fairy hands to have been more delicate or finely flavored. . . . Savannah might be called the city of the gushing springs; there can not be, in the whole world, a more beautiful city than Savannah!

—Fredrika Bremer (1853)

Quail is the favorite game bird of Savannah and the Low Country. In fact, it is a staple on most tables and is served grilled, stuffed, or sautéed at breakfast, lunch, or dinner.

3

Planning Your Trip to Savannah

In the pages that follow, we've compiled everything you need to know to handle the practical details of planning your trip: a calendar of events, visitor information, and more.

1 Visitor Information

For advance reading and planning, contact the **Division of Tourism,** Georgia Department of Industry, Trade & Tourism, P.O. Box 1776, Atlanta, GA 30301-1776 (© **800/VISIT-GA** or 404/962-4000; www.georgiaonmymind.com). Ask for information on your specific interests, as well as a calendar of events (Jan–June or July–Dec).

2 When to Go

CLIMATE

The average high and low temperatures in Savannah show Low Country coastal areas to be warmer year-round than farther inland. Winter temperatures seldom drop below freezing. Spring and fall are the longest seasons, and the wettest months are December to April.

Spring is a spectacular time to visit Savannah. Many areas become a riot of color as azaleas, dogwoods, and camellias burst into bloom.

Savannah Average Temperatures & Rainfall

	Jan	Feb	Mar	Apr	May	June	July	Aug	Sept	Oct	Nov	Dec
High (°F)	60	62	70	78	84	89	91	90	85	78	70	62
High (°C)	17	17	21	26	29	32	33	32	29	26	21	17
Low (°F)	38	41	48	55	63	69	72	72	68	57	57	41
Low (°C)	3	5	9	13	17	21	22	22	20	14	14	5
Rain (in.)	3.6	3.2	3.8	3.0	4.1	5.7	6.4	7.5	4.5	2.4	2.2	3.0

SAVANNAH CALENDAR OF EVENTS

February

Wormsloe Colonial Faire and Muster. Wormsloe was the Colonial fortified home of Noble Jones, one of Georgia's first colonists. Costumed demonstrators portray skills used by those early settlers. Tickets cost $2 for adults, $1 for children. Call ☎ **912/353-3023** or go to www.wormsloe.org. First Saturday and Sunday in February.

Savannah Irish Festival. This Irish heritage celebration promises fun for the entire family, with music, dancing, and food. There's a children's stage and a main stage. Contact the Irish Committee of Savannah at ☎ **912/232-3448 or go to** www.savannahirish.com. Mid-February.

March

St. Patrick's Day Celebration on the River. The river flows green and so does the beer in one of the largest celebrations held on River Street each year. Enjoy live entertainment, lots of food, and tons of fun. Contact the Savannah Waterfront Association at ☎ **912/234-0295** or www.savriverstreet.com. St. Patrick's Day weekend.

Savannah Music Festival. Featuring everything from indigenous music from the South to world premieres, this annual music festival attracts fans from all over America. Chamber music and even ballet troupes perform before an appreciative audience. For more information, call ☎ **912/525-5050** or visit www.savannahmusic festival.org. Begins mid-March and lasts 17 days.

Savannah Tour of Homes. During this annual festival, now more than 70 years old, each day a different district of historic Savannah is featured on a tour, including private homes and gardens not available to visitors the rest of the year. For more information, call ☎ **912/234-8054** or visit www.savannahtourofhomes.org. Late March and through the first week of April.

May

Memorial Day at Old Fort Jackson. The commemoration includes a flag-raising ceremony and a memorial service featuring "Taps." Contact the Coastal Heritage Society at ☎ **912/944-0456.** Late May.

June

Juneteenth. This event highlights the contributions of more than 200,000 African-Americans who fought for their freedom and that of future generations. This event is a celebration of the Emancipation Proclamation. Although this promise of freedom was announced in January, it was not until the middle of June (actual date unknown) that the news reached Savannah, thus prompting the remembrance of "Juneteenth." For more information, contact the Coastal Heritage Society at © **912/944-0456.** Mid-June.

September

Savannah Jazz Festival. This festival features national and local jazz and blues legends. A jazz brunch and music at different venues throughout the city are among the highlights. Contact Host South at © **912/356-2399** or www.coastaljazz.com. Mid-September.

November

Crafts Festival & Cane Grinding. More than 75 craftspeople from four states sell and demonstrate their art. Music is provided by the Savannah Folk Music Society. Contact Oatland Island at © **912/897-3773.** Mid-November.

December

Christmas 1864. Fort Jackson hosts the dramatic re-creation of its evacuation on December 20, 1864. More than 60 Civil War re-enactors play the part of Fort Jackson's Confederate defenders, who were preparing to evacuate ahead of Union Gen. William Tecumseh Sherman. Contact Old Fort Jackson at © **912/232-3945.** Early December.

Annual Holiday Tour of Homes. The doors of Savannah's historic homes are opened to the public during the holiday season. Each home is decorated, and a different group of homes is shown every day. Contact the Downtown Neighborhood Association at © **912/236-8362** or visit www.dnaholidaytour.net. Mid-December.

3 Money

You won't have any problem finding ATMs all over the state that are connected to the major national networks. For specific locations of **Cirrus** machines, call © **800/424-7787;** for the **PLUS** network, call © **800/843-7587.**

If you run out of funds on the road, you can have a friend or relative advance you some money through **MONEYGRAM,** www.moneygram.com, which allows you to transfer funds from one person to another in less than 10 minutes from thousands of locations. An American Express phone representative will give you the names of four or five offices nearby. The service charge is $21.60 for the first $300 sent, with a sliding scale after that.

What Things Cost in Savannah	U.S.$
Taxi from Savannah airport to downtown	20.00
One-way bus fare	.75
Local telephone call	.35
Hyatt Regency Savannah (expensive)	175.00
River Street Inn (moderate)	159.00
Bed & Breakfast Inn (inexpensive)	89.00
Lunch for one at Huey's (moderate)	24.00
Lunch for one at The River Grill (inexpensive)	15.00
Dinner for one, without wine, at the 45 South (very expensive)	55.00
Dinner for one, without wine, at Il Pasticcio (moderate)	30.00
Dinner for one, without wine, at Dockside	16.00
Bottle of beer	4.50
Coca-Cola	1.25
Cup of coffee in a cafe	1.50
Roll of 35mm Kodak film, 36 exposures	7.50
Admission to Telfair Mansion and Art Museum	8.00
Movie ticket	7.00
Theater ticket to Savannah Theater	32.00

4 The Active Vacation Planner

BEACHES   Georgia's beaches don't offer the lights and entertainment or enjoy the fame of those in the Carolinas. But at one time, the Georgia coast was frequented by the likes of the Rockefellers and Vanderbilts; and even though this grand life has faded, the coast remains a quiet retreat for those seeking a true getaway. The Georgia coast is dotted with the Golden Isles: Historic Jekyll Island, luxurious Sea Island, and secluded Cumberland Island are the Eastern Seaboard's best-kept secrets. For information, call ℂ **800/VISIT-GA,** or write the **Division of Tourism,** Georgia Department of Industry, Trade & Tourism, P.O. Box 1776, Atlanta, GA 30301-1776.

CAMPING   For information on Georgia's state parks and their camping facilities, contact the **Georgia Department of Natural**

Resources, Office of Information, 205 Butler St. SE, Suite 1352, Atlanta, GA 30334 (© **800/864-7275,** or 770/389-7275 in Georgia for reservations; http://gastateparks.org). Forty of the state parks in Georgia welcome campers to sites that rent for $10 to $20 per night. Some 25 parks have vacation cottages that rent for $50 to $135 per night. These rates are for the summer and are reduced during other months. Make reservations by calling © **800/864-PARK.** Be aware that some of the Georgia state parks have become privatized; site and cabin rentals could be higher. **Georgia State Parks & Historic Sites** (© **404/656-3530**) can provide additional information, including details on hiking.

FISHING & HUNTING   No license is needed for saltwater fishing, but fishing in Georgia's lakes, streams, and ponds does require a license. Hunting is a sport used to curtail the annual exponential growth of the white-tailed deer population. Wild turkey and quail also abound. To obtain information about hunting and fishing regulations, contact the **Georgia Department of Natural Resources,** Office of Information, 205 Butler St. SE, Suite 1352, Atlanta, GA 30334 (© **800/241-4113;** www.georgiawildlife.com). Many hunting clubs will allow you to join provided that you have references or can be sponsored by a local friend or family member.

GOLF   Golf is *very* big in Georgia. Augusta, an easy drive from Savannah, is home to the venerable Augusta National Golf Club, where the Masters Golf Tournament is played (the club's course is not open to the public). For information on private and public golf courses across the state of Georgia, call © **800/949-4742** or go to www.gsga.org to receive your free guide, *Georgia Golf on My Mind.*

HIKING   For those who want easy hikes, some 40 state parks in Georgia offer trails of varying difficulty. Call © **800/864-PARKS** for more information.

LAKES   Georgia is a virtual land of lakes, providing water, electricity, and recreation. East Georgia's Clarks Hill Lake (the Georgia side of South Carolina's Thurmond Lake); northeast Georgia's Lake Hartwell; and middle Georgia's lakes Oconee, Sinclair, and Lanier are the premier spots for boating and fishing. For more information, contact the **Georgia Department of Natural Resources,** Office of Information, 205 Butler St. SE, Atlanta, GA 30334; or call © **800/241-4113.**

5 Specialized Travel Resources

FOR TRAVELERS WITH DISABILITIES   Many hotels and restaurants in Georgia provide easy access for persons with disabilities, and some display the international wheelchair symbol in their brochures. However, it's always a good idea to call ahead.

The **Georgia Governor's Developmental Disabilities Council** (© 404/657-2126; www.gcdd.org) may also be of help. The Georgia Department of Industry, Trade & Tourism publishes a guide, *Georgia on My Mind,* that lists attractions and accommodations with access for persons with disabilities. To receive a copy, contact **Tour Georgia,** P.O. Box 1776, Atlanta, GA 30301-1776 (© 800/VISIT-GA, ext. 1903).

Many agencies provide advance information to help you plan your trip. One such agency is **Travel Information Service,** Industrial Rehab Program, 1200 W. Tabor Rd., Philadelphia, PA 19141 (© 215/456-9603, or 215/456-9602 for TTY). It answers questions on various destinations and also offers discounts on videos, publications, and programs that it sponsors. For a free copy of *Air Transportation of Handicapped Persons,* published by the U.S. Department of Transportation, write for Free Advisory Circular No. AC12032, Distribution Unit, U.S. Department of Transportation, Publications Division, M-4332, Washington, DC 20590.

Amtrak, with 24 hours' notice, will provide porter service, special seating, and a substantial discount (© 800/USA-RAIL; www.amtrak.com).

Many travel agencies offer customized tours and itineraries for travelers with disabilities. **Flying Wheels Travel** (© 507/451-5005; www.flyingwheelstravel.com) offers escorted tours and cruises that emphasize sports and private tours in minivans with lifts. **Access-Able Travel Source** (© 303/232-2979; www.access-able.com) offers extensive access information and advice for those with disabilities traveling around the world. **Accessible Journeys** (© 800/846-4537 or 610/521-0339; www.disabilitytravel.com) caters specifically to slow walkers and wheelchair travelers and their families and friends.

Avis Rent a Car has an "Avis Access" program that offers such services as a dedicated 24-hour toll-free number (© 888/879-4273) for customers with special travel needs; special car features such as swivel seats, spinner knobs, and hand controls; and accessible bus service.

Organizations that offer assistance to disabled travelers include **MossRehab** (www.mossresourcenet.org), which provides a library of accessible-travel resources online; **SATH (Society for Accessible Travel & Hospitality;** ✆ **212/447-7284;** www.sath.org; annual membership fees: $45 adults, $30 seniors and students), which offers a wealth of travel resources for people with all types of disabilities and informed recommendations on destinations, access guides, travel agents, tour operators, vehicle rentals, and companion services; and the **American Foundation for the Blind (AFB;** ✆ **800/232-5463;** www.afb.org), a referral resource for the blind or visually impaired that includes information on traveling with Seeing Eye dogs.

For more information specifically targeted to travelers with disabilities, the community website **iCan** (www.icanonline.net/channels/travel/index.cfm) has destination guides and several regular columns on accessible travel. Also check out the quarterly magazine **Emerging Horizons** ($14.95 per year, $19.95 outside the U.S.; www.emerginghorizons.com); and *Open World* magazine, published by SATH (see above; subscription: $13 per year, $21 outside the U.S.).

FOR GAY & LESBIAN TRAVELERS   Homophobia is rampant in "Red State" Georgia, which does not approve, according to voter turnout, of same-sex marriages. Nor does it approve, in the words of one gay bartender, "of homosexuals in general." That having been said, Savannah and Atlanta are the most gay-friendly places to travel in Georgia. Even so, open displays of affection between same-sex couples may be met with glares of hostility. In other words, Georgia is a long way from New York's Chelsea district.

The **International Gay and Lesbian Travel Association (IGLTA;** ✆ **800/448-8550** or 954/776-2626; www.iglta.org) is the trade association for the gay and lesbian travel industry, and offers an online directory of gay- and lesbian-friendly travel businesses; go to their website and click on "Members."

Many agencies offer tours and travel itineraries specifically for gay and lesbian travelers. **Above and Beyond Tours** (✆ **800/397-2681;** www.abovebeyondtours.com) is the exclusive gay and lesbian tour operator for United Airlines. **Now, Voyager** (✆ **800/255-6951;** www.nowvoyager.com) is a well-known San Francisco–based gay-owned and -operated travel service.

FOR SENIORS   Nearly all major U.S. hotel and motel chains now offer a senior's discount, so ask for the reduction *when you make the reservation;* there may be restrictions during peak days. Then be sure to carry proof of your age (driver's license, passport, and so on) when you check in. Among the chains that offer the best discounts are **Marriott Hotels** (© 800/228-9290; www.marriott.com) for those 62 and older; and **La Quinta Inns** (© 800/531-5900; www.lq.com) for ages 55 and older.

You can save sightseeing dollars if you're 62 or older by picking up a **Golden Age Passport** from any federally operated park, recreation area, or monument.

Elderhostel (© 877/426-8056; www.elderhostel.org) provides stimulating vacations at moderate prices for those over 55, with a balanced mix of learning, field trips, and free time for sightseeing.

One organization for seniors offers a wide variety of travel benefits: **AARP,** 601 E St. NW, Washington, DC 20049 (© 888/687-2277).

FAMILY TRAVEL   All Georgia visitor centers offer discount coupons for families as well as the *Atlanta Street Map & Visitors Guide.* Families might also pick up the book *A Guide for Family Activities,* by Denise Black, with a host of ideas and activities for children in the metro Atlanta area. Another local guide is called *Fun Family Vacations—Southeast.*

6 Getting There

BY PLANE   Depending on where you are coming from, many visitors fly first to Atlanta's **Hartsfield International Airport,** 13 miles south of downtown Atlanta off I-85 and I-285. From Atlanta, there are many connecting flights into Savannah. There are also direct flights into Savannah on many airlines.

BY TRAIN   Amtrak (© 800/USA-RAIL; www.amtrak.com) has stops in Atlanta and Savannah. Be sure to ask about Amtrak's money-saving "All Aboard America" regional fares or any other current fare specials. Amtrak also offers attractively priced rail/drive packages in the Carolinas and Georgia.

BY CAR   Georgia is crisscrossed by major interstate highways: I-75 bisects the state from Dalton in the north to Valdosta in the south; I-95 runs north-south along the Eastern Seaboard. The major east-west routes are I-16, running between Macon and Savannah; and I-20, running from Augusta through Atlanta and into Alabama. I-85 runs northeast-southwest in the northern half of the state.

In addition to the interstates, U.S. 84 cuts across the southern part of the state from the Alabama state line through Valdosta and Waycross, and eventually connects to I-95 south of Savannah.

The state-run welcome centers at all major points of entry are staffed with knowledgeable, helpful Georgians who can often advise you as to timesaving routes. The speed limit varies from 55 to 70 mph and the seat-belt law is strictly enforced.

Here is a list of approximate mileages to Savannah from other major cities in the East: Atlanta, GA 248 miles; Charleston, SC 107 miles; Charlotte, NC 252 miles; Jackson, FL 138 miles; Richmond, VA 467 miles; Orlando, FL 278 miles; New York, NY 815 miles; and Washington, DC 579 miles.

For 24-hour road conditions, call © **404/656-5267. AAA** services are available in Savannah.

BY BUS **Greyhound/Trailways** (© **800/231-2222;** www. greyhound.com) has good direct service to major cities in Georgia from out of state, including Savannah, with connections to almost any destination.

FAST FACTS: Georgia

Emergencies Dial © **911** for police, ambulance, paramedics, and fire department. Travelers Aid can also be helpful—check local telephone directories.

Liquor Laws If you're 21 or over, you can buy alcoholic beverages in package stores between 8am and midnight (except on Sun, election days, Thanksgiving, and Christmas).

Newspapers/Magazines The *Savannah Morning News* is the major newspaper of the city, carrying international and national news as well as regional coverage.

Police In an emergency, call © **911** (no coin required).

Taxes Georgia has a 6% sales tax.

Time Zone Georgia is in the Eastern Standard Time zone and goes on daylight saving time in spring.

4

Getting to Know Savannah

Savannah is to Georgia what Charleston is to South Carolina—Georgia's grandest, most historic, and most intriguing city to visit. In fact, it's one of the 10 most historic cities of America.

Because much of the interest focuses on the easily walkable historic core, getting the hang of navigating Savannah comes relatively easy for most visitors from more congested urban areas.

Even more than Charlestonians, the people of Savannah are noted for their old-fashioned Southern hospitality. You'll frequently hear them say, "Y'all come back, you hear?"

1 Orientation

ARRIVING

BY PLANE   **Savannah Hilton Head International Airport** is about 8 miles west of downtown, just off I-16. **American** (© 800/433-7300; www.aa.com), **Delta** (© 800/221-1212; www.delta.com), **United** (© 800/241/6522; www.united.com), and **US Airways** (© 800/428-4322; www.usairways.com) have flights from Atlanta and Charlotte, with connections from other points.

BY CAR   From north or south, I-95 passes 10 miles west of Savannah, with several exits to the city, and U.S. 17 runs through the city. From the west, I-16 ends in downtown Savannah, and U.S. 80 also runs through the city from east to west. American Automobile Association services are available through the **AAA Auto Club South,** 712 Mall Blvd., Savannah, GA 31406 (© **912/352-8222;** www.aaa.com).

BY TRAIN   The **train station** is at 2611 Seaboard Coastline Dr. (© **912/234-2611**), some 4 miles southwest of downtown; cab fare into the city is around $5. For **Amtrak** schedule and fare information, contact © **800/USA-RAIL** (www.amtrak.com).

VISITOR INFORMATION

The **Savannah Information Visitor Center,** 301 Martin Luther King Jr. Blvd., Savannah, GA 31401 (© **912/944-0455**), is open

Monday to Friday 8:30am to 5pm and Saturday and Sunday 9am to 5pm. The staff is friendly and efficient. The center offers an audiovisual presentation ($4 adults, $1 children), organized tours, and self-guided walking, driving, or bike tours with excellent maps, cassette tapes, and brochures.

Tourist information is also available from the **Savannah Area Convention & Visitors Bureau,** 101 E. Bay St., Savannah, GA 31402 (*©* **877/SAVANNAH** or 912/644-6401; www.savannahvisit.com).

For everything you might want to know about The Book, check out the Internet site **www.midnightinthegarden.com**.

CITY LAYOUT

Every other street—north, south, west, and east—is punctuated by greenery. The grid of 24 scenic squares was laid out in 1733 by Gen. James Oglethorpe, the founder of Georgia. The design—still in use—has been called "one of the world's most revered city plans." It's said that if Savannah didn't have its history and architecture, it would be worth a visit just to see the city layout.

Bull Street is the dividing line between east and west. On the south side are odd-numbered buildings, on the north side even-numbered buildings.

NEIGHBORHOODS IN BRIEF

Historic District   The Historic District—the real reason to visit Savannah—takes in both the riverfront and the City Market, described below. It's bordered by the Savannah River and Forsyth Park at Gaston Street and Montgomery and Price streets. Within its borders are more than 2,350 architecturally and historically significant buildings in a 2½-square-mile area. About 75% of these buildings have been restored.

Riverfront   In this popular tourist district, River Street borders the Savannah River. Once lined with warehouses holding King Cotton, it has been subjected to massive urban renewal into a row of restaurants, art galleries, shops, and bars. The source of the area's growth was the river, which offered a prime shipping avenue for New World goods shipped to European ports. In 1818, about half of Savannah was quarantined during a yellow-fever epidemic. River Street never fully recovered and fell into disrepair until its rediscovery in the mid-1970s. The urban-renewal project stabilized the downtown and revitalized the Historic District. Stroll the bluffs along the river on the old passageway of alleys, cobblestone walkways, and bridges known as **Factors Walk.**

Greater Savannah

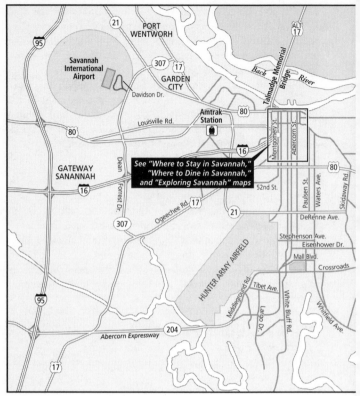

City Market   Two blocks from River Street and bordering the Savannah River, the City Market was the former social and business mecca of Savannah. Since the late 18th century, it has known fires and various devastations, including the threat of demolition. But in a major move, the city of Savannah decided to save the district. Today, former decaying warehouses are filled with restaurants and shops offering everything from antiques to collectibles, including many Savannah-made products. And everything from seafood and pizza to French and Italian cuisine is served here. Live music often fills the nighttime air. Some of the best jazz in the city is presented here in various clubs. The market lies at Jefferson and West Julian streets, bounded by Franklin Square on its western flank and Ellis Square on its eastern.

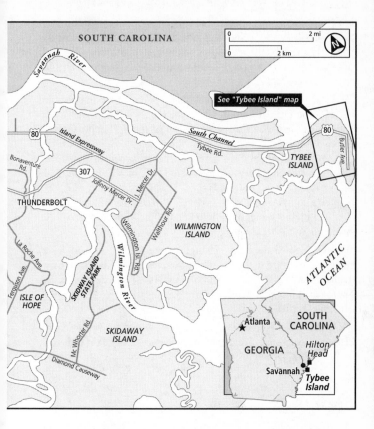

Victorian District The Victorian District, south of the Historic District, holds some of the finest examples of post–Civil War architecture in the Deep South. The district is bounded by Martin Luther King Jr. Boulevard and by East Broad, Gwinnett, and Anderson streets. Houses in the district are characterized by gingerbread trim, stained-glass windows, and imaginative architectural details. In all, the district encompasses an area of nearly 50 blocks, spread across some 165 acres. The entire district was listed on the National Register of Historic Places in 1974. Most of the two-story homes are wood frame and were constructed in the late 1800s on brick foundations. The district, overflowing from the historic inner core, became the first suburb of Savannah.

2 Getting Around

The grid-shaped Historic District is best seen on foot—the real point of your visit is to take leisurely strolls with frequent stops in the many squares.

BY CAR Though you can reach many points of interest outside the Historic District by bus, your own wheels will be much more convenient, and they're absolutely essential for sightseeing outside the city proper.

All major car-rental firms have branches in Savannah and at the airport, including **Hertz** (© **800/654-3131,** or 912/964-9595 at the airport); **Avis** (© **800/831-2847**), with locations at 422 Airways Ave. (© 912/964-1781) and at 2215 Travis Field Rd. (© 912/964-0234); and **Budget** (© **800/527-0700**), with offices at 7070 Abercorn St. (© 912/966-1771).

BY BUS You'll need exact change for the $1 fare, plus $1 for a transfer. For route and schedule information, call **Chatham Area Transit (CAT)** at © **912/233-5767.** A free CAT shuttle departs the Savannah Visitor's Center and makes several stops around the Historic District.

BY TAXI The base rate for taxis is 60¢, with a $1.20 additional charge for each mile. For 24-hour taxi service, call **Adam Cab Co.** at © **912/927-7466.**

FAST FACTS: Savannah

American Express There is no American Express office in Savannah, but cardholders can obtain assistance by calling © **800/221-7282.**

Dentist Call **Abercorn South Side Dental**, 11139 Abercorn St., Suite 8 (© **912/925-9190**), for complete dental care and emergencies, Monday to Friday 8:30am to 3pm.

Drugstore Drugstores are scattered throughout Savannah. One with longer hours is **CVS,** 11607 Abercorn St. (© **912/925-5568**), open Monday to Saturday 8am to midnight and Sunday 10am to 8pm.

Emergencies Dial © **911** for police, ambulance, or fire emergencies.

Hospitals There are 24-hour emergency-room services at **Candler General Hospital,** 5353 Reynolds St. (© **912/819-6000**); and at the **Memorial Medical Center,** 4700 Waters Ave. (© **912/ 350-8390**).

Newspapers The *Savannah Morning News* is a daily filled with information about local cultural and entertainment events. The *Savannah Tribune* and the *Herald of Savannah* are geared to the African-American community.

Police In an emergency, call © **911.**

Post Office Post offices and sub-post offices are centrally located and open Monday to Friday 8am to 4:30pm. The main office is at 2 N. Fahm St. (at the intersection of Fahm and Bay sts.; © **912/235-4666**).

Safety Although it's reasonably safe to explore the Historic and Victorian districts during the day, the situation changes at night. The clubs along the riverfront, both bars and restaurants, report very little crime. However, muggings and drug dealing are common in the poorer neighborhoods of Savannah.

Taxes Savannah has a 6% sales tax and tacks on a 6% accommodations tax (room or occupancy tax) to your hotel bill.

Transit Information Call **Chatham Area Transit** at © **912/ 233-5767.**

Weather Call © **912/964-1700.**

5

Where to Stay in Savannah

The undisputed stars of Savannah lodging are the small inns in the Historic District, most in restored homes that have been renovated with modern conveniences while retaining their original charm.

A note on rates: Because many of Savannah's historic inns are in converted former residences, price ranges can vary greatly. Keep in mind that a very expensive hotel might also have some smaller, more moderately priced units. So it pays to ask. Advance reservations are necessary in most cases, since many of the best properties are small.

MAKING RESERVATIONS

You may make your reservations by telephone, mail, fax, and, in many cases, the Internet. If you're booking into a chain hotel, such as a Hilton, you can easily make your reservations by calling their toll-free phone numbers.

You can usually cancel a room reservation 1 week ahead of time and get a full refund. A few places will return your money up to 3 days before the reservation date; others won't return any of your deposit, even if you can cancel far in advance. It's best to clarify this issue when you make your reservation. If you are booking by mail, include a stamped, self-addressed envelope with your payment so that the hotel can easily send you a receipt and confirmation.

If you arrive without a reservation, begin your search for a room as early in the day as possible. If you arrive late at night and without a reservation, you may have to take what you can get, often in a price range much higher than you'd like to pay.

1 Along the Riverfront

EXPENSIVE

Hyatt Regency Savannah 𝄐 There was an outcry from Savannah's historic preservation movement when this place went up in 1981. Boxy and massively bulky, it stands in unpleasant contrast to the restored warehouses flanking it along the banks of the Savannah River. Today it is grudgingly accepted as the biggest and flashiest

Where to Stay in Savannah

Azalea Inn **29**

Ballastone Inn **15**

Baymont Inn & Suites **28**

Bed & Breakfast Inn **22**

Catherine Ward House Inn **23**

Clubhouse Inn **28**

Courtyard Savannah Historic District **17**

Days Inn & Suites Historic District **1**

East Bay Inn **8**

Eliza Thompson House **20**

Fairfield Inn by Marriott **28**

Foley House Inn **16**

The Forsyth Park Inn **25**

Gaston Gallery Bed & Breakfast **30**

The Gastonian **31**

Hamilton Turner Inn **19**

Hampton Inn Historic District **9**

Hilton Savannah DeSoto **18**

Homewood Suites by Hilton **29**

Hyatt Regency Savannah **2**

Kehoe House **12**

Magnolia Place Inn **24**

Marriott Riverfront Hotel **6**

The Marshall House **11**

Master's Inn Suites,
   Savannah Midtown **32**

The Mulberry Inn **7**

Olde Georgian Inn **23**

Olde Harbour Inn **5**

Park Avenue Manor **27**

Planters Inn **10**

The President's Quarters Inn **14**

River Street Inn **3**

17 Hundred 90 **13**

Westin Savannah Harbor
   Golf Resort and Spa **4**

Whitaker-Huntington Inn **26**

Wingate Inn **21**

> ### *Tips* **Savannah's Fluctuating Room Rates**
>
> Savannah's hotel and B&B rates are like the weather—subject to change. Most establishments rate their room prices based on high and low seasons. **High season** is from April to October. In addition, the rates may vary if you stay during a weekday or if you stay over a weekend. You will find that the cheapest rates will usually be on weekdays during **low season,** which is January, February, and sometimes late August.

---

hotel in town. It has a soaring atrium as well as glass-sided elevators. The comfortable rooms, often with paper-thin walls, are international and modern in their feel, all with good-size bathrooms with tub/shower combinations and some with balconies overlooking the atrium. Room prices vary according to their views—units without a view are quite a bargain. Chances are you'll find better food by dining outside the hotel at one of the independent restaurants recommended in this guide.

2 W. Bay St., Savannah, GA 31401. ✆ **800/223-1234** or 912/238-1234. Fax 912/944-3678. www.hyatt.com. 347 units. $175–$265 double; $315–$665 suite. AE, DC, DISC, MC, V. Parking $15. **Amenities:** Restaurant; bar; indoor pool; fitness center; limited room service; laundry service/dry cleaning; nonsmoking rooms; rooms for those w/limited mobility. *In room:* A/C, TV, dataport, hair dryer, iron/ironing board, safe.

Marriott Riverfront Hotel ⚿
At least the massive modern bulk of this place is far away enough from the 19th-century restored warehouses of River Street not to clash with them aesthetically. Towering eight stories, with an angular facade sheathed in orange and yellow brick, it doesn't quite succeed at being a top-rated luxury palace but nonetheless attracts lots of corporate business and conventions. Its comfortable, modern guest rooms aren't style-setters but are generous in space, with bathrooms containing tub/shower combinations, a generous supply of towels, and enough space to store your stuff.

100 General McIntosh Blvd., Savannah, GA 31401. ✆ **800/228-9290** or 912/233-7722. Fax 912/233-3765. www.marriott.com. 379 units. $160–$200 double; from $250 suite. Children 12 and under stay free in parent's room. AE, DC, DISC, MC, V. Parking $10. **Amenities:** Restaurant; bar; lounge; 2 pools (1 indoor); fitness center; Jacuzzi; limited room service; laundry service/dry cleaning; nonsmoking rooms; rooms for those w/limited mobility. *In room:* A/C, TV, dataport, coffeemaker, hair dryer, iron/ironing board.

Westin Savannah Harbor Golf Resort & Spa ⚿
Savannah's largest hotel was opened in 1999 in a 16-story blockbuster format

that dwarfs the city's existing B&Bs. It rises somewhat jarringly from what were, until the late 1990s, sandy, scrub-covered flatlands on the swampy, far side of the river from Savannah's historic core. Conceived as part of a massive resort development project, it includes a Greenbrier Spa and a golf course that is home to the PGA TOUR's Champions Tour Liberty Mutual Legends of Golf 2003–2006. The Westin derives the bulk of its business from corporate groups who arrive for conventions throughout the year. It's the newest and largest of the four large-scale hotels that dominate the city's convention business, yet despite a worthy collection (more than 250 pieces) of contemporary art that accents the labyrinth of high-ceilinged public rooms here, there's something a bit sterile, even lifeless, about this relatively anonymous blockbuster. Compounding the problem is its isolated position, both geographically and emotionally, from the bustle, grace, and charm of central Savannah—this in spite of cross-river shuttle ferries that deposit clients into the center of the River Street bar and restaurant frenzy. The most elaborate guest rooms are on the two top floors, and contain extras and comforts designated as Club Level. Otherwise, rooms are comfortable but bland, outfitted with pale colors and conservative furnishings. All units contain well-kept bathrooms with tub/shower combinations.

One Resort Dr., P.O. Box 427, Savannah, GA 31421. © **800/WESTIN-1** or 912/201-2000. Fax 912/201-2001. www.westinsavannah.com. 403 units. $239–$299 double; $325–$800 suite. Water taxis, free for hotel guests, $1 round-trip for everyone else, shuttle across the river to Rousakis Plaza, on River St., at 15-min. intervals. From I-95 and Savannah International Airport take exit 17A to I-16 toward Savannah. Follow sign for Rte. 17(Talmadge Bridge). Take Hutchinson Island exit onto Resort Dr. **Amenities:** 2 restaurants; bar; 2 outdoor pools; 18-hole golf course; 4 tennis courts; fitness center; Jacuzzi; sauna; beauty treatments; 24-hr. room service; babysitting; laundry service/dry cleaning; nonsmoking rooms; rooms for those w/limited mobility. *In room:* A/C, TV, dataport, minibar, coffeemaker, hair dryer, safe, iron/ironing board.

MODERATE

Olde Harbour Inn ⚐ The neighborhood has been gentrified and the interior of this place is well furnished, but you still get a whiff of riverfront seediness as you approach from Factors Walk. It was built in 1892 as a warehouse for oil, and its masonry bulk is camouflaged with shutters, awnings, and touches of wrought iron. Inside, a labyrinth of passages leads to small but comfortable suites, many of which reveal the building's massive timbers and structural iron brackets and offer views of the river. Some decors feature the original brick, painted white. Each unit contains a well-maintained bathroom with a tub/shower combination along with its own kitchen—useful for an extended stay. Despite the overlay of chintz, you'll have a constant sense of the building's thick-walled bulk. Breakfast is the only meal served.

508 E. Factors Walk, Savannah, GA 31401. (800/553-6533 or 912/234-4100. Fax 912/233-5979. www.oldeharbourinn.com. 24 units. $169–$279 suite. Rates include continental breakfast. AE, DC, DISC, MC, V. **Amenities:** Breakfast room; nonsmoking rooms. *In room:* A/C, TV, dataport, kitchenette (in some), coffeemaker, hair dryer, iron/ironing board, safe.

River Street Inn ⭑⭑ *Kids* When Liverpool-based ships were moored on the nearby river, this building stored massive amounts of cotton produced by upriver plantations. After the boll weevil decimated the cotton industry, it functioned as an icehouse, a storage area for fresh vegetables, and (at its lowest point) the headquarters of an insurance company. Its two lowest floors, built in 1817, were made of ballast stones carried in the holds of ships from faraway England.

In 1986, a group of investors poured millions into the building's development as one of the linchpins of Savannah's River District, adding a well-upholstered colonial pizzazz to the public areas and converting the building's warren of brick-lined storerooms into some of the most comfortable and well-managed rooms in town. All units have neatly kept bathrooms with tub/shower combinations. Breakfast is served in **Huey's** (see chapter 6, "Where to Dine in Savannah"). A wine-and-cheese reception is held Monday through Saturday, and turndown service is offered each evening.

124 E. Bay St., Savannah, GA 31401. (800/253-4229 or 912/234-6400. Fax 912/234-1478. www.riverstreetinn.com. 86 units. $159–$229 double; $275 suite. Children 13 and under stay free in parent's room. AE, DC, MC, V. Parking $6. **Amenities:** Restaurant; lounge; Jacuzzi; nonsmoking rooms. *In room:* A/C, TV, dataport, hair dryer.

IN THE HISTORIC DISTRICT
VERY EXPENSIVE

Ballastone Inn ⭑⭑ This glamorous, inner-city B&B occupies a dignified 1838 building separated from the Juliette Gordon Low House (home of the founder of the Girl Scouts of America) by a formal garden; it's richly decorated with all the hardwoods, elaborate draperies, and antique furniture you'd expect. For a brief period (only long enough to add a hint of spiciness), the place functioned as a bordello *and* a branch office for the Girl Scouts (now next door).

There's an elevator, unusual for Savannah B&Bs, but no closets (they were taxed as extra rooms in the old days and so were never added); there are many unusual furnishings—cachepots filled with scented potpourri, and art objects—that would thrill the heart of any decorator. A full-service bar area is tucked into a corner of what was originally a double parlor. The four suites are in a clapboard town house a 5-minute walk away and staffed with live-in receptionists. Every unit has a well-maintained bathroom with a tub/shower combination. A yearlong refurbishment project in 1997 resulted in AAA four-diamond distinction.

14 E. Oglethorpe Ave., Savannah, GA 31401. ℂ **800/822-4553** or 912/236-1484. Fax 912/236-4626. www.ballastone.com. 16 units. $215–$375 double; $395 suite. Rates include full breakfast, afternoon tea, and evening hors d'oeuvres. AE, MC, V. Free parking. No children. **Amenities:** Breakfast room; lounge; spa treatments; all nonsmoking rooms. *In room:* A/C, TV, hair dryer, fireplace (in some).

The Gastonian ✦✦ One of the two or three posh B&Bs in Savannah, the Gastonian incorporates a pair of Italianate Regency buildings constructed in 1868 by the same unknown architect. Hard times began with the 1929 stock market crash—the buildings were divided into apartments for the payment of back taxes. In 1984, the Lineberger family, who were visiting from California, saw the place and fell in love with it. They poured $2 million into restoring it. Today everything is a testimonial to Victorian charm, except for a skillfully crafted serpentine bridge connecting the two buildings curving above a semitropical garden. The guest rooms are appropriately plush, comfortable, cozy, and beautifully furnished. Each unit comes with a well-kept bathroom with a tub/shower combination. The Gastonian has received the AAA's Four Diamond Award for excellence.

220 E. Gaston St., Savannah, GA 31401. (C) **800/322-6603** or 912/232-2869. Fax 912/232-0710. www.gastonian.com. 17 units. $195–$415 double; $395 suite. Rates include full breakfast. AE, DISC, MC, V. No children under 12. **Amenities:** Breakfast room; lounge; nonsmoking rooms. *In room:* A/C, TV, dataport, hair dryer.

Hamilton-Turner Inn 🐪🐪 In its way, this is one of the most noteworthy B&Bs in Savannah, boasting a unique (and sometimes bizarre) pedigree that's unlike any other in town. It was built for the then-astronomical price of $100,000 by a local power broker, Samuel Hamilton, in 1873. Mayor of Savannah, president of the Shriners, and owner of the local electrical company, the waterworks, the icehouse, and the town's biggest "fancy goods store," with a reputation as a blockade-runner during the Civil War, he was one of the inspirations for Margaret Mitchell's character of Rhett Butler in *Gone With the Wind.* His four-story French Empire house was almost obscenely ostentatious at the time, and today, with more than 10,000 square feet, it's the largest upscale B&B (in terms of square footage) in Savannah.

Most of the modern-day notoriety associated with this place came from its portrayal, in John Berendt's *Midnight in the Garden of Good and Evil,* as the party house of Savannah's favorite rakish twosome, Joe and Mandy Odom. Long after all that died down, in 1997, the building was acquired by native Savannahians Charles and Sue Strickland, who poured money and a strong dose of respectability back into the place, restoring it to a grandiose testimonial to a robber-baron's Gilded Age fortune in the Deep South. Guest rooms—most of them with 14-foot ceilings, fireplaces, and tub/shower combinations—are outfitted with Empire, Eastlake, and/or Renaissance Revival antiques and a kind of dignified, slightly chilly-looking grandeur. The staff, some remaining from the Joe and Mandy era, maintain a healthy perspective on the building's infamy and larger-than-life past. Breakfasts are full and prolonged Southern rituals, including everything from grits to quiche. An English-inspired high tea, served every afternoon from 4 to 5pm, is included in the price. In a radically different context from the much-battered and much-abused venue of yesteryear, this is now one of the few AAA Four Diamond Award B&Bs in Savannah.

330 Abercorn St., Savannah, GA 31401-4636. ℭ 888/448-8849 or 912/233-1833. www.hamilton-turnerinn.com. 17 units. $169–$358 double. Rates include full breakfast. Free parking. AE, DC, DISC, MC, V. **Amenities:** Breakfast room; all non-smoking rooms; 1 room for those w/limited mobility. *In room:* A/C, TV.

Kehoe House 𝖔𝖔𝖔   The Kehoe was built in 1892. In the 1950s, after the place had been converted into a funeral parlor, its owners tried to tear down the nearby Davenport House to build a parking lot. The resulting outrage led to the founding of the Historic Savannah Foundation and the salvation of most of the neighborhood's remaining historic buildings.

Today, the place functions as a spectacularly opulent B&B, with a collection of fabrics and furniture that's almost forbiddingly valuable. However, it lacks the warmth and welcome of the Ballastone. This isn't a place for children—the ideal guest will tread softly on floors that are considered models of historic authenticity and flawless taste. Breakfast and afternoon tea are part of the ritual that has seduced such clients as Tom Hanks, who stayed in room 301 during the filming of *Forrest Gump*. Guest rooms are spacious, with the typical 12-foot ceilings. Each is tastefully furnished in English period antiques and equipped with a well-kept bathroom containing a tub/shower combination. Owners Rob and Jane Sales and Kathy Medlock acquired the Kehoe in 1997 and immediately renovated the back garden and expanded the guest parking area. Amenities include a concierge and twice-daily maid service with turndown.

123 Habersham St., Savannah, GA 31401. ℭ 800/820-1020 or 912/232-1020. Fax 912/231-0208. www.kehoehouse.com. 13 units. $179–$295 double; $275–$325 suite. Rates include full breakfast, evening tea, and hors d'oeuvres. AE, DISC, MC, V. **Amenities:** Breakfast room; lounge; all nonsmoking rooms; rooms for those w/limited mobility. *In room:* A/C, TV, dataport, hair dryer.

Magnolia Place Inn 𝖔   This building was begun in 1878 on a desirable plot overlooking Forsyth Square and completed 4 years later by a family who'd been forced off their upriver plantation after the Civil War for nonpayment of taxes. A forebear had represented South Carolina at the signing of the Declaration of Independence, and so the Second Empire ("steamboat Gothic") house was designed to be as grand as funds would allow. The result includes the most endearing front steps in town (Neiman Marcus once asked to display them as a backdrop for one of its catalogs), verandas worthy of a Mississippi steamer, and an oval skylight (an "oculus") that illuminates a graceful staircase ascending to the dignified guest rooms. Each contains a beautifully maintained bathroom with tub/shower combination.

503 Whitaker St., Savannah, GA 31401. © 800/238-7674 outside Georgia, or 912/236-7674. Fax 912/236-1145. www.magnoliaplaceinn.com. 13 units. $185–$295 double. Rates include full breakfast, afternoon tea, and evening hors d'oeuvres. AE, DC, DISC, MC, V. Free parking. No children under 12. **Amenities:** Breakfast room; lounge; Jacuzzi; breakfast-only room service. *In room:* A/C, TV, hair dryer.

EXPENSIVE

Azalea Inn   The furnishings of this B&B are a bit richer, its colors a bit more evocative, and its decor more appealingly cluttered than those of many of its nearby competitors. The setting is a circa 1889 Italianate house less than 2 blocks east of Forsyth Park, within a garden that has a swimming pool. It was originally built for Capt. Walter Coney, an army officer whose fortune derived from a then-flourishing maritime supply company. Guest rooms are furnished with period antiques, and each comes with a different Victorian-era decor. Especially appealing is the Gentleman's Parlor, a ground-floor guest room once dominated by men discussing manly things, which still carries a hint of the bourbon and cigars consumed liberally within its confines. More frilly and feminine is the Magnolia Room, where white walls offset a four-poster bed with upholsteries depicting—you guessed it—magnolia blossoms. Newest of all is the Captain's Room, with a massive four-poster and a newly built deck overlooking the swimming pool. Some of the guest rooms have fireplaces, and all have bathrooms, most of them with showers. A hand-painted mural on the wall of the dining room—site of morning breakfasts—depicts the history of Savannah. There's usually someone on hand to deliver a cold or warm (nonalcoholic) drink, depending on the season, to guests whenever one is needed.

217 E. Huntingdon St., Savannah, GA 31401. © 800/582-3823 or 912/236-2707. www.azaleainn.com. 9 units. $160–$260 double. Rates include full breakfast. MC, V. No children under 12. **Amenities:** Outdoor pool; nonsmoking rooms. *In room:* A/C, TV, hair dryer, iron/ironing board.

Catherine Ward House Inn   *Finds*   The restoration of this house has won several civic awards, and it's so evocative of Savannah's "carpenter Gothic" Victorian revival that Clint Eastwood inserted a long, graceful shot of its exterior in *Midnight in the Garden of Good and Evil.* Built by a sea captain for his wife (Catherine Ward) in 1886, a short walk from Forsyth Park, it offers one of the most lavishly decorated interiors of any B&B in Savannah, but at prices significantly lower than those offered at better-known B&Bs

a few blocks away. Alan Williams, the owner and innkeeper, maintains a policy that discourages children under 16 and that stresses a gay-friendly but even-handed approach to a diverse clientele. Breakfast is relatively elaborate, served on fine porcelain in a grandly outfitted dining room. A garden in back encourages languid, sun-dappled conversation. Each midsize guest room is richly decorated and equipped with a well-kept bathroom with a tub/shower combination.

118 E. Waldburg St., Savannah, GA 31401. (✆ 912/234-8564. Fax 912/231-8007. www.catherinewardhouseinn.com. 10 units. $149–$335 double. Rates include full breakfast. DISC, MC, V. **Amenities:** Breakfast room; lounge; tennis courts (nearby); laundry service/dry cleaning; nonsmoking rooms. *In room:* A/C, TV, dataport, hair dryer.

East Bay Inn ☆

Though the views from its windows might be uninspired, the East Bay is conveniently located near the bars and attractions of the riverfront. It was built in 1853 as a cotton warehouse; green awnings and potted geraniums disguise the building's once-utilitarian design. A cozy lobby contains Chippendale furnishings and elaborate moldings. The guest rooms have queen-size four-poster beds, reproductions of antiques, and neatly kept bathrooms with tub/shower combinations. The hotel frequently houses tour groups from Europe and South America. In the cellar is **Skyler's** (✆ 912/232-3955), an independently managed restaurant specializing in European and Asian cuisine.

225 E. Bay St., Savannah, GA 31401. (✆ 800/500-1225 or 912/238-1225. Fax 912/232-2709. www.eastbayinn.com. 28 units. $149–$210 double. Rates include continental breakfast. AE, DC, DISC, MC, V. **Amenities:** Breakfast room; nonsmoking rooms. *In room:* A/C, TV, dataport, coffeemaker, hair dryer, iron/ironing board, safe, bathrobes.

Eliza Thompson House ☆☆

Many newer and less well-funded B&Bs attempt to re-create this inn's patina of historicity (around 1847), often with less success. It's set on a distinguished tree-lined street whose weather-beaten cobblestones demonstrate their long-ago craftsmanship. The wrought-iron accents and meticulously maintained details of its shutter-accented façade imply enormous care on the part of its owners. And inside, high ceilings, elaborate cove moldings, and well-chosen antiques imply a mixture of genteel propriety and discreetly romantic potential. Historical references abound within rich but understated interiors, and decorator wannabes often salivate at the ideas they garner for historic projects of their own. About half the rooms in the stately-looking inn are within the main house; the remainder lie within a much-restored and very tasteful building in back that was originally conceived as a stable and carriage house. Linking the two buildings is one of the largest and most lavishly landscaped courtyards in the city's historic core. In the words of a writer from *Georgia Magazine*, "Like its namesake, the Eliza Thompson House is a hospitable hostess."

5 W. Jones St., Savannah, GA 31401. ℂ **912/236-3620.** Fax 912/238-1920. www.elizathompsonhouse.com. 25 units. $149–$269 double. Rates include continental breakfast. AE, DC, DISC, MC, V. **Amenities:** Breakfast room; lounge; nonsmoking rooms. *In room:* A/C, TV, dataport, hair dryer, iron/ironing board, bathrobes.

Foley House Inn ⟨⟩   Decorated with all the care of a private home, this small B&B occupies a brick-sided house built in 1896. Its owners doubled its size by acquiring the simpler white-fronted house next door, whose pedigree predates its neighbors by half a century. Guest rooms are neatly furnished and contain well-kept bathrooms with tub/shower combinations. The staff will regale you with tales of the original residents of both houses—one was a notorious turn-of-the-century suicide. Breakfast and afternoon hors d'oeuvres, tea, and cordials are served in a large, verdant space formed by the two houses' connected gardens.

The inn is the recipient of the AAA's Four Diamonds Award and has been featured on HGTV's "Great Homes Across America." Enjoy home-baked sweets every afternoon in the lounge; wine and homemade appetizers are served from 5:30 to 6:30pm.

14 W. Hull St., Savannah, GA 31401. ℂ **800/647-3708** or 912/232-6622. Fax 912/231-1218. www.foleyinn.com. 18 units. $200–$345 double. Rates include full breakfast, afternoon hors d'oeuvres, tea, and cordials. AE, MC, V. No children under 12. **Amenities:** Breakfast room; laundry service; nonsmoking rooms. *In room:* A/C, TV, dataport, hair dryer, safe, Jacuzzi (in some).

Hilton Savannah DeSoto ⟨⟩   The name still evokes a bit of glamour—built in 1890, this hotel was for generations the city's grandest. In 1967, thousands of wedding receptions, Kiwanis meetings, and debutante parties later, the building was demolished and rebuilt in a bland modern format. It's a well-managed commercial hotel, renovated by new owners in 1995. The guest rooms are conservatively modern and reached after registering in a stone-sheathed lobby whose decor was partly inspired by an 18th-century Colonial drawing room. All units contain well-maintained bathrooms with tub/shower combinations. Despite the absence of antique charm, many guests like this place for its polite efficiency and modernism.

15 E. Liberty St. (P.O. Box 8207), Savannah, GA 31412. ℂ **800/426-8483** or 912/232-9000. Fax 912/232-6018. www.hilton.com. 246 units. $99–$279 double. AE, DC, DISC, MC, V. **Amenities:** 2 restaurants; bar; pool; fitness center; limited room service;

massage; babysitting; laundry service/dry cleaning; nonsmoking rooms; rooms for those w/limited mobility. *In room:* A/C, TV, dataport, hair dryer, iron/ironing board.

The Mulberry Inn *(Kids*
Locals point with pride to the Mulberry as a sophisticated adaptation of what might've been a derelict building into a surprisingly elegant hotel. Built in 1868 as a stable and cotton warehouse, it was converted in 1982 into a simple hotel, and in the 1990s it received a radical upgrade and a dash of decorator-inspired Chippendale glamour. Today, its lobby looks like that of a grand hotel in London, and the guest rooms, though small, have a formal decor (think English country house with a Southern accent). Each unit includes a well-kept bathroom with a tub/shower combination. The hotel's brick-covered patio, with fountains, trailing ivy, and wrought-iron furniture, evokes the best aspects of New Orleans.

601 E. Bay St., Savannah, GA 31401. © **877/468-1200** or 912/238-1200. Fax 912/236-2184. www.savannahhotel.com. 145 units. $179–$269 double; $229–$269 suite. Children under 18 stay free in parent's room. AE, DC, DISC, MC, V. Parking $8. **Amenities:** Restaurant; lounge; outdoor pool; fitness center; Jacuzzi; children's activities; limited room service; nonsmoking rooms; rooms for those w/limited mobility. *In room:* A/C, TV, dataport, fridge, microwave, coffeemaker, hair dryer, iron/ironing board, safe.

Olde Georgian Inn *(Finds*
Small-scale, with a vivid sense that you're a paying guest in the carefully furnished home of a family devoted to Old South nostalgia, this B&B occupies a clapboard-sided Victorian house built in 1890. Set within 2 blocks of the western flank of Forsyth Park, behind a bow-fronted facade adorned with intricate decorative detailing, it's loaded with a sense of Victorian propriety, graced with an occasional tribute to works by African-American artists, and flooded with sunlight from big windows. Guest rooms have heart pine floors and a mixture of 19th- or early-20th-century antiques and latter-day reproductions. Each guest room has a fireplace, all have showers, and about half have tub/shower combinations. If you have pets, children under 12, or the propensity to carouse late into the night, consider a stay in the carriage house, since none of those things are tolerated within the main house. The carriage house contains a loft bedroom with a queen-size four-poster bed and access to a private rooftop deck. It also offers its own washer and dryer, a kitchen, and a living area downstairs with a queen-size pullout sofa bed along with a half-bathroom.

212 W. Hall St., Savannah, GA 31401-5521. © **800/835-6831** or 912/236-2911. www.oldegeorgianinn.com. 4 units, 1 carriage house. $145–$195 double; $175–$225 carriage house. Rates include full breakfast. AE, MC, V. **Amenities:** Breakfast room; all nonsmoking rooms. *In room:* A/C, TV, fireplace.

Whitaker-Huntington Inn 🏛 Dignified and permeated with a sense of decency and Southern honor, this house was built in 1883 for a member of the eight-member Confederate delegation that had surrendered the city of Savannah to General Sherman in December 1864. Later, a local cotton merchant who served a 4-year term as the city's mayor owned it. In 1923, the doctor who was using the house as the base for his medical practice added an all-brick addition onto the house's backside. Today, the much-restored interior boasts 12-foot ceilings, period antiques, Oriental carpets, and pine floors—all of it gracefully arranged for a look that's faithful to the original decorative theme but a lot more comfortable than it was in the building's original days. Each of the three units is a two-bedroom suite, each with at least one bathroom (one unit has two), and two of them with kitchenettes. All units are equipped with tub/shower combinations. There's also a resident ghost.

601 Whitaker St., Savannah, GA 31401-5543. 📞 **877/232-8911** or 912/232-8911. Fax 912/234-1540. www.whinn.com. 4 units. $125–$275 double. Rates include continental breakfast. AE, DISC, MC, V. **Amenities:** Breakfast room; laundry service; all nonsmoking rooms. *In room:* TV, dataport, kitchenette, coffeemaker, iron/ironing board.

MODERATE

Days Inn & Suites Historic District *Value* One of the best and most affordable deals for those seeking a central location in the historic core is this seven-story modern chain-run hotel; it is much better than your typical Days Inn, which can be quite dreary. The hotel lies in an attractive area of live Georgia oaks between River Street and the Old City Market, convenient to many attractions. Many of Savannah's best-known restaurants, such as The Olde Pink House, lie within a short walk. Guest rooms are midsize and attractively and comfortably furnished, each with a first-rate bathroom with tub/shower combination. Guests from all over the world meet each other at the cafe/coffee shop on-site or else around the pool. For those willing to spend extra money, several spacious apartment suites are available.

201 W. Bay St., Savannah, GA 31491. 📞 **912/236-4400.** Fax 912/232-2725. www.daysinn.com. 314 units. $62–$90 double; $102–$150 suite. AE, DC, DISC, MC, V. Free parking. **Amenities:** Cafe/coffee shop; outdoor pool; health club privileges; room service (7am–noon). *In room:* A/C, TV, kitchenettes in some.

The Forsyth Park Inn 🏛 One of the grandest houses on the western flank of Forsyth Park is this yellow frame place built in the 1890s by a sea captain (Aaron Flynt, aka Rudder Churchill). A richly detailed staircase winds upstairs from a paneled vestibule, and the Queen Anne decor of the formal robin's-egg-blue salon extends through the rest of the house. Guest rooms have oak paneling and oversize doors that are testimonials to turn-of-the-century craftsmanship. The more expensive rooms, including one in what used to be the dining room, are among the largest in town. All units contain well-kept bathrooms with tub/shower combinations. Home-baked breads and pastries are breakfast staples. Don't expect frivolity: The inn is just a bit staid.

102 W. Hall St., Savannah, GA 31401. ℭ **912/233-6800.** Fax 912/233-6804. www.forsythparkinn.com. 11 units, 1 cottage with kitchenette. $130–$225 double; $185 cottage. Rates include full breakfast. AE, DISC, MC, V. **Amenities:** Breakfast room; lounge; nonsmoking rooms. *In room:* A/C, TV, bathrobes.

Gaston Gallery Bed & Breakfast   This major investment in period restoration was built as two separate houses united by a shared Italianate facade. In 1997, a lavish reunification of the two houses was undertaken. Today, the unified building bears the distinction of having the city's longest and most stately front porch (called a gallery in Savannah) and inner ceilings that are almost dizzyingly high. Each unit is beautifully furnished and is equipped with a well-maintained bathroom containing a tub/shower combination. The breakfasts are social events, each featuring a different dish each day, like curried eggs or Southern grits casserole. Wine and cheese are served every day at 5pm or upon your arrival, according to your wishes.

211 E. Gaston St., Savannah, GA 31401. ℭ **800/671-0716** or 912/238-3294. Fax 912/238-4064. www.gastongallery.com. 15 units. $90–$175 double. AE, DISC, MC, V. **Amenities:** Breakfast room; lounge; nonsmoking rooms; 1 room for those w/limited mobility. *In room:* TV, fireplace (in some), ceiling fans.

Hampton Inn Historic District ⰲ *Kids*   This is the most appealing of the city's middle-bracket large-scale hotels. Opened in 1997, it rises seven redbrick stories above the busy traffic of historic Bay Street, across from Savannah's Riverwalk and some of the city's most animated nightclubs. Its big-windowed lobby was designed to mimic an 18th-century Savannah salon, thanks to the recycling of heart pine flooring from an old sawmill in central Georgia and the use of antique Savannah bricks. Comfortably formal seating arrangements, a blazing fireplace, and an antique bar add cozy touches. The guest rooms are simple and comfortable, with flowered upholstery, wall-to-wall carpeting, and medium-size tiled bathrooms with tub/shower combinations. On the roof are a small pool and sun deck supplemented by an exercise room on the seventh floor. There's no restaurant, but many eateries are a short walk away.

201 E. Bay St., Savannah, GA. ℭ **800/426-7866** or 912/232-9700. Fax 912/ 231-0440. www.hampton-inn.com. 144 units. $140–$210 double. AE, DC, DISC, MC, V. Parking $8. **Amenities:** Breakfast room; lounge; rooftop pool; laundry service/dry cleaning; nonsmoking rooms; rooms for those w/limited mobility. *In room:* A/C, TV, dataport, coffeemaker, hair dryer, iron/ironing board.

The Marshall House   Some aspects of this hotel—especially the second-story cast-iron veranda that juts above the sidewalk—might remind you of a 19th-century hotel in the French Quarter of New Orleans. It originally opened in 1851 as the then-finest hotel in Savannah. In 1864-65, it functioned as a Union Army hospital, before housing such luminaries as Conrad Aiken and Joel Chandler Harris, author of *Stories of Uncle Remus.* After a ratty-looking decline, it closed—some people thought permanently—in 1957. In 1999, it reopened as a "boutique-style" inn. Despite the fact that this place has some of the trappings of an upscale B&B, don't think that it will provide the intimacy or exclusivity of, say, the Foley House. There's something a bit superficial about the glamour here, and some aspects evoke a busy motel, albeit with Colonial-era reproductions in the public areas that are more elegant than usual. Guest rooms succeed at being mass-production-style cozy without being particularly opulent. Each is sheathed in one of three standardized possibilities: yellow with pinewood furniture, green with wrought-iron furniture, and blue with white-painted furniture. Seven of the largest and most historically evocative rooms in the hotel are on the second floor, overlooking noisy Broughton Street, and are prefaced with wrought-iron verandas with wrought-iron furniture. All rooms contain neatly kept bathrooms with shower units. The bar contains exposed brick, green leather upholstery, and a very Southern clientele. The 45 Bistro, set beneath the glassed-in roof of what used to be the hotel's rear stable yard, is a restaurant serving Southern and international cuisine.

123 E. Broughton St., Savannah, GA 31401. ℭ **800/589-6304** or 912/644-7896. Fax 912/234-3334. www.marshallhouse.com. 68 units. $169–$189 double; $199–$219 suite. AE, DC, DISC, MC, V. Rates include continental breakfast at 45 Bistro. **Amenities:** Restaurant; bar; nonsmoking rooms. *In room:* A/C, TV, hair dryer.

Park Avenue Manor   Historic and cozy, this is Savannah's premier gay-friendly guesthouse. An 1897 Victorian B&B, it has an old-fashioned charm with antiques, double staircases, two formal parlors, and angel ceiling borders. Many accommodations have four-poster beds with antiques, silk carpets, porcelains, working fireplaces, and period prints. All units contain neatly kept bathrooms with shower units. The small-scale inn has a well-rehearsed management style and an emphasis on irreverently offbeat Savannah. Many straight clients also book here, as the place is noted not only for its comfort but for its warm welcome and one of the best Southern breakfasts served in town. The guesthouse was created in 1997, when a pair of Victorian houses were "sewn" together into a tasteful whole. A favorite is the Robert E. Lee Room with a large bay window.

107–109 W. Park Ave., Savannah, GA 31401. ℂ 912/233-0352. 4 units. $99–$125 double; $170 suite. MC, V. **Amenities:** Breakfast room; lounge; tennis courts (nearby); nonsmoking rooms. *In room:* A/C, TV, hair dryer, no phone.

Planters Inn   This small European-style inn is more businesslike than the average Savannah B&B. Built adjacent to Reynolds Square in 1912 as a seven-story brown brick tower, it boasts a lobby with elaborate millwork, a scattering of Chippendale reproductions, and an honor bar (sign for whatever drink you consume). The guest rooms are comfortably outfitted with four-poster beds and flowery fabrics; they're rather dignified and formal. Each unit contains a neatly kept bathroom with a tub/shower combination. The Planters Inn is not associated with the well-recommended Planters Tavern (which stands next door and is separate).

29 Abercorn St., Savannah, GA 31401. ℂ **800/554-1187** or 912/232-5678. Fax 912/232-8893. www.plantersinnsavannah.com. 59 units. $115–$195 double. Rates include continental breakfast. AE, DC, MC, V. Parking $6.95. **Amenities:** Breakfast room; lounge; nonsmoking rooms. *In room:* A/C, TV, dataport, coffeemaker, hair dryer.

The President's Quarters Inn ★★   This inn has many appealing aspects. The guest rooms and bathrooms (each with a tub/shower combination) are among the largest and most comfortable of any inn in Savannah. The inn manages to combine the charm of a B&B with the efficiency of a much larger place. It has appealed to guests as diverse as the former president of Ireland and numbers of Hollywood actors. Each unit is named after a U.S. president who visited Savannah during his term in office.

225 E. President St., Savannah, GA 31401. ℂ **888/592-1812** or 912/233-1600. Fax 912/238-0849. www.presidentsquarters.com. 19 units. $137–$167 double; $187–$235 suite. Rates include breakfast. AE, DISC, MC, V. Free parking on premises. **Amenities:** Lounge; limited room service. *In room:* A/C, TV, dataport, hair dryer, fridge, bathrobes, fireplace.

17 Hundred 90 ★   The oldest inn in Savannah is located within a small but dignified clapboard-sided house built in the year that gave the establishment its name. Reminiscent of the kind of clapboard-sided sea captain's house you might have expected in New England, this is a cozy, personalized, and charming inn decorated to emulate a well-appointed private home. There's a fireplace in 11 of the 13 smallish but charming guest rooms. The sounds of conversation and laughter emanate from a basement-level restaurant with a beamed ceiling and the exposed original brickwork, giving you the vivid sense that the inn is also a hardworking, sometimes harddrinking bar and restaurant frequented by locals as well as visitors. The staff isn't shy about referring to a resident ghost, the unhappy victim of an early 19th-century love affair that ended in suicide. Rich in associations of both requited and unrequited love, it's the kind of place that encourages romantic fancies and attachments, hopefully to the person you brought with you. The inn is run by The Presidents Quarters, to which all calls are directed.

307 E. President St., Savannah, GA 31401. ℭ **877/468-1200** or 912/238-1200. Fax 912/236-2184. www.17hundred90.com. 14 units. $129–$169 double. Rates include full breakfast. AE, MC, V. **Amenities:** Restaurant; bar; limited room service; nonsmoking rooms. *In room:* A/C, TV, dataport, minibar, coffeemaker, hair dryer.

INEXPENSIVE

Bed & Breakfast Inn ⊀ *Value* Adjacent to Chatham Square, in the oldest part of historic Savannah, this is a dignified stone-fronted town house built in 1853. You climb a gracefully curved front stoop to reach the cool, high-ceilinged interior, outfitted with a combination of antique and reproduction furniture. All of the good-size comfortable and tastefully furnished units contain well-kept bathrooms with tub/shower combinations. There's no smoking.

117 W. Gordon St. (at Chatham Sq.), Savannah, GA 31401. ℭ **888/238-0518** or 912/238-0518. Fax 912/233-2537. www.savannahbnb.com. 18 units. $89–$169 double. Rates include full breakfast. AE, DISC, MC, V. **Amenities:** Breakfast room; lounge; nonsmoking rooms. *In room:* A/C, TV, hair dryer, iron/ironing board, fireplaces (in some).

Courtyard Savannah Historic District ⊀ *Value* One of the newest places at which to stay in the Historic District, this well-run chain hotel stands across from the visitor center and enjoys one of the town's best locations. Its spacious guest rooms are spread across five floors and are comfortably furnished and well-equipped, though with the aura of a first-class motel. Bathrooms are tiled and midsize, each with a tub/shower combination. The desk staff is helpful in directing you to the best sports nearby, including golf courses and even horseback riding and jet-skiing. They will also advise you on the best restaurants in Savannah, many of which lie within walking distance of the front door. On-site is The Courtyard Café, serving American-style cuisine at breakfast and again at dinnertime.

415 W. Liberty St., Savannah, GA 31401. © **800/321-2211** or 912/790-8287. Fax 912/790-8288. 158 units. $139–$169 double; $169 suite. AE, DC, MC, V. Parking $10. **Amenities:** Restaurant; bar; outdoor pool; whirlpool; fitness center; nonsmoking rooms; rooms for those w/limited mobility. *In room:* A/C, TV, dataport, coffeemaker, hair dryer, iron/ironing board.

Fairfield Inn by Marriott   Not quite as good as Marriott's other recommended motel (above), this reliable budget hotel offers standard but comfortably appointed guest rooms, with large, well-lit desks and well-kept bathrooms containing tub/shower combinations. Health-club privileges are available nearby, as are several good moderately priced restaurants.

2 Lee Blvd. (at Abercorn Rd.), Savannah, GA 31405. © **800/228-2800** or 912/353-7100. www.marriott.com. 135 units. $59–$109 double. Rates include continental breakfast. Children 17 and under stay free in parent's room. AE, DC, DISC, MC, V. Free parking. From I-16, take exit 34A to I-516 East, then turn right on Abercorn St. and go right again on Lee Blvd. **Amenities:** Breakfast room; lounge; outdoor pool; nonsmoking rooms; rooms for those w/limited mobility. *In room:* A/C, TV, dataport, coffeemaker, hair dryer, iron/ironing board.

2 Nearby Hotels & Inns

MODERATE

Baymont Inn & Suites   This motor lodge, one of the best in the Savannah area, appeals to motorists drawn to its location 6 miles from historic Bay Street in the Southside district. The location is also convenient for day trips to Hilton Head, lying only 18 miles to the north. A modern three-story structure, the inn offers attractively furnished and good-sized guest rooms, with bathrooms containing tub/shower combinations. Each room features such extras as ergonomic chairs, free bottled water, and free cable TV, with pay-for-view movies and Nintendo. Many families visiting relatives at the adjacent Hunter Army Airfield lodge here. Several affordable restaurants are nearby, but the hotel staff fills you up with complimentary morning treats such as waffles and French toast before you head out for the day. The hotel has such features as a senior discount program, interior-corridor room entrances, free local calls, and 24-hour staffed front desk and switchboard personnel.

8484 Abercorn St., Savannah, GA 31406. © **912/927-7600.** Fax 912/927-6392. www.baymontinn.com. 103 units. $55 double. Rates include continental breakfast. Children under 18 stay free in parent's room. AE, DC, DISC, MC, V. **Amenities:** Outdoor pool; nonsmoking rooms; rooms for those w/limited mobility. *In room:* A/C, TV, coffeemaker, hair dryer, iron/ironing board.

Clubhouse Inn & Suites ✿ 𝒱𝑎𝑙𝑢𝑒   One of the better deals in Savannah, this newly renovated property, with its upgraded decor and furnishings, offers first-class comfort but charges moderate prices. Guest rooms are large and well-furnished. The suites don't cost a lot more, so these upgraded and oversized units may be the way to go. To make the suites even more attractive, a small kitchenette is included in each, with such extras as a microwave, dishware, and utensils for cooking light meals. Each unit comes with a tiled bathroom with tub/shower combination.

Many of the guest rooms open onto balconies. A generous buffet breakfast, complete with such Southern favorites as biscuits and gravy, along with plenty of pancakes, bacon, and sausage, greets guests every morning. A Club Lounge overlooks an outdoor courtyard and pool area.

6800 Abercorn St., Savannah, GA 31405. © **800/258-2466** or 912/356-1234. www.clubhouseinn.com. 138 units. $74–$84 double; $89–$99 suite. Rates include buffet breakfast. Children under 18 stay free in parent's room. AE, DC, DISC, MC, V. **Amenities:** Outdoor pool; health club privileges; business services; 24-hr. free coffee and tea; coin laundry. *In room:* A/C, TV, dataport, kitchenette in suite, hair dryer, iron/ironing board.

Homewood Suites by Hilton   Built in 1990 about a 6-mile drive south of Savannah's historic core, this is a blandly modern member of a nationwide chain, wherein each unit is a suite with either one or two bedrooms. Favored by business travelers who sometimes opt to stay in larger-than-usual quarters on extended business trips, it occupies a commercial neighborhood with suburban-style traffic and plenty of nearby restaurants and shopping malls. An evening cocktail party, hosted by the manager, takes the edge off the sense of anonymity that sometimes prevails here, but if you're looking for space to move around within a modern, uncontroversial setting, this place might be fine for you. Each unit, regardless of its size, has a fully equipped kitchen with a microwave, full-size refrigerator, and cooking utensils. Bathrooms are tiled, each with a tub/shower combination.

5820 White Bluff Rd., Savannah, GA 31405-5523. © **912/353-8500.** Fax 912/354-3821. www.homewood-suites.com. 106 units. $109–$169 double. AE, DC, DISC, MC, V. **Amenities:** Restaurant; pool; gym; Jacuzzi; all nonsmoking rooms. *In room:* A/C, TV, kitchen, hair dryer, iron/ironing board.

Master's Inn Suites, Savannah Midtown   If it's raining hard, and if every inn in the city's historic core is fully booked, and if you have no other option, you might stay in this modern hotel, built in

1983, where you can sustain life in between the visits you'll make, 7 miles north, to Historic Savannah. Each unit is divided by a lattice into a sleeping area and, on its other side, a sitting area where there's a small refrigerator, a coffeemaker, and a microwave—a somewhat uninspired setup which isn't by anyone's evaluation a genuine "suite," despite the large signs on the building's exterior advertising accommodations as such. Guest rooms have either two double beds or a king-size bed. Bathrooms are modern, tiled, and motel-style in their design, each with a tub/shower combination. At the center of the hotel is a glass-roofed atrium with a scattering of plants, and outside in the garden is a swimming pool.

7110 Hodgson Memorial Dr. Savannah, GA 31406. © **912/354-8560.** Fax 912/356-1438. www.mastersinn.com. 51 units. $90–$225 double. Rates include continental breakfast. AE, DC, DISC, MC, V. **Amenities:** Pool; gym; Jacuzzi; sauna; 24-hr. room service; laundry/dry cleaning; nonsmoking rooms; rooms for those w/limited mobility;. *In room:* A/C, TV, dataport, fridge, microwave, coffeemaker, hair dryer, iron/ironing board.

Wingate Inn   This is one of the newer and more comfortable hotels in the shopping-mall zone south of Savannah. Although the distance to the city's historic core is about 8 miles, part of the transit is via interstate highways, sometimes (if traffic is light) only about 18 minutes away. Built in a four-story brick-and-stucco format in 1999, with a bit of architectural flair, the inn offers comfortable, family-friendly rooms outfitted with modern furniture that carries no pretensions of Southern Colonial plantation life. (This might be a relief after too heavy a dose of that style in other modern hotels nearby.) Each unit has a modern-looking bathroom with a tub/shower combination, in some cases with whirlpool jets.

11 Gateway Blvd. E., Savannah, GA 31419. © **912/925-2525.** Fax 912/925-7904. 101 units. $69–$129 double. Rates include continental breakfast. AE, DC, DISC, MC, V. **Amenities:** Pool; gym; spa; Jacuzzi; nonsmoking rooms; rooms for those w/limited mobility. *In room:* A/C, TV, dataport; kitchenette, fridge, microwave, coffeemaker, hair dryer, iron, safe.

6

Where to Dine in Savannah

Savannah is known for the excellence of its seafood restaurants. They're among the best in Georgia, rivaled only by those in Atlanta. The best dining is in the Historic District, along River Street, bordering the water. However, locals also like to escape the city and head for the seafood places on Tybee and other offshore islands.

Some of Savannah's restaurants, like **Elizabeth on 37th,** are ranked among the finest in the South. And others, like **Mrs. Wilkes' Dining Room,** are places to go for real Southern fare—from collard greens and fried okra to fried chicken, corn bread, and hot biscuits.

1 Along or Near the Riverfront

EXPENSIVE

The Chart House Ⓕ STEAK/SEAFOOD Overlooking the Savannah River and Riverfront Plaza, "the home of the mud pie" is part of a nationwide chain—and one of the better ones. It's housed in a building that predates 1790, reputed to be the oldest masonry structure in Georgia and once a sugar-and-cotton warehouse. You can enjoy a view of passing ships on the outside deck, perhaps ordering an appetizer and a drink before dinner. The bar is one of the most atmospheric along the riverfront. As in all Chart Houses, the prime rib is slow-roasted and served au jus. The steaks from corn-fed beef are aged and hand-cut on the premises before being charcoal-grilled. The most expensive item is lobster. You may prefer one of the fresh catches of the day, which can be grilled to your specifications.

202 W. Bay St. Ⓒ **912/234-6686.** Reservations recommended. Main courses $22–$40. AE, DC, DISC, MC, V. Mon–Fri 5–10pm; Sat 5–10:30pm; Sun 5–9pm.

River House Seafood Ⓕ SEAFOOD/AMERICAN Try for a view of the river if one of the tables is available. Sometimes they aren't, as this place seats some 250 patrons on a busy night in one of its four dining rooms with exposed brick. The restaurant is installed in an 1850 antebellum King Cotton warehouse which has been successfully converted. As you dig into the homemade bread, baked

Where to Dine in Savannah

Savannah River

W. River St.
Factors' Walk
W. Bay St.
Franklin Square
W. Bryan St. Ellis Square
Johnson Square
Reynolds Square
W. Congress St.
W. Broughton St.
Zulby St.
W. State St.
President Telfair Square St.
Wright Square
Oglethorpe Square
Columbia Square
Greene Square President St.
Grey-hound Station
W. York St.
W. York St.
E. York St.
W. Oglethorpe Ave.
E. Oglethorpe Ave.
Elbert Square
Civic Center
Orleans Square
Chippewa Square
W. Hull St.
Colonial Park Cemetery
E. Hull St.
Crawford Square
W. Perry St.
Perry La.
E. Perry St.
W. Liberty St.
E. Liberty St.
Louisville Rd.
W. Harris St.
Pulaski Square
Madison Square
Lafayette Square
Troup Square
E. Harris St.
W. Charlton St.
E. Charlton St.
W. Jones St.
E. Jones St.
Atlanta ★ GEORGIA Savannah
Chatham Square
Monterrey Square
W. Taylor St.
Calhoun Square
Whitfield Square
E. Taylor St.
W. Gordon St.
E. Gordon St.
W. Gaston St.
Forsyth Park
E. Gaston St.

Factors' Walk
E. River St.
Emmet Park
E. Bay St.
E. Bryan St.
Warren Square
Washington Square
E. Congress St.
E. Broughton St.
E. State St.

Barnes Restaurant **24**
Belford's **6**
Bistro Savannah **4**
Café at City Market **7**
Casbah **16**
The Chart House **9**
Clary's Café **23**
Dockside Seafood Restaurant
  & Steakhouse **10**
Elizabeth on 37th **25**
45 South **19**
Garibaldi's **5**
Gottlieb's Restaurant
  and Dessert Bar **14**
Huey's **1**
Il Pasticcio **15**
Johnny Harris Restaurant **26**

The Lady & Sons **2**
Moon River Brewing Company **13**
Mrs. Wilkes' Dining Room **22**
Musashi **24**
The Olde Pink House Restaurant **17**
Pearl's Saltwater Grille **26**
The River Grill **11**
River House Seafood **12**
Sapphire Grill **8**
Savannah Steak House **3**
Seasons in Savannah **6**
17 Hundred 90 **20**
Shrimp Factory **18**
Toucan Café **24**
Tubby's Tank House **1**
Wall's **21**

61

right on the premises, you can watch local and merchant ships go by. There is a freshness to all the dishes, which are full of flavor. Daily specials supplement the regular menu items.

Many patrons drop in for lunch to sample some of the best sandwiches in town, from an oyster po'boy to a barbecued chicken club. At night the repertoire broadens with such offerings as a delectable lobster bisque with crab as an appetizer, or else one dozen fresh oysters—steamed or raw. Main courses, which come with a house Caesar salad, include our favorites—blackened mahimahi with four pepper herbs, or a shrimp-and-oyster combo. We are especially impressed with one dish—chicken breast Marsala sautéed with shitake mushrooms and served with demi-glaze buttermilk whipped potatoes.

125 W. River St. ✆ 912/234-1900. Reservations advised. Lunch sandwiches $8.25–$11. Lunch specials $9.50–$11. Dinner main courses $23–$29. AE, DC, DISC, MC, V. Mon–Thurs 11am–10pm; Fri–Sat 11am–11pm.

MODERATE

Bistro Savannah ✿✿ SOUTHERN FUSION   This is the most eclectic bistro in town, attracting serious Savannah foodies. Count on something different every night. Cajun and Southern cuisine we're used to, but how many chefs prepare a Southern cuisine with Thai overtones? Some readers of the Zagat Survey have hailed this bistro as the number-one restaurant in Georgia, but that's going too far in enthusiasm. The chef makes the best coastal seafood bouillabaisse in town, and he excels in other specialties as well, namely crisp pecan chicken with blackberry bourbon sauce, one of the delights of Southern cuisine. On different occasions we've been impressed with the barbecued black grouper and the crispy roast duck with Bing cherries and orange marmalade, each dish perfectly seasoned. Naturally, being from Savannah, the cooks excel at shrimp 'n' grits. The atmosphere is cozy with exposed brick and comfortable seating, along with some of the best service in town.

309 W. Congress St. ✆ 912/233-6266. Reservations required. Main courses $15–$24. AE, MC, V. Sun–Thurs 5:30-10:30pm; Fri–Sat 5:30–11pm.

Huey's ✿ CAJUN/CREOLE   At first glance, this casual place overlooking the Savannah River seems little different from the other restored warehouses. But you'll discover it's special when you taste the food, created under the direction of Louisiana-born Mike Jones. He even manages to please visitors from New Orleans—and that's saying a lot. The place is often packed. Breakfast begins with such dishes as a Creole omelet, followed by an oyster po'boy for lunch. It's at dinner, however, that the kitchen really shines, producing jambalaya with andouille sausage, crayfish étouffée, and crab-and-shrimp au gratin (with Louisiana crabmeat and Georgia shrimp). The soups are homemade and the appetizers distinctive. A jazz brunch is featured Saturday and Sunday 8am to 3pm. The bar next door offers live entertainment.

In the River Street Inn, 115 E. River St. © **912/234-7385.** Reservations recommended. Sandwiches $6–$10. Main courses $12–$22. AE, DISC, MC, V. Mon–Thurs 7am–10pm; Fri 7am–11pm; Sat 8am–11pm; Sun 8am–10pm.

INEXPENSIVE

Dockside Seafood Restaurant & Steakhouse *(Kids* SEAFOOD/STEAK

An inviting family-oriented restaurant, this eatery is in a building constructed in 1792 by Capt. William Taylor, a ship's chandler. It is the oldest existing commercial building and the oldest existing stone-and-masonry building in Georgia. Everything on the menu is familiar fare, which is why its patrons come here.

If you drop in for lunch, you'll find an array of barbecued pork sandwiches, burgers, Philly steak, shrimp salads, and Cajun shrimp po'boys. The dinner menu is more extensive, although sandwiches are still featured as well as a children's menu. The chef's specialty is a potato cheese soup, although you can order a selection of oysters and shrimp as well. Pasta, such as shrimp and scallop Parmesan, is a regular item, and you can create your own salad, a full meal with pita bread. Choices for your salad topping range from grilled mahimahi to grilled chicken. The steamer is active all night turning out the likes of a Low Country shrimp boil, among its other selections. A specialty in the evening is a Savannah steam pot for two with shrimp cocktails, soup, salads, a basket of hush puppies, and a cast iron pot full of crab legs, shrimp, sausage, corn on the cob, and potatoes. All the steaks are hand cut and really succulent, ranging from top sirloin to blackened rib-eye. Every night a "Southern dessert of the day" is featured; ask your waiter.

201 W. River St. © **912/236-9253.** Lunch $7.95–$27; main courses $7.45–$34. AE, DC, DISC, MC, V. Daily 11am–9:30pm; Sat–Sun closes at 10pm. Closed Thanksgiving and Christmas.

The Lady & Sons *(★* SOUTHERN

Paula Deen started this place in 1989 with $200, the help of her sons, and a 1910 structure. Today, she runs one of Savannah's most celebrated restaurants. Her first cookbook, *The Lady & Sons Savannah Country Cookbook*

(Random House), is in its second printing (John Berendt wrote the introduction); and her second, *The Lady & Sons Too,* was published in 2000. Paula has yet a third best-selling cookbook, *The Lady & Sons Just Desserts,* and also hosts a top-rated cooking show, *Paula's Home Cooking,* on the Food Network. A fourth cookbook will premier in the spring of 2005. One taste of the food and you'll understand the roots of her success. Menu items like crab cakes (one Maryland visitor claimed they were the best he'd ever eaten), crab burgers, and several creative varieties of shrimp best exhibit her style. The locals love her buffets, which are very Southern. With fried chicken, meatloaf, collard greens, beef stew, "creamed" potatoes, or macaroni and cheese, this buffet is more aptly described as "more-than-you-can-eat."

Lunches are busy with a loyal following; dinners are casual and inventive. The aphrodisiac dish has to be the oyster shooters—half a dozen raw oysters, each served in a shot glass. Paula's signature dish, chicken potpie topped with puff pastry, looks so attractive you'll have reservations about eating it: Maybe that's why *Southern Living* used a picture of it in their magazine. Be careful not to fill up on the cheese biscuits and hoecakes that constantly land on your table. If for some reason you don't want a glorious glass of syrup-sweet tea, you'd better ask for unsweetened. But why rob yourself of the complete experience?

120 W. Congress St. ✆ **912/233-2600.** www.ladyandsons.com. Reservations recommended for dinner. Main courses $6–$13 lunch, $18–$24 dinner; all-you-can-eat buffet $13 lunch, $17 dinner; $15 Sun buffet. AE, DISC, MC, V. Mon–Sat 11am–3pm; Mon–Thurs 5–9pm; Fri–Sat 5–10pm; Sun 11am–5pm (buffet only).

The River Grill SEAFOOD   Its decor was modeled after a barn somewhere on the panhandle of Texas; the recorded music might remind you of the country-western tunes they play at this place's namesake in Houston. The seafood here is fresh and tender. Examples are fresh stuffed flounder topped with a lobster brandy sauce or the delicious homemade crab cakes. Appetizers feature a warm crab-and-artichoke dip and oysters Rockefeller. Steaks and seafood include grilled swordfish, battered shrimp platters, and at least five kinds of Angus beef.

21 E. River St. ✆ **912/234-5588.** Main courses $7.95–$30. AE, DISC, MC, V. Sun–Thurs 11am–10pm; Fri–Sat 11am–11pm.

Shrimp Factory *Value* SEAFOOD   Exposed old brick and wooden plank floors form a setting for harborside dining in a circa-1850 cotton warehouse. Lots of folks drop in before dinner to watch the boats pass by, perhaps enjoying a glass of Chatham Artillery punch in a souvenir snifter. Yes, the place is touristy, never more so than when it welcomes tour buses. A salad bar rests next to a miniature shrimp boat, and fresh seafood comes from local waters. A specialty, pine bark stew, is served in a little iron pot with a bottle of sherry on the side; it's a potage of five seafoods simmered with fresh herbs but minus the pine bark. Other dishes include peeled shrimp, shucked oysters, Maine lobsters, sirloin steaks, and various fish filets.

313 E. River St. (2 blocks east of the Hyatt). © 912/236-4229. Reservations not accepted. Main courses $6.25–$15 lunch, $19–$28 dinner. AE, DC, DISC, MC, V. Mon–Thurs 11am–10pm; Fri–Sat 11am–11pm; Sun noon–10pm.

Tubby's Tank House SEAFOOD   Hungry diners flock here for the fresh fish. This old-brick building has a nautical decor, a casual atmosphere, and an outdoor deck for river views. The menu is corny—appetizers, for example—are called "Tubby's Teasers"—but the food is affordable, good, and wholesome. Oysters Savannah is a favorite appetizer, baked with andouille sausage and Parmesan. Lemon garlic shrimp is another savory opening. The chefs make the best crab stew along River Street. When we drop in, we generally opt for grilled fresh fish of the day. It's grilled to perfection over an open flame, and served with fresh steamed vegetables and your choice of a starch such as fettuccine Alfredo. Families like to order the seafood baskets, or else one of the steam pots served with hush puppies. The most savory kettle of fish is the Low Country platter with steamed oysters, rock shrimp, steamed shrimp, snow crab, deviled crab, sausage, and corn on the cob. A limited number of steak and chicken dishes are offered, including charbroiled chicken breast and a 14-ounce rib-eye.

115 E. River St. © 912/233-0770. Main courses $6.95–$28. AE, MC, V. Daily 11am–10pm. Closed Thanksgiving and Christmas.

2 In the Historic District

VERY EXPENSIVE

45 South ⓐⓐ INTERNATIONAL   Recommended by such magazines as *Food & Wine, Southern Living,* and even *Playboy,* this is a ritzy choice. The food has been called "gourmet Southern," and the ever-changing menu is likely to feature smoked North Carolina trout, rack of lamb flavored with crushed sesame seeds, grilled venison with au gratin of sweet potatoes, chicken breast with truffled pâté, or sliced breast of pheasant with foie gras. Appetizers might include everything from South Carolina quail to crab cakes. Among the most expensive restaurants in Savannah, it's softly lit with elegantly set tables and a cozy bar. The service is impeccable.

20 E. Broad St. ℂ **912/233-1881.** Reservations suggested. Jackets advised. Main courses $26–$45. AE, MC, V. Mon–Thurs 6–9pm; Fri–Sat 6–9:30pm.

Gottlieb's Restaurant & Dessert Bar 𝒻𝒻 SEAFOOD/AMERICAN

In what used to be the old McCrory's Department Store, a casual, contemporary eatery has opened and has already been discovered by Savannah foodies. The original brass railings of the department store are still intact, although the decor is modern, softly lit by Chinese lanterns. The appeal of this restaurant is its market-fresh ingredients, which are deftly handled by a skilled kitchen staff. Whenever possible, fresh local ingredients, including fish harvested off the Georgia coast, are used. Sesame-crusted yellowfin tuna with sweet-and-sour peppers might win your heart. It's served on a bed of cauliflower purée. Fire-roasted Long Island Peking duck is yet another temptation, resting under a sweet potato crust. In harmonious flavors, slow-roasted tomato and shallot ravioli comes with asparagus and local butterbeans. Since the restaurant uses dessert in its name, you know you're heading for some specialties. The sweets are freshly made and changed daily. Count on some of the best cakes in town based on original recipes from a bakery that flourished in Savannah in 1884.

1 W. Broughton St. ℂ **912/234-7447.** Reservations required. Main courses $22–$42. AE, DC, MC, V. Tues–Fri 5:30–10pm; Sat 5–10pm.

Sapphire Grill 𝒻 AMERICAN/LOW COUNTRY

One of the city's most consistently stylish restaurants evokes a low-key, counterculture bistro, but its cuisine is grander and more cutting-edge than its industrial-looking decor and its level of hipness would imply. Christopher Nason is the owner and the most talked-about chef of the moment in Savannah, preparing what he defines as a "coastal cuisine" based on seafood hauled in, usually on the day of its preparation, from nearby waters. If you opt for a table here, you won't be alone: Scads of media and cinematic personalities will have preceded you. Collectively, they add an urban gloss of the type you might expect to see in Los Angeles. Launch your repast with a "firecracker salad"—that is, roasted red peppers and a red chile- and-shallot vinaigrette—or crisp fried green tomatoes, perhaps tuna medallions, or even James Island littleneck clams tossed in a foie gras butter, each beginning course a delectable choice. The chef is justifiably proud of such signature dishes as duck served with roasted tomato cannelloni or grilled prime tenderloin of beef with dauphinoise potatoes. The local black grouper is flavored with lemon coriander, and a double-cut pork loin chop is one of the most elegant versions of this dish in Savannah. Each day the chef serves a tasting menu—based on the market price—that includes an appetizer, salad, main course, and confection. Ask about it, as it might be your best dining bet.

110 W. Congress St. ✆ **912/443-9962.** Reservations recommended. Main courses $19–$28. AE, DC, MC, V. Sun–Thurs 6–10:30pm; Fri–Sat 5:30–11:30pm.

EXPENSIVE

17 Hundred 90 🐸 INTERNATIONAL   In the brick-lined cellar of Savannah's oldest inn (p. 55), this place evokes a seafaring tavern along the coast of New England. Many visitors opt for a drink at the woodsy-looking bar in a separate back room before heading down the slightly claustrophobic corridor to the nautically inspired dining room. Students of paranormal psychology remain alert to the ghost rumored to wander through this place, site of Savannah's most famous 18th-century suicide. Lunch might be the quiche of the day with salad, Southern-style blue crab cakes, or a choice of salads and sandwiches. Dinners are more formal, featuring crab bisque, snapper Parmesan, steaks, and bourbon-flavored chicken. The cooking is of a high standard.

307 E. President St. ✆ **912/236-7122.** Reservations recommended. Main courses $20–$27. AE, DISC, MC, V. Mon–Fri 11:30am–2pm and daily 6–10pm.

The Olde Pink House Restaurant 🐸🐸 SEAFOOD/AMERICAN
Built in 1771 and glowing pink (its antique bricks show through a protective covering of stucco), this house has functioned as a private home, a bank, a tearoom, and headquarters for one of Sherman's generals. Today, its interior is severe and dignified, with stiff-backed chairs, bare wooden floors, and an 18th-century aura similar to what you'd find in Williamsburg, Virginia. The cuisine is richly steeped in the traditions of the Low Country and includes crispy scored flounder with apricot sauce, steak au poivre, black grouper stuffed with blue crab and drenched in Vidalia onion sauce, and grilled tenderloin of pork crusted with almonds and molasses. You can enjoy your meal in the candlelit dining rooms or in Planters Tavern.

23 Abercorn St. ✆ **912/232-4286.** Reservations recommended. Main courses $15–$30. AE, MC, V. Sun–Thurs 5:30–10:30pm; Fri–Sat 5:30–11pm.

MODERATE

Casbah MOROCCAN   With its North African theme, this restaurant, a dining oddity for Savannah, offers a lush and sensual atmosphere. Brocade tapestries on the wall and tented velvet ceilings create the aura; fortune-tellers predict your future and belly dancers entertain you. It has all that *faux* "Come with me to the Casbah" allure.

You can feast on exotic specialties. We like to start with a festival of Moroccan salads. Ask your server about the day's selection. One tantalizing appetizer is Cornish Hen Bastila—served boneless and mixed with onions, parsley, spiced eggs, and toasted almonds in a pastry baked and garnished with cinnamon and powdered sugar. It's more economical to order the three-course Moroccan Diaffa dinner, in which you select your appetizer, main course, and dessert, finishing off with hot mint tea. For main courses you're taken on an "Arabian Nights" tour, and can order such dishes as chicken and caramelized apricots dipped in a honey-nutmeg sauce. Our favorite is spicy roast lamb, served oven roasted and very tender with saffron rice and a choice of vegetables. If you like kabobs, you can opt for the Sultan's Feast with an assortment of chicken, beef, and lamb kabobs.

118 E. Broughton St. ✆ **912/234-6168.** Reservations recommended. Main courses $15–$22; 3-course menu $27. AE, DC, DISC, MC, V. Daily 5:30–10:30pm.

Il Pasticcio ITALIAN   This restaurant is one of the city's most popular dining spots. With its big windows and high ceiling, it has a definite postmodern, big-city style. A rotisserie turns out specialties. Many locals come here just for the pasta dishes, all homemade and served with savory sauces. Begin with *carpaccio* (thinly sliced beef tenderloin) or a tricolor salad of radicchio, endive, and arugula. Main dishes are likely to feature a mixed grilled seafood platter or grilled fish steak with tricolor roasted sweet peppers.

2 E. Broughton St. (corner of Bull and Broughton sts.). ✆ **912/231-8888.** Main courses $15–$28. AE, DC, DISC, M, V. Mon–Thurs 5:30–10pm; Fri–Sat 5:30–11:30pm.

Pearl's Saltwater Grille SEAFOOD/AMERICAN   "Let's not cook tonight and go to Pearl's," is often heard in local homes. Visitors know they'll get good food and plenty of it, everything from fresh seafood to perfectly grilled steaks. Dress is casual, and service is good unless the waitstaff is too rushed when all the tables are full. "This is where I take my guests from the north to show them how we eat in Savannah," one patron informed us. "We have better restaurants here than in New Orleans. Of course, I've never been to Louisiana, but that's what my friends tell me."

The cuisine may not be inspired here, but it's good and most filling, beginning with fresh hush puppies with sweetened butter. Many diners arrive early for more than one drink at the bar before proceeding to table. On our last visit, we noticed many families dining here. Southern-style vegetables accompany the main courses, and locals refer to them as "sides." Favorite dishes include shrimp and crab au gratin with a rich white sauce, and a shrimp trio—fried shrimp, garlic shrimp, and shrimp wrapped in bacon. Other good-tasting dishes include barbecued pork chops and pepper steak.

7000 La Roche Ave. ✆ **912/352-8221**. Reservations not accepted. Main courses $12–$20. AE, DC, DISC, MC, V. Sun–Thurs 5–10pm; Fri–Sat 5–10:30pm.

INEXPENSIVE

Barnes Restaurant ✦ *Kids* BARBECUE/LOW COUNTRY
This casual, family-style restaurant is very affordable. Local hotels and B&Bs often refer their economy-minded guests to this joint for its generous helpings and good food. A tradition since 1975, it is typical of many in the South, serving barbecue dinners, oyster po'boys, and fried catfish. "These dishes are popular," a waiter confided, "because it's what the customers want to eat day after day." From hand-cut and freshly battered onion rings to deviled and pan-seared crab cakes, the starters are spicy openings. The sandwiches are among the best in the area, including fish sandwiches, chicken sandwiches, and crab burgers. The spare ribs are slowly smoked over oak or hickory wood, and chicken is crispy and tasty outside, tender and moist inside as it emerges from the rotisserie. A children's menu is also offered.

5320 Waters Ave. at 68th St. ✆ **912/354-8745**. Main courses $3.30–$15. AE, DC, DISC, MC, V. Sun–Thurs 10:30am–10pm; Fri–Sat 10:30am–10:30pm. Closed Thanksgiving and Christmas.

Clary's Café ✦ *Value* AMERICAN
Clary's Café has been a Savannah tradition since 1903, though the ambience today, under the devilish direction of Michael Faber, is decidedly 1950s. The place was famous long before it was featured in *Midnight in the Garden of Good and Evil* in its former role as Clary's drugstore, where regulars like eccentric flea-collar inventor Luther Driggers breakfasted and lunched. John Berendt and the fabled Lady Chablis were once frequent patrons. Begin your day with the classic Hoppel

(Kids) Family-Friendly Restaurants

Barnes Restaurant (p.69)   A casual restaurant with generous helpings and good food. From hand-cut and freshly battered onion rings to deviled and pan-seared crab cakes, the starters are spicy. The sandwiches are among the best in the area. A children's menu is also offered.

Café at City Market (p. 72)   Right in the bustle of market life, with outdoor sidewalk cafe tables, this place offers food that's tasty and affordable, with a good children's menu. Their soups are the best in the market area. Pizzas are cooked to perfection.

Dockside Seafood Restaurant & Steakhouse (p. 63)   An inviting eatery in a building constructed in 1792. Everything on the menu is familiar fare; a children's menu at lunch and dinner includes barbecued pork sandwiches, burgers, Philly steak, shrimp salads, and Cajun shrimp po'boys.

Mrs. Wilkes' Dining Room (p. 71)   Since your kid didn't grow up in the era of the boardinghouse, here's a chance to experience a long-faded American dining custom. It's an all-you-can-eat, family-style place. Your kid might balk at the okra and collards, but go for the corn on the cob and barbecued chicken.

Wall's (p. 71)   If your kid is from the North and has never tasted Southern barbecue, take him or her here. There is no finer introduction. Even the booths are plastic. Spare ribs and barbecue sandwiches are the hearty fare, but there's also a vegetable plate for the non-meat eater in the family.

Poppel (scrambled eggs with chunks of kosher salami, potatoes, onions, and green peppers) and go on from there. Fresh salads, New York–style sandwiches, and stir-fries, along with grandmother's homemade chicken soup and flame-broiled burgers, are served throughout the day, giving way in the evening to chicken potpie, stuffed pork loin, or planked fish (a filet of red snapper—broiled, grilled, or blackened).

404 Abercorn St. (at Jones St.). ⓒ **912/233-0402.** Breakfast $3.95–$7.95; main courses $5.95–$7.95. AE, DC, DISC, MC, V. Daily 8am–4pm.

Mrs. Wilkes' Dining Room 🍴 *Kids* SOUTHERN   Remember the days of the boardinghouse, when everybody sat together, and belly-busting food was served in big dishes at the center of the table? Before her death in late 2002 at the age of 95, Sema Wilkes had served breakfast and lunch to locals and travelers in just that manner since the 1940s. Bruce Willis, Demi Moore, and Clint Eastwood are among the long list of celebrities who've dined here. The tradition continues. Expect to find a long line of people patiently waiting for a seat at one of the long tables in the basement dining room of this 1870 brick house with curving steps and cast-iron trim.

Mrs. Wilkes believed in freshness and planned her daily menu around the seasons. Your food will be a reflection of the cuisine Savannah residents have enjoyed for generations—fried or barbecued chicken, red rice and sausage, black-eyed peas, corn on the cob, squash and yams, okra, corn bread, and collard greens.

107 W. Jones St. (west of Bull St.). ✆ **912/232-5997.** www.mrswilkes.com. Reservations not accepted. Lunch $13. No credit cards. Mon–Fri 11:30am–2pm.

Wall's *Kids* BARBECUE   This is the first choice for anyone seeking the best barbecue in Savannah. Southern barbecue aficionados have built-in radar to find a place like this. Once they see the plastic booths, bibs, Styrofoam cartons, and canned drinks from a fridge, they'll know they've found home. Like all barbecue joints, the place is aggressively casual. Spare ribs and barbecue sandwiches star on the menu. Deviled crabs are the only non-barbecue item, though a vegetable plate of four non-meat items is also served.

515 E. York Lane (between York St. and Oglethorpe Ave.). ✆ **912/232-9754.** Reservations not accepted. Main courses $6.50–$10. No credit cards. Wed 11am–5pm; Thurs–Sat 11am–9pm.

3 In & Around the City Market

EXPENSIVE

Belford's 🍴 LOW COUNTRY   This restaurant keeps alive the tradition of offering good food in the area of the old City Market. The setting is nostalgic, with hardwood floors, dark-wood paneling, glass-topped tables, black-and-white tablecloths, high ceilings, and a patio. The cooks prepare a daily crab stew that is excellent, along with such other favorites as fried calamari or crab cakes, the latter served with a spicy tomato jam and lemon aioli. A trio of pastas is featured daily, our favorite always being the lobster and wild mushroom ravioli served with a spicy calamari salad and a balsamic brown butter sauce.

For your main course, there is an array of delights, perhaps herb-encrusted sea bass with fresh herbs which has been pan sautéed and finished off with a savory crab *beurre blanc*. It's served with buttermilk mashed potatoes. The hazelnut red snapper is also a temptation, served with prawns and lump crabmeat in a hazelnut liqueur sauce and a side of apple chutney. Shrimp, greens, 'n' grits is a favorite with smoked bacon, green onions, and a chardonnay butter sauce. The kitchen also turns out a succulent rosemary-marinated rack of lamb with roasted garlic mashed potatoes and a spicy bell pepper jelly, along with a garlic-and-thyme crusted double-cut pork chop served with caramelized apple slices and a Jack Daniel's sauce.

315 W. St. Julian St. ℭ **912/233-2626.** Reservations recommended. Breakfast buffet $5.95–$13; lunch $6.95–$11; Sun brunch $7–$13; main courses $17–$33. AE, DC, DISC, MC, V. Mon–Sat 8am–11am; daily 11:30am–3pm and 6–10pm. Closed Thanksgiving, Christmas Eve (night), and Christmas.

MODERATE

Garibaldi's ITALIAN   Many of the city's art-conscious students appreciate this Italian cafe because of the fanciful murals adorning its walls. (Painted by the owner's daughter, their theme is "The Jungles of Italy.") If you're looking for a quiet, contemplative evening, we advise you to go elsewhere—the setting is loud and convivial during the early evening and even louder later at night. Designed as a fire station in 1871, the cafe boasts the original pressed-tin ceiling.

Menu items include roasted red peppers with goat-cheese croutons on a bed of wild lettuces, crispy calamari, artichoke hearts with aioli, about a dozen kinds of pasta, and a repertoire of Italian-inspired chicken, veal, and seafood dishes. Daily specials change frequently but sometimes include duck Garibaldi, king-crab fettuccine, and a choice of lusciously fattening desserts.

315 W. Congress St. ℭ **912/232-7118.** Reservations recommended. Main courses $12–$28. AE, MC, V. Sun–Thurs 5:30–10:30pm; Fri–Sat 5:30–11pm.

INEXPENSIVE

Café at City Market ⟨⟨ (Kids) CONTINENTAL/SEAFOOD Right in the bustle of market life, with sidewalk cafe tables, this lively place evokes a Continental bistro. The owner and chef, Matt Maher, shops the market for the freshest of ingredients, which he fashions into the dishes of the day. The food is good and affordable, making it a family favorite. The children's menu is also alluring. You can dine inside as well, enjoying the tasteful ambience of brick walls and casual furnishings. Their soups are the best in the market area, especially their chicken and okra gumbo, and their cream of tomato dill. Appetizers are good, if not overly familiar, including smoked Norwegian salmon or a spinach artichoke dip. If you're dropping in for lunch, you can always partake of the soup and sandwich of the day. Their salads and pizzas are cooked to perfection. Pizzas come with imaginative toppings such as black beans, spicy sausage, smoked mozzarella, and a tomato and cilantro sauce. Steaks and seafood dominate the menu after 6pm. We recently devoured the 12-ounce rib-eye, grilled before a quick brandy flambé, then served au jus with braised wild mushrooms and buttermilk mashed potatoes. The grilled fresh yellowfin tuna had just the right touch: Creole seasonings served over rice. Fresh fruit sorbet and peppermint ice cream are made exclusively for the cafe, or you can order the fresh baked dessert selections prepared daily.

224 W. St. Julian St. © **912/236-7133**. Lunch $4–$9.95; main courses $7.95–$23. AE, DC, DISC, MC, V. Daily 11:30am–5pm and 6–10pm. Closed Christmas.

Moon River Brewing Company AMERICAN/LOW COUNTRY
This welcoming place, a local favorite, successfully combines a restaurant and a bar with a brewpub. You get a "Cheers"-like atmosphere as well as good food, affordable prices, and fresh ingredients. A local critic called the kitchen a "boiling pot of diversity," and so it is, offering a wide range of dishes. The atmosphere is pubby; the brewing company's dark woods and huge brewing tanks behind glass walls can be viewed by customers while they're eating or sampling the suds.

The restaurant is in the former City Hotel Building, where such names as Gen. Winfield Scott, the marquis de Lafayette, and John James Audubon have stayed. Audubon stayed here for 6 months after a gale marooned his boat, and it was at this site that he worked on his book, *Ornithological Biographies.*

The kitchen is big on crab, evoked by such appetizers as fried crabmeat, stuffed shrimp, or crab cakes. There is always a delectable array of soups, sandwiches, and salads made fresh daily. A perfectly seasoned, 16-ounce grilled rib-eye is served, as well as those local favorites: platters of fried catfish, shrimp 'n' grits, or chicken and sausage Creole. One reliable bet is the catch of the day. Ask the waiter what's on the grill, and tell him or her how you'd like it cooked.

21 W. Bay St. © **912/447-0943**. Reservations not required. Main courses $5–$17. AE, DC, DISC, MC, V. Mon–Thurs noon–11pm; Fri–Sat 11am–midnight; Sun 11am–10pm.

4 In the Victorian District

VERY EXPENSIVE

Elizabeth on 37th ✿✿ MODERN SOUTHERN   This restaurant is frequently cited as the most glamorous and upscale in town. It's housed in a palatial, neoclassical-style 1900 villa ringed with semitropical landscaping and cascades of Spanish moss. The menu items change with the season and manage to retain their gutsy originality despite an elegant presentation. They may include roast quail with mustard-and-pepper sauce and apricot-pecan chutney, herb-seasoned rack of lamb, or broiled salmon with mustard-garlic glaze. You might begin with grilled eggplant soup, a culinary first for many diners. There's also an impressive wine list, and on Thursday all wines are sold by the glass. The desserts are the best in Savannah.

105 E. 37th St. ✆ **912/236-5547.** www.elizabethon37th.com. Reservations required. Main courses $23–$36. AE, DC, DISC, MC, V. Daily 6–10pm.

5 On the South Side

MODERATE

Johnny Harris Restaurant ✿ AMERICAN   Started as a roadside diner in 1924, Johnny Harris is Savannah's oldest continuously operated restaurant. The place has a lingering aura of the 1950s and features all that great food so beloved back in the days of Elvis and Marilyn: barbecue, charbroiled steaks, and seafood. The barbecued pork is especially savory and the prime rib tender. Colonel Sanders never came close to equaling the fried chicken here. Guests can dine in the "kitchen" or in the main dining room, and dance under the "stars" in the main dining room on Friday and Saturday nights, when there's live entertainment. The place will make you nostalgic.

1651 E. Victory Dr. (Hwy. 80). ✆ **912/354-7810.** Reservations recommended. Lunch items $8–$10; dinner main courses $11–$26. AE, DC, DISC, MC, V. Mon–Thurs 11:30am–9:30pm; Fri–Sat 11:30am–10:30pm.

Musashi ✿ (Value) JAPANESE   This was the first Japanese restaurant to open in Savannah, and since that time it's won several local awards, including "Best Lunch Under $5," "Best Oriental Food," and *Savannah Magazine*'s "Best of the Best." Chefs emerge with flashing knives to massacre slices of delicate shrimp, seafood, chicken, and steak. Musashi specializes in the *teppanyaki* style of cooking, and is it ever good! Many locals had never tasted Japanese food until this place opened. The usual starters, such as shrimp appetizer, Musashi soup (clear broth with green onions and mushrooms), and a Japanese salad with ginger dressing, will get you going. The sesame chicken and the sirloin strip steak are cooked to perfection, as are several combination dishes; the best is the shrimp and scallops.

7312 Hodgson Memorial Dr. ℭ 912/352-2128. Reservations recommended. Lunch $4.50–$11; main courses $12–$30. AE, DC, DISC, MC, V. Mon–Fri 11:30am–2pm; Sat noon–2pm; Mon–Thurs 5:30–10pm; Fri 5:30–10:30pm; Sat 5–11pm; Sun 4:30–9pm. Closed Thanksgiving and Christmas.

INEXPENSIVE

Toucan Café INTERNATIONAL/FUSION   This is one of the most sophisticated cafes in town, with a festive atmosphere that ranges in spirit from the Greek islands to the West Indies. You get everything here from down-home taste to exotic flavors. The cafe opened in 1994, in a hole in the wall, and has been attracting a loyal following ever since. In 1998 the owners, Nancy and Steve Magulias, moved into larger quarters to better accommodate their growing number of fans. The decor alone sets the mood with its lime green, shocking pink, and bright yellow—very Jamaican.

The kitchen is known for turning out the best Havana black bean soup in Savannah, and the salads are worth a visit here, especially the Toucan Caesar with tomatoes, red onions, and freshly grated Parmesan cheese topped with either chicken or salmon. Many dishes appeal to the vegetarian, such as the black bean burger. Their lunch sandwiches are the best on the south side. The dinner menu is truly excellent if you launch yourself with the grilled eggplant with tomatoes, provolone, creamy feta, and mousalada over marinara, or the crawfish quesadilla. The Hellenic stuffed chicken with feta cheese and spinach is a main dish specialty, or you may prefer shrimp farfalle with mushrooms, artichokes, and tomatoes in a basil cream with bow-tie pasta. The sesame-encrusted tuna is presented atop soba noodles, and it's divinely wedded to shavings of marinated ginger in a lime *beurre blanc* sauce. Who can resist the coconut kiwi layer cake?

531 Stephenson Ave. ℭ 912/352-2233. Reservations recommended. Lunch $5.25–$12; main courses $6.95–$21. AE, DISC, MC, V. Mon–Sat 11:30am–2:30pm; Tues–Thurs 5–9pm; Fri–Sat 5–10pm.

7

Exploring Savannah

The very name evokes a romantic antebellum aura. Savannah is the city that General Sherman gave President Lincoln as a Christmas present. Crowds flock here to search for Forrest Gump's bench and other nonhistorical monuments, as well as to visit the Juliette Gordon Low Birthplace, the National Center of the Girl Scouts of the U.S.A.

The city, founded in 1733 by Gen. James Oglethorpe as Georgia's first settlement, is located 18 miles inland from the Atlantic on the Savannah River at the South Carolina border. A deep channel connects Savannah to the ocean, attracting massive freighters to the terminals at the Georgia Ports Authority. Visitors can almost touch the ships as they make their way up the river. Lined with classy nightspots and upscale restaurants, as well as a few rough pubs and artsy boutiques, cobblestone River Street has become a hub for tourists.

Savannah's historic sites rival those of Charleston, but paramount on the list are characters and dwellings from John Berendt's bestseller, *Midnight in the Garden of Good and Evil.* Ironically, a city that built its claim on historical prominence has become a gathering place for the curious, who flock to Club One, a popular gay nightspot that hosts a nightly transvestite show sometimes featuring the Lady Chablis, one of Berendt's main characters. Visitors also dine at Clary's Café and gawk at Mercer House, where the shooting described in Berendt's book took place. Oglethorpe would be appalled.

SIGHTSEEING SUGGESTIONS

If You Have 1 Day

Don't set foot outside the Historic District—even there, you won't see it all. Go to the Savannah Visitor Information Center for a general orientation and a viewing of the 15-minute video presentation. Pick up a free map before going to an adjacent building to see the Savannah History Museum. Then set out on our *Midnight in the Garden of Good and Evil* walking tour (see chapter 8), viewing sites like Mercer House, featured in The Book and The Film. Later, dine along River Street and relax at one of the riverfront pubs or take a harbor cruise if it's offered.

If You Have 2 Days

See Day 1 above. Spend Day 2 exploring historic River Street, a 9-block plaza facing the Savannah River, with shops, restaurants, galleries, and pubs. Take our Historic Savannah walking tour, which encompasses the City Market with its City Market Arts Center, home of some 30 working artists.

If You Have 3 Days

Spend Days 1 and 2 as above. On Day 3, stroll the Bull Street corridor with its shops, galleries, museums, and beautiful squares, and pay a visit to some of the elegant historic inns, all unique, perhaps deciding where you'd like to stay on your next visit to Savannah. Sit back and enjoy a leisurely horse-and-carriage tour (perhaps take an evening ghost tour) to see Savannah in a different light. You'll especially enjoy this tour in the evening as the lights come on in the houses.

If You Have 4 Days

Spend Days, 1, 2, and 3 as recommended above. On Day 4, start your morning at the Telfair Mansion and Art Museum, the oldest public art museum in the South. If you have time, walk about 6 blocks and also see the historic Owens-Thomas House and Museum, where Lafayette spent the night in 1825. In the afternoon, venture about 2 miles out of town to see Old Fort Jackson, Georgia's oldest standing fort. To top off your day, return to the city and enjoy a martini in the Bonaventure Cemetery (take note—it closes at 5pm).

If You Have 5 Days

Spend Days 1, 2, 3, and 4 as recommended above. On Day 5, travel a little under 2 hours southeast of Savannah to Jekyll Island, where you can spend the day in the former playground of millionaires like the Vanderbilts, Rockefellers, Morgans, and Pulitzers. Stop by the Museum Visitors Center and learn about Jekyll Island's history through exhibits, artifacts, and displays. The museum's Historical Landmark District Tour begins here. You have a choice of several restaurants at the Jekyll Island Club Hotel—you can eat like the Rockefellers in the Grand Dining Room, or just grab a deli sandwich at the Café Solterra. Specialty boat tours as well as carriage tours are available to enhance your day on the island.

1 Historic Homes

Andrew Low House   After her marriage, Juliette Low (see above) lived in this 1848 house, and it was here that she actually founded the Girl Scouts. She died on the premises in 1927. The classic mid-19th-century house facing Lafayette Square is of stucco over brick with elaborate ironwork, shuttered piazzas, carved woodwork, and crystal chandeliers. William Makepeace Thackeray visited here twice (the desk at which he worked is in one of the bedrooms), and Robert E. Lee was entertained at a gala reception in the double parlors in 1870.

329 Abercorn St. ✆ **912/233-6854.** Admission $7 adults; $4.50 students, children 6–12, and Girl Scouts; free for children 5 and under. Mon–Wed and Fri–Sat 10am–4:30pm; Sun noon–4pm. Closed major holidays.

Davenport House Museum   This is where seven determined women started the Savannah restoration movement in 1954. They raised $22,500, a tidy sum back then, and purchased the house, saving it from demolition and a future as a parking lot. They then established the Historic Savannah Foundation, and the whole city was spared. Constructed between 1815 and 1820 by master builder Isaiah Davenport, this is one of the truly great Federal-style houses in the United States, with delicate ironwork and a handsome elliptical stairway.

119 Habersham St. ✆ **912/236-8097.** www.davenportsavga.com. Admission $7 adults, $3.50 children 6–18, free for children 5 and under. Mon–Sat 10am–4pm; Sun 1–4pm. Closed major holidays.

Juliette Gordon Low's Birthplace   Juliette Gordon Low—the founder of the Girl Scouts—lived in this Regency-style house that's now maintained both as a memorial to her and as a National Program Center. The Victorian additions to the 1818–21 house were made in 1886, just before Juliette Gordon married William Mackay Low.

10 E. Oglethorpe Ave. ✆ **912/233-4501.** Admission $8 adults, $6 children 18 and under. Mon–Tues and Thurs–Sat 10am–4pm; Sun 12:30–4:30pm. Closed major holidays and some Sun Dec–Jan.

Green-Meldrim Home   This impressive house was built on Madison Square for cotton merchant Charles Green, but its moment in history arrived when it became the Savannah headquarters of Gen. William Tecumseh Sherman at the end of his 1864 "March to the Sea." It was from this Gothic-style house that the general sent his now infamous (at least in Savannah) Christmas

Savannah Attractions

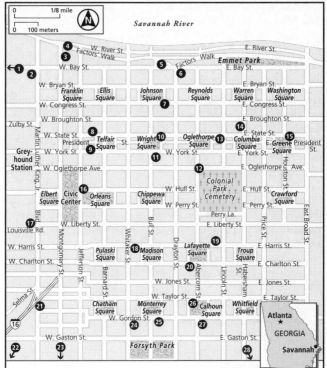

Andrew Low House **20**
Cathedral of St. John the Baptist **19**
Chamber of Commerce **6**
Christ Episcopal Church **7**
Colonial Park Cemetery **12**
Davenport House Museum **14**
Factors' Walk **4**
First African Baptist Church **3**
First Bryan Baptist Church **1**
Green-Meldrim Home **18**
Juliette Gordon Low's Birthplace **11**
Laurel Grove-South Cemetery **22**
Lutheran Church of the Ascension **10**
Massie Heritage Interpretation
   Center **27**
Mercer House **24**

Municipal Auditorium **16**
Nicholsonboro Baptist Church **23**
Owen-Thomas House & Museum **13**
Ralph Mark Gilbert Civil Rights
   Museum **21**
Savannah History Museum **17**
Savannah Visitor Center **17**
Second African Baptist Church **15**
Ships of the Sea Maritime Museum **2**
Telfair Mansion & Art Museum **8**
Temple Mickve Israel **25**
Trinity Unity Methodist Church **9**
U.S. Customs House **5**
Wesley Monumental Methodist
   Church **26**
Wormsloe State Historic Site **28**

telegram to President Lincoln, offering him the city as a Christmas gift. Now the Parish House for St. John's Episcopal Church, the house is open to the public. The former kitchen, servants' quarters, and stable are used as a rectory for the church.

14 W. Macon St. ✆ **912/233-3845.** Admission $5 adults, $3 children. Tues, Thurs, and Fri 10am–4pm; Sat 10am–1pm.

2 The Best Museums

Owens-Thomas House and Museum 𝕬   Famed as a place where Lafayette spent the night in 1825, this house evokes the heyday of Savannah's golden age. It was designed in 1816 by English architect William Jay, who captured the grace of Georgian Bath in England and the splendor of Regency London. The place has been called a "jewel box." You can visit not only the bedchambers and kitchen but also the garden and the drawing and dining rooms. Adapted from the original slave quarters and stable, the Carriage House Visitors' Center opened in 1995.

124 Abercorn St. ✆ **912/233-9743.** Admission $8 adults, $4 students, $2 children 6–12, free for children 5 and under. Mon noon–5pm; Tues–Sat 10am–5pm; Sun 1–5pm.

Savannah History Museum   Housed in the restored train shed of the old Central Georgia Railway station, this museum is a good introduction to the city. In the theater, *The Siege of Savannah* is replayed. An exhibition hall displays memorabilia from every era of Savannah's history.

303 Martin Luther King Jr. Blvd. ✆ **912/238-1779.** Admission $4 adults, $3.50 seniors and students, $3 children ages 6–11, free for children under 6. Mon–Fri 8:30am–5pm; Sat–Sun 9am–5pm.

Ships of the Sea Maritime Museum *Kids*   This museum has intricately constructed models of seagoing vessels, from Viking warships right up to today's nuclear-powered ships. In models ranging from the size of your fist to 8 feet in length, you can see such famous ships as the *Mayflower* and the *Savannah,* the first steamship to cross the Atlantic. More than 75 ships are in the museum's ship-in-a-bottle collection, most of them constructed by Peter Barlow, a retired British Royal Naval commander. The museum is located in the Scarbrough house, designed by William Jay and built in 1819.

41 Martin Luther King Jr. Blvd. ✆ **912/232-1511.** www.shipsofthesea.org. Admission $7 adults, $5 children 8–12, free for children 7 and under. Tues–Sun 10am–5pm. Closed major holidays.

Telfair Mansion and Art Museum ℛ   The oldest public art museum in the South, housing a collection of both American and European paintings, was designed and built by William Jay in 1819. He was a young English architect noted for introducing the Regency style to America. The house was built for Alexander Telfair, son of Edward Telfair, the governor of Georgia. A sculpture gallery and rotunda were added in 1883, and Jefferson Davis, former president of the Confederacy, attended the formal opening in 1886. William Jay's period rooms have been restored, and the Octagon Room and Dining Room are particularly outstanding. The "Bird Girl" sculpture pictured on the cover of *Midnight in the Garden of Good and Evil* is now located here.

121 Bernard St. ℂ **912/232-1177.** Admission $8 adults, $2 students, $1 children 6–12, free for children 5 and under. Mon noon–5pm; Tues–Sat 10am–5pm; Sun 1–5pm.

3 Historic Churches & Synagogues

For other historic churches, see "Black History Sights," later in this chapter.

Cathedral of St. John the Baptist   This is the oldest Catholic church in Georgia and the seat of the Diocese of Savannah. Organized in 1799, it was the first house of worship built on Liberty Square. In 1876 the first rendition of this current Victorian Gothic cathedral was constructed but destroyed by fire in 1898. Based on original designs, the cathedral was rebuilt. Over the past several years, the cathedral has undergone massive renovations. Today its twin spires and chiming bells make it one of Savannah's most notable landmarks. Inside you can view its marble railings, murals, Persian rugs, stained-glass windows from Austria, large carved wooden Stations of the Cross, and a solid white 2,081-pipe Noack tracker organ.

223 E. Harris St. ℂ **912/233-4709.** Self-guided tours Mon–Fri 9–11:30am and 12:30–5pm.

Christ Episcopal Church   Savannah was founded as a Church of England settlement, and its center of religious life was this church, the first established in the colony. It was known as the "Mother Church of Georgia." The present building on this site is in the style of an early Greek Revival public building, having been designed by James H. Cooper in 1838. The church was nearly destroyed by fire in 1898, but was rebuilt within its original walls. Famous clergy in the history of this church include John Wesley and George Whitehead. The first Sunday school conducted in Georgia was held at this church, as was the first hymnal in English. Its 1819 Revere Bell is one of the rarest in the country. The bell bears this ominous engraving: "The living to the church I call, and to the grave I summon all."

28 Bull St. ⓒ **912/232-4131.** Free tours Wed and Fri 10:30am and 3:30pm.

Lutheran Church of the Ascension   Few churches in Georgia have had the bizarre history of this landmark. Its origins are in 1734, when Austrians emigrating from Salzburg founded the church. They came to settle in Savannah a year after Oglethorpe landed. Although most of the Salzburgers settled in a community called Ebenezer outside Savannah, not all of them did. The Rev. Johann Bolzius, who had created the Ebenezer New Jerusalem Lutheran Church, came back to Savannah in 1741 to create this church for the Salzburgers who had settled in the historic core. A wooden structure originally stood on this site, but in 1844 it was replaced by a Greek Revival church. Thirty-five years later, architect George B. Clarke added the second floor and the medieval-style turrets. Today it's a fine example of the Grecian Doric style that swept eastern America.

When General Sherman invaded Savannah in 1864, the church pew cushions were used as beds for his soldiers, the pews themselves for firewood. The church was turned into a hospital for the sick and wounded. Although the building was damaged, it was not destroyed. Today it's known for its spectacular "Ascension Window" inside the sanctuary behind the pulpit, and for its rose window featuring Martin Luther and his coat-of-arms in front of the building.

120 Bull St. on Wright Sq. ⓒ **912/232-4151.** Mon–Fri 9am–1pm.

Temple Mickve Israel   At Monterrey Square, this temple is Georgia's oldest Jewish congregation and the third oldest congregation in the U.S. It is the nation's only Gothic synagogue (ca. 1878) and was designed by architect Henry G. Harrison, who had previously designed only Christian churches. Its founding members were Spanish, Portuguese, and German Jews who came to Savannah in 1733 to escape persecution in their homelands. With them, the group carried a precious relic, the *Sepah Torah,* the oldest Torah in America. The temple today houses a museum with more than 1,800 historical artifacts on view, including portraits, religious objects, documents, and letters to the congregations from presidents George Washington, Thomas Jefferson, and James Madison.

20 E. Gordon St. (on Monterrey Sq.). ⓒ **912/233-1547.** $3 donation suggested. Tours (and museum hours) Mon–Fri 10am–noon and 2–4pm. Closed major Jewish holidays.

Gateway to Historic Savannah

On a bluff above the river, **Factors Walk** and **Factors Row** are arrays of red-brick structures named for the "cotton factors," brokers who graded or "factored" in these buildings in the heyday of the 19th-century King Cotton economy. The men who performed this duty were called "Factors." To build these structures, the architects had to contend with a bluff rising sharply from the river. On the bluff they designed a series of multi-tiered buildings of ballast stone and brick hauled across the Atlantic. Their buildings rose vertically rather than horizontally, as did most warehouses of the time.

Most of the warehouses along Factors Walk were filled with either rice or cotton, two flourishing industries at the time. During Savannah's peak as a seaport, ships from all over the world docked adjacent to the row of warehouses so their exports could be directly loaded into their holds.

The rows of warehouses were made accessible by a network of iron bridgeways over cobblestone ramps. Today this section, lying between Bull and East Broad streets, is filled with many fine shops and restaurants. Ramps lead from the Bay Street level down the bluff to River Street, which you can promenade after checking out Factors Row and Factors Walk.

Trinity United Methodist Church   This church, dedicated in 1848, is known as the "Mother Church of Savannah Methodism." It is hardly the most opulent church in Savannah, but it holds a fascination for students of architecture. It is known for its hand-hewn pine on its interior. It was constructed of stucco over Savannah gray brick, and its interior design is evocative of the Wesley Chapel in London. The Savannah gray brick used to build the church is no longer in existence. The formula for the brick died with its inventor.
225 W. President St. ⓒ **912/233-4766.** Daily Apr–Nov 11am–1:30pm.

Wesley Monumental Methodist Church   Built between 1876 and 1890, this Gothic Revival church is a memorial to John and Charles Wesley, the founders of Methodism. It was based on designs for Queen's Kirk in Amsterdam and holds 1,000 parishioners surrounded by stained-glass windows dedicated to the historic figures of Methodism. The church took a long time to erect because of the financial problems in the Reconstruction era and a catastrophic outbreak of yellow fever in Savannah.

429 Abercorn St. ✆ **912/232-0191.** Mon–Fri 9am–5pm.

4 The Forts: Civil War Memories

Old Fort Jackson   About 2½ miles east of the center of Savannah via the Islands Expressway is Georgia's oldest standing fort, with a 9-foot-deep tidal moat around its brick walls. In 1775, an earthen battery was built here. The original brick fort was begun in 1808 and manned during the War of 1812. It was enlarged and strengthened between 1845 and 1860 and saw its greatest use as headquarters for the Confederate river defenses during the Civil War. Its arched rooms, designed to support the weight of heavy cannons mounted above, hold 13 exhibit areas.

1 Fort Jackson Rd. ✆ **912/232-3945.** Admission $4 adults, $3 children 6–18 and seniors, free for children 5 and under. Daily 9am–5pm.

Fort McAllister   Lying 10 miles southwest on U.S. 17, on the banks of the Great Ogeechee River, is a restored Confederate earthwork fortification. Constructed in 1861–62, it withstood nearly 2 years of bombardments before it finally fell on December 13, 1864, in a bayonet charge that ended General Sherman's infamous "March to the Sea." There's a visitor center with historic exhibits and also walking trails and campsites.

Richmond Hill. ✆ **912/727-2339.** Admission $2.50 adults, $2 seniors, $1.50 children over 5. Tues–Sat 8am–5pm.

Fort Pulaski   This national monument is 15 miles east of Savannah off U.S. 80 on Cockspur and McQueen islands at the very mouth of the Savannah River. It cost $1 million and took 25 tons of brick and 18 years of toil to finish. Yet it was captured in just 30 hours by Union forces. Completed in 1847 with walls 7½ feet thick, it was occupied by Confederate forces at the beginning of the war. However, on April 11, 1862, defense strategy changed worldwide when Union cannons, firing from more than a mile away on Tybee Island, overcame the masonry fortification. The effectiveness of rifled cannon (firing a heavier, bullet-shaped projectile with great accuracy at longer range) was clearly demonstrated. The new Union weapon marked the end of the era of masonry fortifications. The fort was pentagonally shaped, with galleries and drawbridges crossing the moat. You can still find shells from 1862 imbedded in the walls. There are exhibits of the fort's history in the visitor center.

Cockspur and McQueen islands. ℭ **912/786-5787**. Admission $3, free for children 16 and under. Daily 9am–7pm. Closed Christmas.

5 Spooky Cemeteries

Colonial Park Cemetery The oldest burial ground (ca. 1750) in Savannah is filled with magnolia trees and is such a beautiful setting the city turned it into a park in 1986. Many distinguished Georgians are buried here, none more famous than the two duelers who fought one of the most famous battles of insults in the state.

Button Gwinnett, one of the signers of the Declaration of Independence, is buried here. He died of wounds suffered in a duel with Gen. Lachlan McIntosh, another Georgia hero.

The feud between the two generals stemmed from insults leveled against Gwinnett after the abortive Georgia invasion of Florida in 1777. Infuriated, Gwinnett challenged McIntosh to a duel on what is now the cemetery grounds. Both men were shot in the thigh, at which point their seconds stopped the duel. McIntosh, though injured, had only sustained a flesh wound. Gwinnett's injury was far more serious, and he died 3 days after being taken to a hospital. McIntosh was tried for murder but acquitted. Mrs. Gwinnett refused to condemn McIntosh for the death of her husband.

Nonetheless, other members of the Savannah colony turned on McIntosh, who left the city to take a command under George Washington.

In time, he redeemed himself by leading troops successfully at the Battle of Savannah in 1779. He became an esteemed citizen of Savannah in his later years. Those two enemies, Gwinnett and McIntosh, are buried very near each other. The cemetery, at the corner of Oglethorpe and Abercorn streets, is open during daylight hours.

Laurel Grove-South Cemetery Many of the city's most prominent African Americans are buried in this cemetery, one of the oldest black cemeteries in America. Both antebellum plantation slaves and free blacks during the Reconstruction era were buried here, including Andrew Bryan (1716–1812), a pioneer Baptist preacher in the area.

West end of 37th St. ℭ **912/651-6772**. Free admission. Daily 9am–5pm.

Moments   Martinis in the Cemetery

All fans of *Midnight in the Garden of Good and Evil* must pay a visit to the now world-famous **Bonaventure Cemetery,** filled with obelisks and columns and dense shrubbery and moss-draped trees. Bonaventure is open daily 8am to 5pm. You get there by taking Wheaton Street east out of downtown to Skidaway to Bonaventure Road. (You don't want to approach it by boat like Minerva the "voodoo priestess" and John Berendt did—and certainly not at any time near midnight.)

This cemetery lies on the grounds of what was once a great oak-shaded plantation, built by Col. John Mulryne. In the late 1700s, the mansion caught fire during a formal dinner party; reportedly, the host quite calmly led his guests from the dining room and into the garden, where they settled in to finish eating while the house burned to the ground in front of them. When dinner was finished, the host and the guests threw their crystal glasses against the trunk of an old oak tree. It's said that on still nights you can still hear the laughter and the crashing of the crystal. In The Book, Mary Harty called the ruins the "scene of the Eternal Party. What better place, in Savannah, to rest in peace for all time—where the party goes on and on."

6 Black History Sights

For a preview of a famous cemetery of African Americans, refer to "Spooky Cemeteries" above.

First African Baptist Church   This was the first African Baptist church built in America. It was established by George Leile, a slave whose master allowed him to preach to other slaves when they made visits to plantations along the Savannah River. Leile was granted his freedom in 1777 and later raised some $1,500 to purchase the present church from a white congregation. The black congregation rebuilt the church brick by brick, and it became the first brick building in Georgia to be owned by African Americans. The pews on either side of the organ are the work of African slaves.

23 Montgomery St., Franklin Sq. ⓒ **912/233-6597.** Sun worship 8:30am and 11:30am.

It was at the cemetery that John Berendt had martinis in silver goblets with Miss Harty, while they sat on the bench-gravestone of poet **Conrad Aiken.** She pointed out to the writer the double gravestone bearing the names of Dr. William F. Aiken and his wife, Anna, parents of Conrad. They both died on February 27, 1901, when Dr. Aiken killed his wife and then himself. The Aikens are buried in Lot 78. Songwriter **Johnny Mercer** is also buried in Lot 49H.

But not **Danny Hansford,** the blond hustler of The Book. You can find his grave at Lot 6, Block G-8 in the Greenwich Cemetery, next to Bonaventure. After entering Bonaventure, turn left immediately and take the straight path to Greenwich. Eventually you'll see a small granite tile:

DANNY LEWLS HANSFORD
MARCH 1, 1960
MAY 2, 1981

Incidentally, **Jim Williams** is buried in Gordon, Georgia, a 3½-hour drive northwest of Savannah.

The "Bird Girl" statue, made famous by its appearance on the cover of The Book, now resides at the Telfair Museum.

Nicholsonboro Baptist Church   This church serves as a monument to an African-American community founded during the Reconstruction days by 200 former slaves who relocated to Nicholsonboro from St. Catherine's Island. Eighteen settlers signed a $5,000 mortgage for 200 acres of land, paying it off in 5 years and receiving title. For a time they thrived as a fishing and farming community before falling on hard times. Eventually their economic base all but disappeared. Today this small clapboard church serves as a memorial to those early strugglers. Some of the original pews and a porcelain doorknob remain from the original church that had no electricity but was warmed by a wooden stove. In 1978 the church was placed on the National Register of Historic Places. The current Nicholsonboro Baptist Church (ca. 1890) is adjacent to the original structure and holds weekly services.

13319 White Bluff Rd. (℃ **912/921-0566.** Tours available by appointment only. Take Bull St. south until it runs into White Bluff Rd.

Ralph Mark Gilbert Civil Rights Museum   Close to the Savannah Visitor Information Center, this pioneer museum opened in 1996. It's dedicated to the life and service of African Americans and their contributions to the civil rights movement in Savannah. Dr. Gilbert died in 1956 but was a leader in early efforts to gain educational, social, and political equity for African Americans in Savannah.

460 Martin Luther King Jr. Blvd. ℭ **912/231-8900**. Admission $4 adults, $3 seniors, $2 children. Mon–Sat 9am–5pm.

St. Phillip Monumental A.M.E. Church   This was the first African Methodist Church to be established in Savannah. It was organized by the Rev. A. L. Stanford in June 1865, the year the Civil War ended. The original church was destroyed by a storm in 1896, but was rebuilt into the church standing today.

1112 Jefferson St. ℭ **912/233-8547**. Mon–Fri 9am–5pm.

Second African Baptist Church   This early African-American church (ca. 1802) was known for training more ministers—black or white—than any other church in the country. Two historic events took place here. In 1864 Gen. William Tecumseh Sherman read the Emancipation Proclamation to Savannah citizens, promising the newly freed slaves 40 acres and a mule. Dr. Martin Luther King, Jr., proclaimed his "I Have a Dream" sermon here before the famous march on Washington in 1963.

123 Houston St. ℭ **912/233-6163**. Mon–Fri 10am–2pm.

First Bryan Baptist Church   When a congregation of slaves obtained a lot on Bryan Street to build this place of worship, it became the oldest parcel of real estate in America owned by blacks. As such, it has figured greatly over the years into the history of Savannah. In 1788 the Rev. Andrew Bryan, a slave, was ordained as minister. With his preaching, Bryan aroused the fear of plantation owners, who tried to prevent him from holding meetings. Somehow Bryan managed to hold his devout group of followers together.

A slave insurrection in Haiti set off fears in Low Country plantations. Bryan and his brother, Sampson, were beaten savagely and imprisoned, and their meeting house was taken away. Sympathetic white preachers intervened and secured their release. After the pastor's "owner," Jonathan Bryan, died, Andrew Bryan was able to purchase his freedom for 50 pounds sterling. He and his brother restored their church for African Americans. The former slave lived until 1812. In 1873 his church was torn down, and John Hogg designed a new church at this site.

559 W. Bryan St. ✆ **912/232-5526.** Free tours by appointment only.

7 Literary Landmarks

Long before John Berendt's *Midnight in the Garden of Good and Evil,* other writers were associated with Savannah.

Chief of these was **Flannery O'Connor** (1924–64), one of the South's greatest writers, author of *Wise Blood* (1952) and *The Violent Bear It Away* (1960). She was also known for her short stories, including the collection *A Good Man Is Hard to Find* (1955). She won the O. Henry Award three times. Between October and May, an association dedicated to her holds readings, films, and lectures about her and other Southern writers. You can visit the **Flannery O'Connor Childhood Home,** 207 E. Charlton St. (✆ **912/233-6014**). The house is open only Saturday and Sunday from 1 to 4pm. Admission is free.

Conrad Aiken (1889–1973), the American poet, critic, writer, and Pulitzer Prize winner, was also born in Savannah. He lived at 228 (for the first 11 years of his life) and at 230 E. Oglethorpe Ave. (for the last 11 years of his life). In *Midnight in the Garden of Good and Evil,* Mary Harty and its author sipped martinis at the bench-shaped tombstone of Aiken in Bonaventure Cemetery (see "Martinis in the Cemetery," above).

The **Mercer House,** 429 Bull St., featured in The Book, has been restored and is now open to the public as the **Mercer House Williams Museum** (✆ **877/430-6352;** www.mercerhouse.com; Mon–Tues and Thurs–Sat 10:30am–3:40pm, Sun 12:30–4pm; closed Wed and off-season; $12.50 per person) (it's the primary residence of Jim Williams's sister Dorothy Kingery and her family). Although many of its most elegant contents were auctioned off at Sotheby's in October 2000 for $1 million—including the Anatolian carpet upon which the hapless Danny Hansford is reputed to have fallen after being shot—furniture and art from the private collection of Jim Williams are on display .

Visitors can also shop for books, decorative accessories, and antiques (some from Willams's antiques store and country home) at the **Carriage House Shop,** located directly behind the Mercer House at 430 Whitaker St. Mon–Fri 10am–4:30pm, Sat 10am–5pm, Sun 10:30am–4pm).

8 Especially for Kids

Much of Savannah is kid-friendly, including walks along the waterfront and across the cobblestones of the Historic District. Kids particularly enjoy such recently previewed attractions as the **Ships of the Sea Maritime Museum** and the **Civil War forts** on the outskirts. They're especially fond of the beaches at Tybee Island; see chapter 11. Here's one more sight of interest.

Massie Heritage Interpretation Center Here's a stop in the Historic District for the kids. Geared to school-age children, the center features various exhibits about Savannah, including such subjects as the city's Greek, Roman, and Gothic architecture; the Victorian era; and a history of public education. Other exhibits include a period costume room and a 19th-century classroom, where children can experience a classroom environment from days gone by.

207 E. Gordon St. ✆ **912/201-5070.** Admission $3. Mon–Fri 9am–4pm.

9 Organized Tours

If it's a *Midnight in the Garden of Good and Evil* tour you seek, then you've obviously come to the right place. Virtually every tour group in town offers tours of the *Midnight* sites, many of which are included on their regular agenda. Note that some tour outfits will accommodate only groups, so if you're traveling alone or as a pair, be sure to make that known when you make your tour reservations.

A delightful way to see Savannah is by horse-drawn carriage. An authentic antique carriage carries you over cobblestone streets as the coachman spins a tale of the town's history. The 1-hour tour ($19 for adults, $8 for children 5–11) covers 15 of the 20 squares. Reservations are required, so contact **Carriage Tours of Savannah** at ✆ **912/236-6756.**

Old Town Trolley Tours (✆ **912/233-0083**) operates tours of the Historic District, with pickups at most downtown inns and hotels ($20 for adults, $10 for children 4–12), as well as a 1-hour **Haunted History** tour detailing Savannah's ghostly past (and present). Call to make reservations for the tours you want to take.

Gray Line Savannah Tours (✆ **912/236-9604**) has joined forces with **Historic Savannah Foundation Tours** to feature narrated bus tours of museums, squares, parks, and homes. Reservations must be made for all tours, and most have starting points at the visitor center and pickup points at various hotels. Tours cost $19 for adults and $8 for children 11 and under.

A Visit to the Old Customs House

This Greek Revival building, designed from 1848 to 1852 by John Norris, is the oldest federal building in Georgia. It is an austere granite temple with a "Tower-of-the-Winds" portico. It lies on historic ground: James Edward Oglethorpe lived in the area, and John Wesley delivered his first sermon in Savannah on this site. Today, if you look across Bay Street near the Savannah City Hall, you'll see cannons presented to the Chatham Artillery in 1791 by George Washington.

A one-story frame house originally stood on the site in 1733 and was rented by Oglethorpe. All the granite from the present building was brought down from New England by sea or rail. The granite columns out front weighed 15 to 20 tons each. It took 30 days to transport each column up the 30-foot bluff from the river to the site of the Customs House. Once there, it took yet another month to move the mammoth pillars into place. The carved capitals were modeled from the pattern of a tobacco leaf.

The Customs House stands at 1 E. Bay St. (© **912/652-4264**), and can be viewed at any time.

Savannah Riverboat Cruises are offered aboard the *Savannah River Queen,* operated by the River Street Riverboat Co., 9 E. River St. (© **800/786-6404** or 912/232-6404). You get a glimpse of Savannah as Oglethorpe saw it back in 1733. You'll see the historic cotton warehouses lining River Street and the statue of the *Waving Girl* as the huge modern freighters see it when they arrive daily in Savannah. Lunch and bar service are available. Adults pay $28, and children 12 and under are charged $17.

Ghost Talk Ghost Walk takes you through Colonial Savannah on a journey filled with stories and legends based on Margaret Debolt's book *Savannah Spectres and Other Strange Tales.* If you're not a believer at the beginning of the guided tour, you may be at the end. The tour starts at Reynolds Square. For information, call © **912/233-3896.** Hours for tour departures can vary. The cost is $10 for adults and $5 for children 12 and under.

Low Country River Excursions, a narrated nature cruise, leaves from the Bull River Marina, 8005 Old Tybee Rd. (U.S. 80 East).

Call ✆ **912/898-9222** for information. Passengers are taken on a 1993 38-foot pontoon boat, *Natures Way,* for an encounter with friendly bottle-nosed dolphins. Both scenery and wildlife unfold during the 90-minute cruise down the Bull River. Trips are possible daily at 2 and 4pm and at sunset spring through fall, weather permitting. Adults pay $15, seniors $12, and children 11 and under $10. There's a 30-passenger limit.

10 Sports & Outdoor Activities

From Hilton Head to the Florida line, the southeast coast of South Carolina and Georgia invite exploration. The area has intrigued visitors since the first European explorers arrived on its shore. Arthur Barlowe, one of the earliest British captains to arrive in the area, proclaimed: "I thinke in all the world the like abundance is not to be found."

Hyperbole or not, the region is for the adventurer, as it's filled with islands, inlets, sounds, and nature refuges.

Recreational opportunities abound, and many outfitters in the Savannah area stand ready to hook you up with the action.

BIKING   Savannah doesn't usually have a lot of heavy traffic except during rush hours, so you can bicycle up and down the streets of the Historic District, visiting as many of the green squares as you wish (note that you must *walk* your bike across the squares). There's no greater city bicycle ride in all the state of Georgia. In lieu of a local bike-rental shop, many inns and hotels will provide bikes for their guests.

CAMPING   The **Bellaire Woods Campground,** 805 Fort Argyle Rd. (✆ **912/748-4000**), is 2½ miles west of I-95, 4½ miles west of U.S. 17, and 12 miles from the Savannah Historic District on the banks of the Ogeechee River. Facilities include full hookups, LP gas service, a store, self-service gas and diesel fuel, a dump station, hot showers, a laundry facility, and a pool. Rates are $30 to $35 for tents or RV hookups.

Open year-round, **Skidaway Island State Park** (✆ **912/598-2300**) offers 88 camping sites with full hookups, costing $24. Upon arrival, you purchase a $2 parking pass valid for your entire stay. The grounds include 1- and 3-mile nature trails, grills, picnic tables, a pool, a bathhouse, and a laundry facility. Also open year-round, the **River's End Campground and RV Park,** Polk Street, Tybee Island (✆ **912/786-5518**), consists of 128 sites featuring full hookups,

Exploring the Savannah National Wildlife Refuge

A 10-minute drive across the river from downtown Savannah delivers you to the wild, even though you can see the city's industrial and port complexes in the background. The **Savannah National Wildlife Refuge** 🐊 (© **912/652-4415**; http://savannah.fws.gov), which overflows into South Carolina, was the site of rice plantations in the 1800s and is today a wide expanse of woodland and marsh, ideal for a scenic drive, a canoe ride, a picnic, and most definitely a look at a variety of animals.

From Savannah, get on U.S. Highway 17A, crossing the Talmadge Bridge. It's about 8 miles to the intersection of highways 17 and 17A, where you turn left toward the airport. You'll see the refuge entrance, marked LAUREL HILL WILDLIFE DRIVE, after going some 2 miles. Inside the gate to the refuge is a visitor center, distributing maps and leaflets.

Laurel Hill Wildlife Drive goes on for 4 miles or so. It's possible to bike along this trail. People come here mainly to spy on the alligators, and sightings are almost guaranteed. However, other creatures in the wild abound, including bald eagles and otters. Hikers can veer off the drive and go along Cistern Trail, leading to Recess Island. Because the trail is marked, there's little danger of getting lost.

Nearly 40 miles of dikes are open to birders and backpackers. Canoeists float along tidal creeks, which are fingers of the Savannah River. Fishing and hunting are allowed under special conditions and in the right seasons. Deer and squirrels are commonplace; rarer is the feral hog known along coastal Georgia and South Carolina.

Visits are possible daily from sunrise to sunset. For more information, write the Savannah National Wildlife Refuge, U.S. Fish & Wildlife Service, Savannah Coastal Refuges, P.O. Box 8487, Savannah, GA 31412.

with groceries and a beach nearby. Tent sites cost $27 to $30 per day and RV sites $34 per day.

DIVING The **Diving Locker-Ski Chalet,** 74 W. Montgomery Cross Rd. (© **912/927-6604**), offers a wide selection of equipment and services for various watersports. Scuba classes cost $230 for a series of weekday evening lessons, and $245 for a series of lessons beginning on Friday evening. A full scuba-gear package, including buoyancy-control device, tank, and wet suit, is included. You must provide your own snorkel, mask, fins, and booties. It's open Monday to Friday 10am to 6pm and Saturday 10am to 5pm.

FISHING Amicks Deep Sea Fishing, 6902 Sand Nettles Dr. (✆ 912/897-6759), offers daily charters featuring a 41-foot 1993 custom-built boat. The rate is $95 per person and includes rod, reel, bait, and tackle. Bring your own lunch, though beer and soda are sold on board. Reservations are recommended, but if you show up 30 minutes before the scheduled departure, there may be space available. The boat departs at 7am and returns at 6pm.

GOLF Bacon Park, Shorty Cooper Drive (✆ 912/354-2625), is a 27-hole course with greens fees of $25 for an 18-hole round, including carts. Golf facilities include a lighted driving range, putting greens, and a pro shop. It's open daily dawn to dusk.

Henderson Golf Club, 1 Henderson Dr. (✆ 912/920-4653), includes an 18-hole championship course, a lighted driving range, a PGA professional staff, and golf instruction and schools. The greens fees are $40 Monday to Friday and $44 Saturday and Sunday. It's open daily 7:30am to 10pm.

Or try the 9-hole **Mary Calder,** West Congress Street (✆ 912/238-7100), where the greens fees are $15 per day Monday to Friday and $17 per day Saturday and Sunday. It's open daily 7:30am to 7pm (to 5:30pm in winter).

IN-LINE SKATING At **Diving Locker-Ski Chalet** (see "Diving," above), skate rentals cost $12 for 4 hours and $20 for a full day; a Friday-to-Monday rental goes for $35.

JOGGING "The most beautiful city to jog in"—that's how the president of the Savannah Striders Club characterizes Savannah. He's correct. The historic avenues provide an exceptional setting for your run. The Convention & Visitors Bureau can provide you with a map outlining three of the Striders Club's routes: Heart of Savannah YMCA Course, 3.1 miles; Symphony Race Course, 5 miles; and the Children's Run Course, 5 miles.

NATURE WATCHES Explore the wetlands with **Palmetto Coast Charters,** Lazaretto Creek Marina, Tybee Island (✆ 912/786-5403). Charters include trips to the Barrier Islands for shell collecting and watches for otter, mink, birds, and other wildlife. The captain is a naturalist and a professor, so he can answer your questions. Palmetto also conducts a daily dolphin watch from 4:30 to 6:30pm, when the shrimp boats come in followed by dolphins. The cost is $125 for up to six people for a minimum of 2 hours, plus $50 for each extra hour.

RECREATIONAL PARKS   **Bacon Park** includes 1,021 acres with archery, golf, tennis, and baseball fields. **Daffin Park,** 1500 E. Victory Dr. (© **912/351-3851**), features playgrounds, tennis, basketball, baseball, a pool, a lake pavilion, and picnic grounds. Both parks are open daily: May to September 8am to 11pm and October to April 8am to 10pm.

Located at Montgomery Cross Road and Sallie Mood Drive, **Lake Mayer Park** (© **912/652-6780**) consists of 75 acres featuring a multitude of activities, such as fishing and boating, lighted jogging and bicycle trails, a playground, tennis courts, and pedal boats.

SAILING   **Sail Harbor,** 618 Wilmington Island Rd. (© **912/ 897-2896**), features the Catalina 25 boat, costing $150 per full day, $100 for an extra day. It's open Tuesday to Saturday 10am to 6pm and Sunday 12:30 to 5:30pm.

8

Savannah Strolls

The only real way to discover Savannah is in your walking shoes. Wear sturdy ones along the often-cobbled streets. Walking is a fun way to encounter the city up close.

WALKING TOUR 1	MIDNIGHT IN THE GARDEN OF GOOD AND EVIL

Start:	Mercer House.
Finish:	Whitefield Square.
Time:	2½ hours.
Best Times:	Any day from 9am to 5pm, when there's less traffic.
Worst Times:	Between 5 and 6:30pm, when stores are closing and traffic is heavier. Also after dark.

At press time, John Berendt's *Midnight in the Garden of Good and Evil* has reached 2.5 million in hardcover sales alone, and the release of the film, directed by Clint Eastwood, spurred renewed interest in The Book, as it's called in Savannah. The film is now shown on television and is available in DVD rental outlets. The tour below assumes that you have read the book and/or have seen the film and are somewhat familiar with the principal characters. *Midnight* is to Savannah what *Gone With the Wind* was (and is) to Atlanta.

You might as well begin at the center of all the excitement, the "scene of the crime," which stands on the southwest corner of Monterey Square:

❶ Mercer House

Begin at 429 Bull St., a splendid Italianate redbrick mansion built around 1860. It was here in May 1981 that wealthy antiques dealer Jim Williams, about 50, fatally shot his lover/assistant, blond "walking streak of sex" Danny Hansford, age 21. Williams claimed that he'd shot Danny in self-defense because Danny was waving a gun around and taking shots. Williams was tried three times in Savannah. He was found guilty twice, though each conviction was overturned; the third time was declared a mistrial because of a hung jury.

Walking Tour: Midnight in the Garden of Good and Evil

1 Mercer House	8 Oglethorpe Club
2 Mercer Carriage Shop	9 Forsyth Parkside Apartments
3 Lee Adler's House	10 Virginia and John Duncan's House
4 Serena Dawes' House	11 Joe Odom's first house
5 Alex Raskin Antiques	12 22 East Jones St.
6 Congregation Mickve Israel	13 Hamilton Turner House
7 Armstrong House	14 Whitefield Square

He finally was acquitted at a fourth trial, held in Augusta, far removed from the intrigues of the Savannah swamps. As a result, Jim Williams became the first person in Georgia to be tried four times for murder.

Mercer House is also where each year Williams gave his legendary Christmas parties—Friday night for the cream of society and Saturday night "for gentlemen only." Note the lavender interior shutters on the second story's right-hand window. They shield from the sun what Williams called his "playroom," site of *trompe l'oeil* baroque-style frescoes and one of Savannah's most valuable pipe organs. The shooting occurred (as you face the house) in Williams's study, illuminated by the ground floor's right-hand window.

In January 1990, Jim Williams died of a heart attack at 59. As recounted in the book, a strange coincidence occurred at this time: Williams died in the room where he'd killed Hansford, and his body was found behind his desk in the exact spot where his body would have been found in 1981 if Hansford had shot at him and not missed.

Though Jacqueline Kennedy Onassis reportedly once offered Williams $2 million for Mercer House, it's today inhabited by Williams's sister, Dorothy Williams Kingery, who allowed Clint Eastwood's film crew complete access—all for a price, mind you, despite her condemnation of the "circus atmosphere" surrounding her brother's trials and the publication of The Book.

And, no, Johnny Mercer never lived in this house, though his great-grandfather built it.

Monterey Square itself is one of the most interesting in Savannah. The statue in this square represents Lady Liberty atop a stone plinth and is dedicated to Casimir Pulaski, the gallant Polish military officer of Revolutionary War fame. He looks back archly over his shoulder at Mercer House. During production of The Film, the statue was removed for restoration, so Clint Eastwood had a plywood, Styrofoam, and plastic copy constructed.

In back of the house still stands:

❷ Mercer House Carriage Shop

It was here, in Mercer House's detached carriage house at 430 Whitaker St., that Williams offered for sale some of the Deep South's finest antiques, lovely pieces that he'd discovered and restored. He even managed to run this business while he was in jail after his second trial. The property is now a shop where you can buy souvenirs related to The Book and Savannah, as well as tickets to tour Mercer House.

Walk back to the front of Mercer House, and proceed north on Bull Street to:

❸ Lee Adler's House

This half of a double town house at 425 Bull St. is the home of Williams's nemesis, antagonistic Lee Adler and his wife, Emma. Though they seemed to always be at odds, the major animosity between Adler and Williams started when Williams (then president of the Telfair museum's board of directors) set about getting Adler kicked off the board. It's said that Williams used to play his thunderous organ to counter Adler's howling dogs. Facing West Wayne Street, this house is where Adler runs his business of restoring historic properties—and where he used binoculars to spy on one of the all-male Christmas parties of his "decadent" neighbor.

Walk south on Bull Street, past Mercer House, and cross West Gordon Street. Here you'll find:

❹ Serena Dawes's House

The former home of Helen Drexel (whose pseudonym in The Book is Serena Dawes) is at 17 W. Gordon St. Known as one of the world's most beautiful women, Drexel was Williams's flamboyant neighbor—called "the soul of pampered self-absorption." On most days, she received guests in her boudoir, where she drank pink ladies or martinis, gossiping indiscreetly and planning her appearances at various parties in the evening. One of her most frequent gentleman callers—to borrow an expression from Tennessee Williams (no relation to Jim)—was Luther Driggers, the inventor of the flea collar, who was said to possess a poison so powerful that it could wipe out the entire city of Savannah.

Walk east on West Gordon Street, to Bull Street. Here you'll find:

❺ Alex Raskin Antiques

Williams often came to this stately building, at 441 Bull St. (© **912/ 232-8205**), constructed between 1860 and 1870 and known as the Noble Hardee Mansion, to shop for antiques. With a shrewd eye for taste and value, he often made purchases from the present owner, Alex Raskin, who's loath to discuss the notoriety surrounding his friend. "He was a neighbor," is all Raskin has to say on the subject.

After a visit, head south from Madison Square along Bull Street, taking a left turn to reach East Jones Street. Along this street lived the author when he first arrived in Savannah, as well as some of the characters associated with The Book.

Walk back to Monterey Square, turn right, and head for the southeast corner of the square, where you'll see:

❻ Congregation Mickve Israel

The third-oldest congregation of Judaism in America, Mickve Israel was established in 1733. The present synagogue was consecrated in 1878. In 1979, on what he called "Flag Day," Williams shocked Savannah by draping a Nazi banner over a balcony at Mercer House, sending ripples of outrage through the city and especially this synagogue. The action wasn't an anti-Semitic act: A film crew was in town shooting a TV movie, *The Trial of Dr. Mudd,* and wanted to use Monterey Square and Mercer House as a backdrop. The people who lived around the square weren't consulted and weren't pleased by the mess and inconvenience, so they asked Williams to intercede. When the producer didn't respond appropriately, Williams decided to ruin their shot (they managed to get the shot anyway).

Williams said that he didn't intend any disrespect to the synagogue: By spoiling the camera's views, he claimed, he had intended merely to teach a lesson to a film crew who, like latter-day carpetbaggers, were trampling on the sensitivities of his beloved Savannah. However, he had no such scruples years later—after his third trial but before his fourth—when a crew came to town to film scenes for *Glory.* He not only didn't interfere with filming but actually opened Mercer House and let the crew use it.

Walk back towards Alex Raskin Antiques and continue south along Bull Street until you reach:

⑦ Armstrong House

After its construction in 1917, this Italian Renaissance palazzo at 447 Bull St. was Savannah's largest and most expensive home. Once owned by Williams, who faithfully restored the building, it housed the collector's antiques business for a year until he sold it to the law firm of Bouhan, Williams, and Levy. Frank "Sonny" Seiler, the colorful attorney who represented Williams in his last three trials, is a partner in this firm. The house, as depicted in The Book, sits with a curving colonnade that reaches "out like a giant paw as if to swat the Oglethorpe Club off its high horse across the street."

Legend has it that George Armstrong built the house to dwarf the Oglethorpe Club in retaliation for being blackballed from the exclusive club. It was here that Berendt met Simon Glover, an 86-year-old singer working as a porter for the law firm. Glover told the author that he earned $10 extra every week by walking a former law partner's deceased dog, Patrick, up and down Bull Street. Though the dog was long buried, many passersby always commented on the good health of the dog and asked about his welfare.

Across from Armstrong House is the:

⑧ Oglethorpe Club

The most exclusive club in Savannah and the oldest gentlemen's club in Georgia is here at 450 Bull St. The club, which Berendt used to visit, attracts the cream of Savannah's blue bloods. Ladies are admitted only if wearing a dress; pantsuits are forbidden.

Facing Forsyth Park, turn right on West Gaston Street, and then turn left on Whitaker Street. Continue down Whitaker until you reach the southwestern corner of Forsyth Park, where you'll see:

⑨ Forsyth Parkside Apartments

It was here, in his second Savannah apartment, that Berendt wrote most of *Midnight.* It was here also that he met the Grand Empress of Savannah, the Lady Chablis. She had just emerged from Dr. Myra Bishop's office across the street where she'd received her latest estrogen shots to make her "body smooth all over." Berendt soon became her "chauffeur" and witnessed several of her scenes, the most outrageous of which was gate-crashing the black debutante ball.

Return to Monterey Square to the north and walk to the far northeast corner, where you'll come to:

⑩ Virginia & John Duncan's House

Owned by John Duncan, professor of local history, and his charming wife, Virginia, this stucco-fronted house at 12 E. Taylor St., between Bull and Drayton streets, was built in 1869, with embellishments added in the 1890s. Long known for the parties given here, this was the setting where Berendt picked up stories and heard local gossip that he later included in the book. Virginia plays a minor role: It was she who, while walking her dog, was the first to detect the swastika banner waving from Jim Williams's balcony at Mercer House.

At the building's street level is **V&J Duncan Antique Maps, Prints, and Books** (𝄏 **912/232-0338**), where antique maps from around the world, as well as from the lowlands around Savannah, are sold. The house's upper floors contain the bed (acquired after her death) where Serena Dawes used to hold court.

Continue north along Bull Street. Heading east, you'll reach:

⑪ Joe Odom's First House

Located at 16 E. Jones St., this was the temporary home of the notorious Joe Odom (tax lawyer, real estate broker, and piano player) when Berendt moved to Savannah. Berendt first came here in the company of Mandy Nichols, Odom's "fourth wife-in-waiting." Odom had an open-door policy: Though this "sentimental gentleman from Georgia" was constantly broke and almost never paid rent (except for a bounced check or two), a party was always going on at his place day or night. Known for living as an uninvited guest in uninhabited residences, Odom once operated the piano jazz bar Sweet Georgia Brown's until it went bankrupt, though it's now immortalized in The Book.

Continue east on East Jones Street until you reach:

⑫ E. Jones St.

This is the carriage house where Berendt first lived in Savannah. It was here that he began to gather information that after 7 years he'd publish in his bestseller. In 1992, his first agent (whose name the author graciously won't reveal) returned the manuscript, claiming that she didn't think she could interest a publisher in "taking a chance on a book of this kind." She believed the book was "too local."

Continue along East Jones Street, heading east until you reach Abercorn Street.

TAKE A BREAK
Clary's Café, 404 Abercorn St., at Jones Street (© **912/233-0402**). Savannah has been enjoying great food and conversation here since 1903. Today, along with flame-broiled burgers, the store carries souvenirs of The Book, not only T-shirts but also postcards of the Lady Chablis. Both Chablis ("My mama took my name from a wine bottle") and Berendt have frequented the place for its good-tasting food. When we last encountered her ladyship here, she informed us that all this "fuss about The Book is helping [her] save up the big ones for [her] retirement one day."

Continue north along Abercorn Street to Lafayette Square and the site of:

⑬ Hamilton-Turner Inn

In The Book, this was Joe Odom's fourth and grandest residence, at 330 Abercorn St. (© **888/448-8849** or 912/233-4800), built in 1873 in the Second Empire style. The exterior remains intact, though the interior has been restored and converted into one of the most charming inns of Savannah (see chapter 5). One of its apartments was once occupied by Mandy Nichols (real name, Nancy Hillis), who used to sing at Sweet Georgia Brown's. Once voted Miss Big Beautiful Woman, she was involved with Joe Odom until she kicked him out.

From Lafayette Square, head east along East Charlton, cutting right along Habersham. This will lead to:

⑭ Whitefield Square

One of Savannah's lovely though overlooked squares, Whitefield was the turf of hustler Danny Hansford. Fiercely territorial, Danny guarded this square as if he owned it. When another hustler once moved in on his territory, Danny beat him so badly that the competition nearly ended up in the hospital. This idyllic-looking verdant square, centered on a gazebo, was named after the Rev. George Whitefield, who in 1738 succeeded John Wesley as the Church of England's minister to the Georgia colony.

At the edge of the square is the redbrick bulk of the **Rose of Sharon,** a retirement home/hospital. Run by the Catholic Sisters of Mercy, it was here that a penniless Joe Odom, suffering from AIDS, came to die, at age 44. It's fitting to end the tour on Danny's once ferociously guarded turf because it's often forgotten that without him, there would have been no murder, no four trials, no book, no millions in royalties and film rights. And Savannah itself would be poorer by some $150 million (the estimate to date of how much tourism revenue the city has generated from Danny's murder and The Book). Not bad for a young man who used to sell himself for $30 a night.

WALKING TOUR 2   HISTORIC SAVANNAH

Start:	River Street.
Finish:	Chippewa Square.
Time:	2½ hours.
Best Times:	Monday through Saturday from 9am to 5pm, when most of the stores and attractions are open. On the first Saturday of each month there's a River Street festival.
Worst Times:	Monday through Saturday after 5pm, when traffic is heavy. On Sunday, there's little life except on the riverfront.

Begin your walk almost where Savannah began, at the port opening onto:

❶ River Street

This street runs along the Savannah River. (Ramps lead down from Bay St.) The cobblestones came from ballast left behind by early sailing ships coming up the Savannah River. In the mid–19th century, the present brick buildings were most often warehouses holding King Cotton.

On your left is **John P. Rousakis Plaza.** A multimillion-dollar restoration has revived the riverfront, now a 9-block area ideal for strolling and watching ships. Some 80 boutiques, galleries, restaurants, pubs, and artists' studios line the riverfront. All the old cotton warehouses have been restored to a rustic beauty. If you happen to be here on the first Saturday of any month, you'll be swept up in a River Street festival, with entertainment, street vendors, sidewalk artists, and craftspeople hustling their achievements.

Near the eastern end of the walk, you'll reach Morrell Park, site of the:

❷ *Waving Girl* Statue

This tribute to Florence Martus (1869–1943) stands at the foot of the East Broad Street ramp. The statue depicts a young girl waving toward the ships in the harbor. It's said that Florence fell in love with a sailor, and she promised to greet every ship until he returned to marry her. For 44 years, she waved a white cloth by day and a lantern by night to every ship entering the harbor past the Elba Island Light, where she lived with her brother. Greatly loved and looked for eagerly by seamen, she never missed an arriving ship (she said that she could "feel" them approaching) and assisted in at least one heroic rescue. Her own sailor never returned.

At the eastern end of the park, take a sharp right and begin your stroll back west along:

❸ Factors Walk

In the 19th century, Factors Walk, between River and Bay streets, was named for the Factors (brokers) who graded the cotton for its quality. Now restored, the walk is filled with specialty shops, often selling antiques. Buildings rise two or three floors above the bluff. The lower floors were cotton and naval warehouses. Connecting bridges lead to upper-level offices opening onto Bay Street.

When you reach Bay Street, turn right and go back to River Street to:

TAKE A BREAK
Wet Willie's, 101 E. River St. (✆ **912/233-5650**), offers an array of frozen alcoholic beverages. Hamburgers, quesadillas, and chicken fingers are also featured.

After refueling, climb the brick stairs up to Bay Street, exiting at the River Street Inn. You'll be at Old City Exchange Hill, site of the:

❹ Savannah Cotton Exchange

The former exchange building now houses the Solomon's Lodge Number 1 of the Free Masons. When it was built in 1887, it was the major center for cotton trading. An example of the Romantic Revival period, it became one of the first buildings in America to use "air rights" and was erected completely over a public street. Its wrought-iron railing honors famous writers and politicians.

Continue down the street, heading west until you reach:

❺ City Hall

City Hall dates from 1905. The two floors of this building open onto the spot where, on May 22, 1819, the S.S. *Savannah* set sail. It became the first steamship to cross the Atlantic.

Continue along Bay Street, and turn left onto Whitaker Street. Go down Whitaker until you reach Congress Street, then turn right. Past the parking garage you will reach:

❻ City Market

The market occupies 4 blocks in the Historic District. Renovated to capture the atmosphere of the past, it's filled with specialty shops, restaurants, bars, and open-air jazz clubs, along with many theme shops, particularly those selling crafts, accessories, and gifts.

❼ City Market Art Center

The center is on the upper floor of a complex of restored feed-and-seed warehouses at the western end of City Market. The Art Center houses the working studios of three dozen of Savannah's finest

1 River Street	**7** City Market
2 *Waving Girl* Statue	**8** Telfair Square
3 Factors Walk	**9** Wright Square
4 Savannah Cotton Exchange	**10** Oglethorpe Square
5 City Hall	**11** Colonial Park Cemetery
6 City Market Art Center	**12** Chippewa Square

artists, including photographers, stained-glass designers, sculptors, painters, woodcarvers, and fiber artists.

When you reach the end of the City Market at Franklin Square, turn left onto Montgomery Street and proceed south. Turn left on State Street and continue east until you reach:

⑧ Telfair Square

Located between York and State streets, it was originally called St. James's Square but was renamed for the Telfair family in 1883. Modern federal buildings are located on two sides of the square. It's also home to the **Telfair Mansion and Art Museum,** the Royal Governor's residence from 1760 until the end of the Revolutionary War. Today it's a museum of the arts.

Continue east along President Street until you come to:

⑨ Wright Square

The square was named for Sir James Wright, the third and last colonial governor of Georgia. A large boulder marks the grave of Tomochichi, the Yamacraw Indian chief who befriended Oglethorpe's colonists. A monument here honors William Washington Gordon I, early Georgia financier and founder of the Central Georgia Railway.

Proceeding east from the square (still on President St.), you will come to:

⑩ Oglethorpe Square

Mapped out in 1742, the square between State and York streets honors, of course, Gen. James Oglethorpe, founder of Georgia. The Owens-Thomas House (p. 19) is on the northeast lot of this square.

From Oglethorpe Square, head south along Abercorn until you reach:

⑪ Colonial Park Cemetery

On your left, the cemetery was opened to burials from 1750 to 1850. It became the second public burial ground of Old Savannah, and many famous Georgians were buried here, including Button Gwinnett, a signer of the Declaration of Independence, and Edward Green Malbone, the famous miniature painter. You can wander the grounds from dawn to dusk, exploring the inscriptions on the old tombstones.

From the cemetery, go west this time along East McDonough Street until you reach:

⑫ Chippewa Square

Located along Bull Street, between Perry and Hull streets, the square holds a bronze figure immortalizing General Oglethorpe, done by Daniel Chester French, dean of American sculptors. The square is visited today by hordes not wanting to see Georgia's founder but to sit on the bench where Tom Hanks sat in *Forrest Gump*. The movie bench isn't here, since it was only a prop, but plop yourself down somewhere on the square anyway and have a few minutes of relaxation.

9

Shopping

While you don't go to Savannah solely for the shopping, while you're there, there are some unique shops to browse (especially if you're looking for antiques) and several excellent galleries. Of course, the popular chains and several department stores are represented at the major malls, and outlet shopping is available as well.

River Street is a shopper's delight, with some 9 blocks (including Riverfront Plaza) of interesting shops, offering everything from crafts to clothing to souvenirs. The **City Market,** between Ellis and Franklin squares on West St. Julian Street, boasts art galleries, boutiques, and sidewalk cafes along with a horse-and-carriage ride. Bookstores, boutiques, and antiques shops are also located between Wright Square and Forsyth Park.

Oglethorpe Mall, at 7804 Abercorn St., has more than 100 specialty shops, four major department stores, a Barnes & Noble, and a selection of restaurants and fast-food outlets. The **Savannah Mall,** 14045 Abercorn St., is Savannah's newest shopping center, offering two floors of shopping. Included on the premises is a food court with its own carousel. The anchor stores are Dillard's, Target, and Bass Pro Shops Outdoor World.

Some 30 manufacturer-owned "factory direct" stores offer savings up to 70% at the **Savannah Festival Factory Stores,** Abercorn Street at I-95 (© **912/925-3089**). Shops like T-shirts Plus and the Duckhead Outlet feature name brands of shoes, luggage, gifts, cosmetics, household items, toys, and clothing.

1 Shopping A to Z

ANTIQUES

Abercorn Antique Village   Savannahians come here to shop in a self-described setting of "shabby chic." Vendors featuring some 50 dealers and designers are set up in a historic house, a cottage, and an adjacent carriage house. The "village" is strong on vintage silver, crystal, furniture, linens, clocks, and paintings from the 18th to the 20th centuries. 201 E. 37th St. © **912/233-0064.**

Alex Raskin Antiques   This shop offers a wide array of antiques of varying ages. The selection includes everything from accessories to furniture, rugs, and paintings. 441 Bull St. (in the Noble Hardee Mansion), Monterey Sq. ℭ **912/232-8205.**

Clipper Trading Company   This store imports antique furnishings and decorative accent pieces from Southeast Asia, including China, Myanmar (Burma), and Thailand. To make it easier for you, the collection is arranged by country. Vendors sell rare pieces such as Han Dynasty burial urns (206 B.C.–A.D. 220), Song Dynasty bowls (A.D. 960–1279), and Ming and early Qing Dynasty furniture. Other items of interest are woodcarvings, alabaster Buddha statues, ancestral paintings, and temple objects. 201 W. Broughton St. ℭ **912/238-3660.**

J. D. Weed & Co.   This shop prides itself on providing "that wonderful treasure that combines history and personal satisfaction with rarity and value." If you're looking for a particular item, let the staff know and they'll try to find it for you. 102 W. Victory Dr. ℭ **912/234-8540.**

Memory Lane   More than 8,000 square feet of collectibles can be found here. The store's specialty is a collection of German sleds and wagons. You'll also find glassware, furniture, and pottery. 230 W. Bay St. ℭ **912/232-0975.**

ART & SCULPTURE

Compass Prints, Inc./Ray Ellis Gallery   From 1998 to 2000, Ray Ellis was the artist chosen to paint the official White House Christmas card. All three of his original paintings are part of the permanent White House collection of art. This gallery features Ellis's original watercolors, oils, and bronzes, as well as limited-edition prints, reproductions, art books, and other gift items. 205 W. Congress St. ℭ **912/234-3537.**

Gallery 209   Housed in an 1820s cotton warehouse, this gallery displays two stories of original paintings by local artists, sculpture, woodworking, fiber art, gold and silver jewelry, enamels, photography, batiks, pottery, and stained glass. You'll also find a wide selection of limited-edition reproductions and notecards of local scenes. 209 E. River St. ℭ **912/236-4583.**

John Tucker Fine Arts ℛ   This gallery offers museum-quality pieces by local artists as well as artists from around the world, including Haitian and Mexican craftspeople. The restored 1800s home features 19th- and 20th-century landscapes, marine-art painting, portraits, folk art, and still lifes. 5 W. Charlton St. ℭ **912/231-8161.**

Morning Star Gallery   This gallery features the works of more than 80 artists. Pieces include hand-thrown pottery, metalwork, paintings, prints, woodworks, jewelry, and glass (hand-blown and leaded). 8 E. Liberty St. ℭ **912/233-4307.**

Village Craftsmen   This collective of artisans offers a wide array of handmade crafts, including hand-blown glass, needlework, folk art, limited-edition prints, restored photographs, and hand-thrown pottery. 223 W. River St. ℭ **912/236-7280.**

BAKED GOODS

Baker's Pride Bakery   If it's baked, it's here: a wide range of pastries, rich-tasting cookies, and the town's most delectable and aromatic muffins fresh from the oven. The leading family bakery in Savannah since 1982, the establishment has been expanded to include a dining section for those who want to consume the baked goods on-site. Gathering the makings for a party, we loaded up on such desserts as cream puffs, both Key lime and pecan squares, coconut tarts, date bars, assorted rugelach, éclairs dipped in chocolate, strawberry tarts, and strudel. Kids love the store's gingerbread men, and who can fault the superb macaroons? 840 E. DeRenne Ave. ℭ **912/355-1155.**

BLACKSMITH

Walsh Mountain Ironworks   This is the sales outlet of the most successful and high-profile blacksmith in Savannah. Inventories include house, kitchen, and garden ornaments, many of which have modern, but vaguely Gothic, designs. Among the objects for sale are headboards for beds, garden arbors, trellises, tables, chairs, wine racks, CD racks, and ornamental screens. Prices range from $4 to $1,600, and in some cases require several weeks of waiting. 427 Whitaker St. ℭ **912/239-9818.**

BOOKS

Barnes & Noble   This superstore is located in the Oglethorpe Mall. The store holds many events, including a regular open mic night for poetry readings. 7804 Abercorn St. ℭ **912-353-7757.**

Books-a-Million   This enormous store is located in the Abercorn Plaza. 8108 Abercorn St. ℭ **912-925-8112.**

Book Warehouse   You'll find more than 75,000 titles here, including fiction, cookbooks, children's books, computer manuals, and religious tomes. Prices begin at less than a dollar, and all proceeds are donated to Emory University for cancer research. 11 Gateway Blvd. ℭ **912/927-0824.**

E. Shaver, Bookseller   Housed on the ground floor of a Greek Revival mansion in the Historic District, E. Shaver has been a Savannah institution for more than 25 years. This charming store features 12 rooms of tomes and a friendly, knowledgeable staff. The store specializes in books on architecture, decorative arts, and regional history; children's books; and 17th-, 18th-, and 19th-century maps. 326 Bull St. ✆ **912/234-7257.**

CANDY & OTHER FOODS

Byrd Cookie Company   Located 6 miles from the historic center, this store started as a small, family-run local bakery in 1924. Today it's one of Georgia's leading manufacturers in the gourmet industry. Its retail store and showplace, the mammoth Gourmet Marketplace, has it all, including a complete floral design department, daily in-store sampling displays, custom designs such as gift baskets, nautically themed merchandise and, of course, the entire Byrd Cookie line of products. The food line includes not only cookies and candy, but relishes, jams, preserves, salsas, salad dressings, and other specialty items. 6700 Waters Ave. ✆ **912/355-1716.**

Plantation Sweets Vidalia Onions   Outside Savannah, check out the Vidalia onion specialties offered by the Collins family for more than 50 years. Sample one of the relishes, dressings, or gift items. Call for directions. Rte. 2, Cobbtown. ✆ **800/541-2272.**

River Street Sweets   Begun more than 20 years ago as part of the River Street restoration project, this store offers a wide selection of candies, including pralines, bearclaws, fudge, and chocolates. More than 30 flavors of taffy are made on a machine from the early 1900s. 13 E. River St. ✆ **800/627-6175** or 912/234-4608.

Savannah's Candy Kitchen   Chocolate-dipped Oreos, glazed pecans, pralines, and fudge are only a few of the delectables at this confectionery. While enjoying the candies or ice cream, you can watch the taffy machine in action. The store is so sure you'll be delighted with its offerings that it offers a full money-back guarantee if you're not satisfied. 225 E. River St. ✆ **800/242-7919** or 912/233-8411.

GIFTS & COLLECTIBLES

The Book Gift Shop   At Calhoun Square, this store is the official memorabilia headquarters for *Midnight in the Garden of Good and Evil.* Just about anything you can think of that has to do with The Book can be found here, including The Book (of course), coasters, T-shirts, charms, earrings, golf towels, statues, cookies, bookmarks, music, and DVDs. 127 E. Gordon St. ✆ **912/233-3867.**

Charlotte's Corner   Featuring local items, this shop offers a wide array of gifts and souvenirs. The selection encompasses children's clothing, a few food items, Sheila houses, and Savannah-related books, including guidebooks and Southern cookbooks. 1 W. Liberty St. (at Bull St.). ✆ 912/233-8061.

The Christmas Shop   This shop keeps the Christmas spirit alive all year with a large selection of ornaments, Santas, nutcrackers, and collectibles. Collectors will appreciate the various featured lines, including Dept 56, Polonaise, Christina's World, and Patricia Breen. 307 Bull St. ✆ 912/234-5343.

Enchantments   If you collect bears or dolls, this store has one for you. Its other selections include quality toys and collector's pieces. 407 E. Montgomery Cross Rd. ✆ 912/651-9035.

A Fine Choice   This is one of the best places for high-quality gifts in Savannah. In its gifts and collectibles category, it carries more than 20 different lines of merchandise. Among them are paperweights from Scotland and America, Polish hand-carved wooden boxes, Polish mouth-blown glass, Italian porcelains, Celtic pieces, lead glass "fairies" and angels, and art reproductions. 10 W. State St. ✆ 912/650-1845.

Le Belle Maison   This is one of Savannah's best outlets for gifts from all over the world in all shapes, sizes, and prices. You'll find such delights as bread knives in carved wood *baquette,* terra-cotta dolls dressed in Provençal fabrics (made entirely by hand in Marseille), and handcrafted lamps with mouth-blown glass, along with soaps and shampoos produced from pure botanical essences harvested in Provence. Wood grain soaps, for example, are made from cedar, pine, and sandalwood. It's a delight to breathe the fragrances in this store, including lavender, magnolia, and almond blossom. 230 Bull St. ✆ 912/236-1700.

True Grits   Located along River Street, this outlet welcomes you aggressively to the land of cotton. Civil War books, a display of Civil War swords, even authentic Civil War artifacts keep alive that memory of "The War of Northern Aggression." Naturally there are Confederate T-shirts and such "fun" items as 10-gauge blank-firing cannons. The shop is strong on nautical accessories, including ship bells and models. It also features Southern gourmet food items. 107 E. River St. ✆ 912/234-8006.

HOME FURNISHINGS

Wonderful Things   In an 1880s restored building, this retailer specializes in romantic home decor, including linens, bed products, and furnishings. Items range from a Victorian wicker loveseat and coffee table to candelabras to armoires to drawer liners to bath salts. 115 W. Broughton St. ✆ **912/447-0004.**

JEWELRY & SILVER

Levy Jewelers   Located downtown, this boutique deals mainly in antique jewelry. It offers a large selection of gold, silver, gems, and watches. Among its other items are crystal, china, and gifts. The main store is on Broughton Street, but they also have stores at the Oglethorpe and Savannah malls. 101 E. Broughton St. ✆ **912/233-1163.**

Simply Silver   The specialty here is sterling flatware, ranging from today's designs to discontinued items of yesteryear. The inventory includes new and estate pieces along with a wide array of gift items. 103 W. Liberty St. ✆ **912/238-3652.**

MUSIC

The Folk Traditions Store ⩗   This store sells musical instruments, especially flutes, harps, and banjos, along with printed music. A variety of instruments is provided for you to experience. The store's owner, David Dirlam, takes his music, and especially his instruments, seriously, and is on hand to guide you to the instrument you desire. He specializes in hammered dulcimers. Folk artists view this store as a mecca. 414 Whitaker St. (at Taylor). ✆ **912/341-8898.**

10

Savannah After Dark

River Street, along the Savannah River, is the major after-dark venue. Many night owls stroll the waterfront until they hear the sound of music they like, then follow their ears inside.

In summer, concerts of jazz, Big Band, and Dixieland music fill downtown **Johnson Square** with foot-tapping sounds that thrill both locals and visitors. Some of Savannah's finest musicians perform regularly at this historic site.

1 The Performing Arts

Johnny Mercer Theater, Orleans Square (© 800/537-7894 or 912/236-9536), is home to ballet, musicals, and touring Broadway shows. Call to find out what's being presented at the time of your visit. Tickets range from $25 to $50.

Some of the best entertainment in Savannah is presented at the restored 1921 **Lucas Theatre,** 32 Abercorn St. (© 912/525-5050). The box office is at 216 E. Broughton St.; call 912/525-5050 or 912/525-5040. The Lucas was Savannah's first and only movie palace. The theater shut down in 1976 but was restored and reopened in 2000. It now plays host to everything from jazz bands to dance theater, from concerts by classical artists to ballets such as *Cinderella* by the Ballet Savannah troupe. Depending on the presentation, tickets range from $13 to $35.

Many of these cultural events are sponsored by **SCAD** (www.scad.edu/events/index.html). SCAD, the Savannah College of Art & Design, hosts a wide range of events throughout the year, even sponsoring a Savannah Film Festival in October that attracts filmmakers from around the world. Spring fashion shows and an arts festival are only some of the presentations of this cultural group.

Late September brings the 5-day **Savannah Jazz Festival** ★★ (© 912/232-2222), when nationally known musicians perform around the city.

Savannah Theater, Chippewa Square (© 912/233-7764), presents musical reviews. Tickets are usually $32 for regular admission,

$30 for seniors or students, $15 for ages 12 to 16, and $10 for children 11 and under.

2 Live Music Clubs

Deja Groove   The setting is a severe-looking 19th-century warehouse perched on soaring bulwarks on the sloping embankment between River Walk and the busy traffic of Bay Street. Inside, you'll find an intriguing blend of exposed brick and timber, psychedelic artwork, and a youthful (under 35-ish) sense of hip. There's a dance floor featuring dance music from the '70s and '80s, at least two sprawling bar areas, video games, and about a dozen pool tables, priced at $1 per game. Entrance is usually free, but sometimes a $3 cover charge is levied after 10pm. Hours are Tuesday through Thursday 8:30pm to 3am, Friday and Saturday 8pm to 3am. 301 Williamson St. ✆ 912/644-4566.

Hannah's East ⟨⟩   This club, the most popular in Savannah, is the showcase for jazz greats, including the late Emma Kelly, "The Lady of 6,000 Songs," who appeared in *Midnight in the Garden of Good and Evil.* The current reigning jazz artist holds forth Tuesday through Sunday 6 to 9pm. A Monday special features authentic Dixieland and New Orleans–style jazz, beginning at 6pm. At the Pirates' House, 20 E. Broad St. ✆ 912/233-2225. Cover $5 Fri–Sat after 9pm.

Monkey Bar   This is a "high octane" bar in the Fusion Restaurant, with a self-proclaimed "martini chic" atmosphere and a sort of West Indies decor. Longtime restaurateur and club owner Wendy Snowden is the hostess, welcoming all for a good time. The live music agenda changes every night, ranging from piano music to soul. Sometimes the hottest bands in Savannah can be found rocking away the night here. Drink specials are labeled "Jungle Mai-Tais," "Monkey Shots," or similar, and Monkey Hour with reduced drink prices is from 5 to 8pm. The club opens at 4pm Tuesday through Saturday with no set closing time. 8 E. Broughton St. ✆ 912/232-0755.

Planters Tavern ⟨⟩   This is Savannah's most beloved tavern, graced with a sprawling and convivial bar, a pair of fireplaces, and a decor of antique bricks and carefully polished hardwoods. Because it's in the cellar of the Olde Pink House Restaurant, many diners ask to be served at the tavern's tables. Otherwise, you can sit, drink in hand, listening to the melodies emanating from the sadder-but-wiser pianist. Foremost among the divas who perform is the endearingly elegant Gail Thurmond, one of Savannah's most legendary songstresses, who weaves her enchantment Tuesday through Sunday nights. In the Olde Pink House Restaurant, 23 Abercorn St. © 912/232-4286.

Savannah Blues   The name is so obvious, some club owner had to choose it. Established in 1998, this is the home of the Eric Culberson Blues Band, which has a good local following. Live blues music is featured every night and, as the owner states, "music gets kickin' after 10." Most nights have a theme: Beer Night on Monday, Jam Night on Tuesday, a house band on Wednesday. Happy hour is until 8pm every night. The club is open Monday through Tuesday 7pm to 3am; and Wednesday through Saturday 5pm to 3am. 206 W. St. Julian St. © 912/447-5044. Cover charge for live music, $5 and up.

Velvet Lounge ☆☆   This is Savannah's number-one live music venue, as noted in the city's *Creative Loafing* magazine. It's known as punk-rock heaven to its hundreds of local fans, with a battered but prominent stage for live bands, and a wraparound collection of rock 'n' roll memorabilia and kitsch. Until its current manifestation, it was a hippie-style junk store; now you're likely to find such visiting luminaries as Kevin Spacey, John Cusack, and Tracey Cunningham. Hours are Monday through Saturday from 5pm to 3am. 127 W. Congress St. © 912/236-0665. Cover charge for live music $5–$10, depending on the band.

3 Bar Hoppin' & Pub Crawling

Bernies   This bar and grill, conveniently located on the riverfront, occupies one of the pre–Civil War cotton warehouses and has the ambience of an old portside pub. The bar offers live music, televised sports, and extended late weekend hours. The bartenders claim that their Bloody Mary is the best on River Street; it's presented in a Mason jar and topped with pickled okra. If you're hungry, a light menu features seafood, burgers, and sandwiches. Hours are Monday through Thursday 11am to midnight, Friday through Saturday 11am to 3am, and Sunday noon to midnight. 115 E. River St. © 912/236-1827. www.berniesriverstreet.com/index.html.

Churchill's Pub   If you like a cigar with your martini (the pub has a large selection), this is the place for you. Once the oldest bar in Savannah, it was originally built in England in 1860, dismantled, and shipped to Savannah in the 1920s. A fire in 2003 forced it to move to this new location. On tap are such imported beers as John Courage, Guinness, Dry Blackthorn, and Bass Ale. You can also order pub grub like fish and chips, homemade bangers (English sausage), or shepherd's pie. The pub is open Monday through Saturday 11:30am to 2am and Sunday 5pm to 2am. 13-17 W. Bay St. ✆ **912/232-8501.**

Crystal Beer Parlor   This historic haunt opened its doors in 1933 as a speakeasy and sold huge sandwiches for a dime. Prices have gone up since then, but local affection for this unpretentious place has diminished not one whit. Try to go earlier or later than the peak lunch or dinner hours (if you get there at noon, you'll be in for a lengthy wait). Restaurant owner Conrad Thomson still serves up fried oysters, shrimp-salad sandwiches, crab stew, and chili. The seafood gumbo is one of the best in the southern Atlantic region. A full range of beer and spirits are served. Hours are Monday through Saturday 11am to 9pm. Parking is available in the lot off Jones Street. 301 W. Jones St. (west of Bull St.). ✆ **912/232-1153.**

Kevin Barry's Irish Pub   The place to be on St. Patrick's Day, this waterfront pub rocks all year. Irish folk music will entertain you as you choose from a menu featuring such Irish fare as beef stew, shepherd's pie, and corned beef and cabbage. Many folks come here just to drink, often making a night of it in the convivial atmosphere. Hours are Monday through Friday 4pm to 3am, and Saturday and Sunday 11am to 3pm. 117 W. River St. ✆ **912/233-9626.** www.kevin barrys.com.

Mellow Mushroom   Don't expect grandeur here: This member of a Georgia-based restaurant chain appeals to a funky, irreverent, and sometimes raucous crowd of college students and faded counterculture aficionados from yesterday. Decor includes rambling murals painted with an individualized—and subjective—iconography that might require an explanation from a member of the cheerful waitstaff. There's the cut-off front end of a VW Beetle near the entrance; a limited menu focused on pizzas, salads, and calzones; and a die-hard emphasis on cheap beer, especially Pabst, which sells by the pitcher. Expect lots of SCAD (Savannah College of Art & Design) students; a battered, dimly lit interior; recorded (not live) music; and a vague allegiance to the hard rock, hard drugs, and hard sex fantasies of the early 1970s. Hours are daily 11am to midnight. 11 Liberty St. ✆ **912/495-0705.**

Mercury Lounge   The venue is as hip, counterculture, and artfully kitsch as anything you might expect in Manhattan, with the added benefit of a reputation for the biggest martinis (10 oz.) in town. You'll find the most comfortable barstools anywhere (they're covered in *faux* leopard or zebra); a house band that cranks out their versions of the latest favorites; and, when the band is not performing, a jukebox. Everything is congenially battered, with enough rock and musical memorabilia to please the curators of a hall of fame. Hours are daily from 3pm to 3am. 125 W. Congress St. © 912/447-6952. www.mercuryloungeonline.com.

The Rail Not as aggressively noisy as Club One (see below), the Rail manages to be sophisticated and welcoming of divergent lifestyles. Its name acknowledges the 19th-century day laborers who used to congregate nearby every morning in hopes of being hired for a job on the local railway. Today you can "work the rail" in more comfortable circumstances among some of Savannah's most engaging writers, artists, and eccentrics. Tavernkeepers Trina Marie Brown (from Los Angeles) and Melissa Swanson (from Connecticut) serve snack-style food, but most folks just drink and chat. Hours are Monday through Saturday 3pm to 2:30am. 405 W. Congress St. © 912/238-1311.

Savannah Smiles Near River Street and in back of the Quality Inn, this piano bar not only encourages audience participation, it requires it. A pair of talented musicians duels for the audience's attention as they play old-time favorites. Request a song, and the musicians will do the rest. Savannah Smiles won city awards for best new bar in 2001 and best overall bar in 2002. There are several shows of the "dueling pianos" every night, and an "open mic" night on Sunday. Hours are Wednesday through Saturday 6pm to 3am, Sunday 6pm to 2am. 314 Williamson St. © 912/527-6453. Cover $3–$5 (on some nights, ladies and/or service members get in free).

17 Hundred 90 Lounge This is Savannah's haunted pub. The ghost of Anna Powers, who killed herself by jumping out of the third-floor window onto a brick courtyard, has been spotted wandering about at night. She committed suicide after falling in love with a married sea captain who sailed away. If you don't mind ghosts, this is a cozy bar attached to one of Savannah's most acclaimed restaurants. Happy hour with hors d'oeuvres lasts from 4:30 to 7pm nightly. Hours are Monday through Friday 11am to closing, and weekends 6pm until closing. 307 E. President St. © 912/236-7122.

Six Pence Pub You can drop into this authentic-looking English pub for grub including English fare and homemade soups, salads, and sandwiches. On Sunday an ale-and-mushroom pie is featured. Drinks are discounted during happy hour Monday through Friday 5 to 7pm. Hours are Sunday through Thursday 11:30am to midnight, Friday and Saturday 11:30am to 2am. 245 Bull St. © **912/233-3156.**

Wet Willie's   Few other nightspots in Savannah seem to revel so voluptuously in the effects produced by 190-proof grain alcohol. If you want to get falling-down drunk in a setting that evokes the more sociable aspects of a college fraternity/sorority bash, this is the place. When it's busy, it's loaded with the young, the nubile, and the sexually accessible—a worthy pickup joint if you're straight and not particularly squeamish. If you aren't sure what to order, consider such neon-colored head-spinners as Call-a-Cab, Polar Cappuccino, Monkey Shine, or Shock Treatment. Karaoke is the venue every Monday and Tuesday night; otherwise, it's something of a free-for-all with a Southern accent. Hours are Monday through Thursday 10:30am to 1am, Friday and Saturday 10:30am to 2am, and Sunday 12:30pm to 1am. 101 E. River St. © **912/233-5650.** www.wetwillies.com.

The Zoo   In its way, it's wilder, less inhibited, and a bit more insiderish than even Club One (see below), with which it's frequently compared. One thing it isn't is prissy, as you'll quickly realize after a view of its two-fisted clientele (both male and female) and the staggeringly comprehensive array of almost psychedelic cocktails. (One of the house specials, bluntly identified as a Red-Headed Slut, elevated Jagermeister into something mind-bending for $3–$4, depending on the size.) If there's a genuine fetishist in Savannah, chances are high that you'll find him, her, or it at this ode to Southern heat. Expect a scattering of military men on weekend furlough, women and men of slightly untidy morality, a dance venue that's devoted to trance and techno music upstairs, and more conservative top-40 hits on the street level. Hours are Wednesday through Saturday 9pm to 3am. 121 W. Congress St. © **912/236-6266.** Cover $5–$10 after 10pm.

4 Gay & Lesbian Bars

Chuck's Bar   Most of the bars along Savannah's River Street are mainstream affairs, attracting goodly numbers of tourists, some of whom drink staggering amounts of booze and who seem almost proud of how rowdy they can get. In deliberate contrast, Chuck's usually attracts local members of Savannah's counterculture, including lots of gay folk, who rub elbows in a tucked-away corner of a neighborhood rarely visited by locals. The setting is a dark and shadowy 19th-century warehouse, lined with bricks, just a few steps from the Jefferson Street ramp leading down to the riverfront. Hours are Monday to Saturday from 6pm to 3am. 305 W. River St. ✆ **912/232-1005.**

Club One ✿✿　Club One defines itself as the premier gay bar in a town priding itself on a level of decadence that falls somewhere between New Orleans's and Key West's, and it's the hottest, most amusing spot in town. Patrons include lesbians and gays from the coastal islands; visiting urbanites; and cast and crew of whatever film is being shot in Savannah (Demi Moore and Bruce Willis showed up here in happier times). There's also likely to be a healthy helping of voyeurs who've read *Midnight in the Garden of Good and Evil.*

You pay your admission at the door, showing ID if the attendant asks for it. Wander through the street-level dance bar, trek down to the basement-level video bar for a (less noisy) change of venue, and (if your timing is right) climb one floor above street level for a view of the drag shows. There, a bevy of black and white *artistes* lip-synch the hits of Tina Turner, Gladys Knight, and Bette Midler. Hours are Monday to Saturday 5pm to 3am, and Sunday 5pm to 2am. Shows are nightly at 10:30pm and 12:30am. 1 Jefferson St. ✆ **912/232-0200.** Cover (after 9:30pm) $10 for those 18–20, $5 for those 21 and older.

Faces　Regulars sometimes refer to this neighborhood bar as the gay "Cheers" of Savannah. There's a pool table in back, and the unstudied decor includes battered ceiling beams, semi-rusted license plates, and an utter lack of concern about decorative fashion. Its provenance goes back to 1817, when it was a tavern. If you hear dialogue a bit more insightful than the norm, it might be due to the bar's ownership by a licensed psychologist. Hours are Monday through Saturday 11:30am to 3am, and Sunday 12:30pm to 2am. 17 Lincoln St. ✆ **912/233-3520.**

5 Dinner Cruises

The *Savannah River Queen,* a replica of the boats that once plied this waterway, is a 350-passenger vessel operated by the River Street Riverboat Co., 9 E. River St. (✆ **912/232-6404;** www.savannahriverboat.com). It offers a 2-hour cruise with a prime rib or fish dinner and live entertainment. Reservations are necessary. The fare is $42 for adults and $27 for children 11 and under. Departures are usually daily at 6pm, but the schedule might be curtailed in the colder months.

11

Day Trips & Overnights from Savannah

You can use Savannah as a base, returning to your lodging after local excursions, or embarking from the city to nearby points of interest, including South Carolina's Hilton Head and Daufuskie islands and the quaint Southern town of Beaufort.

We'll start off with a day trip and then move on to travel at greater distances, including a stop at one of the "Golden Islands."

1 Tybee Island ★★

For more than 150 years, **Tybee Island** has lured those who want to go swimming, sailing, fishing, and picnicking. Pronounced "Tie-bee," an Euchee Indian word for "salt," the island offers 5 miles of unspoiled sandy beaches, only 14 miles east of Savannah. From Savannah, take U.S. 80 until you reach the ocean.

VISITOR INFORMATION

The **Tybee Island Visitors Information Center** (© **800/868-BEACH** or 912/786-5444) provides complete information if you plan to spend some time on the island, as opposed to a day trip.

SEEING THE SIGHTS

Consisting of 5 square miles, Tybee was once called the "Playground of the Southeast," hosting millions of beach-loving visitors from across the country. In the early 1900s, Tybrisa Pavilion, on the island's south end, became one of the major summer entertainment pavilions in the South. Benny Goodman, Guy Lombardo, Tommy Dorsey, and Cab Calloway all played here. It burned down in 1967 and was rebuilt in 1996.

Over Tybee's salt marshes and sand dunes have flown the flags of pirates and Spaniards, the English and the French, and the Confederate States of America. A path on the island leads to a clear pasture where John Wesley, founder of the Methodist Church, knelt and declared his faith in the new land.

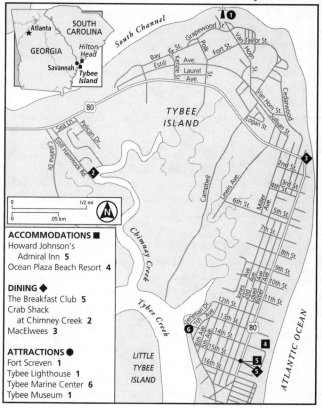

ACCOMMODATIONS ■
Howard Johnson's
  Admiral Inn **5**
Ocean Plaza Beach Resort **4**

DINING ◆
The Breakfast Club **5**
Crab Shack
  at Chimney Creek **2**
MacElwees **3**

ATTRACTIONS ●
Fort Screven **1**
Tybee Lighthouse **1**
Tybee Marine Center **6**
Tybee Museum **1**

Fort Screven, on the northern strip, began as a coastal artillery station and evolved into a training camp for countless troops in both World Wars. Remnants of wartime installations can still be seen. Also in the area is the **Tybee Museum,** housed in what was one of the fort's batteries. Displayed is a collection of photographs, memorabilia, art, and dioramas depicting Tybee from the time the Native Americans inhabited the island through World War II. Across the street is the **Tybee Lighthouse,** built in 1742 and the third oldest lighthouse in America. It's 154 feet tall, and if you're fit you can climb 178 steps to the top. From the panoramic deck you get a sense of the broad and beautiful marshes.

For information about the museum and lighthouse, call ✆ **912/ 786-5801.** Both are open Wednesday to Monday 9am to 5:30pm. Adults pay $5; seniors 62 and older, $4; and children 6 to 17, $4. Kids 5 and under enter free. There are picnic tables here, and access to the beach is easy.

Tybee Marine Center, in the 14th Street parking lot (✆ **912/ 786-5917**), has aquariums with species indigenous to the coast of southern Georgia. Also on display is the usual cast of marine mammals, sharks, and other creatures. Hours are daily 9am to 5pm (closes at noon on Tues). Admission is $4 for adults, $3 for children.

WHERE TO STAY ON TYBEE ISLAND

If you're interested in daily or weekly rentals of a condo or beach house (one or two bedrooms), contact **Tybee Beach Rentals,** P.O. Box 2802, Tybee Island, GA 31328 (✆ **800/755-8562** or 912/786-8805).

Howard Johnson's Admiral Inn *(Kids*   Set within a mixed commercial and residential neighborhood, about a block from the beach, this is a clean and well-managed hotel. With only 41 units, the inn conveys a sense of intimacy. Guest rooms are chain-motel uncontroversial, with the kind of blandly international contemporary furniture you might expect in, say, Florida. The units are large enough to accommodate families. Some have microwaves and minirefrigerators. Some have whirlpool bathtubs; the majority contain tub/shower combinations. Children under 17 stay free. There's no restaurant, but lots of options lie within a short drive.

1501 Butler Ave. (U.S. 80 E.), Tybee Island, GA 31328. ✆ 800/793-7716 or 912/ 786-0700. Fax 912/786-0399. www.tybeehowardjohnson.com. 41 units. $45–$170 double. Off-season discounts. AE, DC, DISC, MC, V. **Amenities:** Outdoor pool; Jacuzzi; 24-hr. room service; babysitting; laundry service/dry cleaning; nonsmoking rooms; rooms for those w/limited mobility. *In room:* A/C, TV, dataport, hair dryer, microwave.

Ocean Plaza Beach Resort *(R*   This hotel has more direct exposure to the beach than any other hotel or motel on Tybee Island. As such, it considers itself among the upscale of the island's resorts, a bit more plush than, say, the also-recommended Howard Johnson's Admiral Inn. Its bar-lounge and restaurant—added in 1999—boast big-windowed views of the sea. Guest rooms are a bit larger than those in some of the hotel's competitors, with blandly international furnishings and sliding glass doors that open onto private balconies. The hotel also has a number of suites, each with a microwave and refrigerator. Bathrooms are standardized and motel-style, with tiled walls and tub/shower combinations. Children under 13 stay free.

1401 Strand Ave., Tybee Island, GA 31328. © 800/215-6370 or 912/786-7777. Fax 912/786-4531. www.oceanplaza.com. 200 units. $80–$190 double. Off-season discounts granted. AE, DC, DISC, MC, V. **Amenities:** Restaurant; bar; 2 pools; 24-hr. room service; nonsmoking rooms; rooms for those w/limited mobility. *In room:* A/C, TV, fridge, coffeemaker, microwave, hair dryer.

WHERE TO DINE ON TYBEE ISLAND

The Crab Shack *Kids* SEAFOOD   This local joint advertises itself as "where the elite eat in their bare feet." Your lunch or dinner might have just arrived off the boat after swimming in the sea only an hour or so earlier. Fat crab is naturally the specialty. It's most often preferred in cakes or can be blended with cheese and seasonings. Boiled shrimp is another popular item. Kids delight in selecting their crabs from a tank. A Low Country boil (a medley of seafood) is a family favorite. The jukebox brings back the 1950s.

40 Estill Hammock Rd. © 912/786-9857. Reservations not accepted. Main courses $7–$35. MC, V. Mon–Thurs 11:30am–10pm; Fri–Sun 11:30am–11pm.

MacElwees SEAFOOD   This restaurant was recently voted number one in Chatham County by *Food & Wine* magazine. Established in 1982, it is imbued with a nautical theme and opens onto ocean views from its location along Highway 80 at the big curve on Tybee Island. It is famous locally for its "beer-battered" shrimp and its raw and steamed oysters. It's also known for grilling the best chicken and serving the best Angus beef on the island. The chef's special appetizer is oysters MacElwee on the half shell, topped with melted cheese, diced onions, bell peppers, and bacon. The crab soup is also an island favorite. The chef does perfectly grilled filet mignon and rib-eye; his specialty is a 10-ounce rib-eye, steak Tybrisa, cooked to your specifications and smothered with fresh crabmeat, scallions, and mushrooms in a peppercorn demi-glaze. The kitchen also turns out succulent pastas such as fettuccine Diane made with shrimp and scallops in a lobster brandy cream sauce.

101 Lovel Ave. © 912/786-4259. Main courses $7–$26. AE, MC, V. Tues–Fri 4–11pm; Sat noon–10pm. Closed Easter, Thanksgiving, and Christmas.

The Breakfast Club *Value* AMERICAN   Established in 1976, this restaurant was selected to cater the wedding of the late John Kennedy, Jr., on Cumberland Island. It's become so successful that lines form around the block daily, and it has won Savannah's "Best Place to Eat Breakfast" contest 11 times. What's the big attraction?

It's the food and affordable prices. The omelets are the best in the area, including a Philly steak omelet with top sirloin tips, sautéed onions, mushrooms, and cream cheese. The waffles are superb; most guests prefer the ones with pecans, although toppings are varied enough to include corned beef hash. If you drop in for lunch, know that the joint has consistently won "Best Burger in Savannah" awards. Expect a half-pound of lean ground beef grilled to perfection and served on a freshly baked bun. Hot daily specials are also featured, including shrimp 'n' grits.

1500 Butler Ave. ⓒ **912/786-5984.** Breakfast and lunch dishes $3.45–$9. DISC, MC, V. Daily 6:30am–12:30pm. Closed Christmas.

Finds **Strolling Around Isle of Hope**

About 10 miles south of downtown Savannah is the community of **Isle of Hope** 👌. First settled in the 1740s, it wasn't until the 1840s that this area became a summer resort for the wealthy. It's now a showcase of rural antebellum life. To reach, drive east from Savannah along Victory Drive to Skidaway Road. Turn right at Skidaway and follow it to LaRoche Avenue. Then take a left and follow LaRoche until it dead-ends on Bluff Drive.

This is the perfect place for a lazy afternoon stroll. The short path is home to authentically restored cottages and beautiful homes, most enshrouded with Spanish moss cascading from the majestic oaks lining the bluff. A favorite of many local landscape artists and Hollywood directors, Bluff Drive affords the best views of the Wilmington River.

As you head back toward Savannah, drive down Skidaway Road. On your left stands **Wormsloe Plantation,** 7601 Skidaway Rd. (ⓒ **912/353-3023**). Wormsloe, originally a silk plantation and home of Noble Jones, isn't much more than a ruin. After you enter the gates, you proceed down an unpaved, oak-lined drive 1½ miles long; the ruins lie approximately a mile down the drive. Because of its strategic location, Wormsloe has been home to forts and garrisons during the Civil and Spanish-American wars. The plantation includes a museum and walking trails. It's open Tuesday to Saturday 9am to 5pm and Sunday 2 to 5:30pm. Admission is $3 for adults and $2 for students 6 to 18; children 5 and under are admitted free.

2 Hilton Head ✫✫

41 miles NE of Savannah

Hilton Head is the largest sea island between New Jersey and Florida and one of America's great resort meccas. Surrounded by the Low Country, where much of the romance, beauty, and graciousness of the Old South survive, its broad white-sand beaches are warmed by the Gulf Stream and fringed with palm trees and rolling dunes. The subtropical climate makes all this beauty the ideal setting for golf and for some of the Southeast's finest saltwater fishing. Far more sophisticated and upscale than Myrtle Beach and the Grand Strand, Hilton Head's "plantations" (as most resort areas here call themselves) offer visitors something of the traditional leisurely lifestyle that's always held sway here.

Although it covers only 42 square miles (it's 12 miles long and 5 miles wide), Hilton Head feels spacious, thanks to judicious planning that began in 1952. And that's a blessing, because about 2.3 million resort guests visit annually (the permanent population is about 35,000). The broad beaches on its ocean side, sea marshes on the sound, and natural wooded areas of live and water oak, pine, bay, and palmetto have all been carefully preserved amid commercial explosion. This lovely setting attracts artists, writers, musicians, theater groups, and craftspeople. The only city (of sorts) is Harbour Town, at Sea Pines Plantation, a Mediterranean-style cluster of shops and restaurants.

ESSENTIALS
GETTING THERE
It's easy to fly into Savannah, rent a car, and drive to Hilton Head (about 65 miles north of Savannah). See chapter 4 for details on all the airlines flying into Savannah. If you're driving from the north, take exit 28 off I-95 South. If you're coming from the south, take exit 8 off I-95 North to U.S. 278 East. U.S. 278 leads over the bridge to the island. It's 52 miles northeast of Savannah and located directly on the Intracoastal Waterway.

VISITOR INFORMATION
The **Island Visitors Information Center** is on U.S. 278 at S.C. 46 (© **843/785-4472;** www.islandvisitorcenter.com), just before you cross the bridge from the mainland. It offers a free *Where to Go* booklet, including a visitor map and guide. Hours are Monday to Saturday from 9:30am to 5:30pm.

The **Hilton Head Visitors and Convention Bureau** (chamber of commerce), 1 Chamber Dr. (② **843/785-3673;** www.hilton headisland.org), offers free maps of the area and will assist you in finding places of interest and outdoor activities. It will even make hotel reservations. It's open Monday to Friday 8:30am to 5:30pm.

GETTING AROUND

U.S. 278 is the divided highway that runs the length of the island.

Yellow Cab (② **877/603-8294**) serves all Hilton Head; they will also pick up passengers from the Savannah Airport but you must make reservations in advance.

SPECIAL EVENTS

The earliest annual event is **Springfest,** a March festival featuring seafood, live music, stage shows, and tennis and golf tournaments. Outstanding PGA golfers also descend on the island in mid-April for the **MCI Heritage Tournament** at the Harbour Town Golf Links. To herald fall, the **Hilton Head Celebrity Golf Tournament** is held on Labor Day weekend at Palmetto Dunes and Sea Pines Plantation.

BEACHES, GOLF, TENNIS & OTHER OUTDOOR PURSUITS

You can have an active vacation here any time of year; Hilton Head's subtropical climate ranges in temperature from the 50s (10°C–15°C) in winter to the mid-80s (around 30°C) in summer. And if you've had your fill of historic sights in Savannah or Charleston, don't worry—the attractions on Hilton Head mainly consist of nature preserves, beaches, and other places to play.

Coastal Discovery Museum, 100 William Hilton Pkwy. (② **843/ 689-6767;** www.coastaldiscovery.org), hosts 12 separate guided tours and cruises. Tours go along island beaches and salt marshes or stop at Native American sites and the ruins of old forts or long-gone plantations. The nature, beach, and history tours generally cost $10 for adults and $5 for children. The dolphin and nature cruise costs $15 per adult, $10 per child. A kayak trip costs $35 per person. Hours are Monday to Saturday 9am to 5pm; Sunday 10am to 3pm. Children can choose from museum items such as shark's teeth with an identification chart, and educational toys.

BEACHES

Travel & Leisure ranked Hilton Head's **beaches** ☆☆☆ as among the most beautiful in the world, and we concur. The sands are extremely firm, providing a sound surface for biking, hiking, jogging, and beach games. In summer, watch for the endangered loggerhead turtles that lumber ashore at night to bury their eggs.

All beaches on Hilton Head are public, but land bordering the beaches is private property. Most beaches are safe, although there's sometimes an undertow at the northern end of the island. Lifeguards are posted only at major beaches, and concessions are available to rent beach chairs, umbrellas, and watersports equipment.

There are four public entrances to Hilton Head's beaches. The main parking and changing areas are on Folly Field Road, off U.S. 278 (the main highway), and at Coligny Circle. Other entrances (signposted) from U.S. 278 lead to Singleton and Bradley beaches.

Most frequently used are **North** and **South Forest** beaches, adjacent to Coligny Circle (enter from Pope Ave. across from Lagoon Rd.). You'll have to use the parking lot opposite the Holiday Inn, paying a $4 daily fee until after 4pm. The adjacent beach park has toilets and a changing area, as well as showers, vending machines, and phones. It's a family favorite.

Of the beaches on the island's north, we prefer **Folly Field Beach.** Toilets, changing facilities, and parking are available.

BIKING

Enjoy Hilton Head's 25 miles of bicycle paths. There are even bike paths running parallel to U.S. 278. Beaches are firm enough to support wheels, and every year, cyclists delight in dodging the waves or racing fast-swimming dolphins in the nearby water.

Most hotels and resorts rent bikes to guests. If yours doesn't, try **Hilton Head Bicycle Company,** off Sea Pines Circle at 112 Arrow Rd. (*©* **843/686-6888**). The cost is $12 per day, but only $18 for 3 days and $25 per week. Baskets, child carriers, locks, and headgear are supplied. The inventory includes cruisers, BMXs, mountain bikes, and tandems. Hours are daily 9am to 5pm.

Another rental place is **South Beach Cycles,** South Beach Marina Village in Sea Pines (*©* **843/671-2453**), offering beach cruisers, tandems, child carriers, and bikes for kids. There's free delivery to Sea Pines. Cost is $10 per half-day, $15 for a full day, or $23 for 3 days. Hours are 9am to 6pm daily.

CRUISES & TOURS

To explore Hilton Head's waters, contact **Adventure Cruises, Inc.,** Shelter Cove Harbour, Suite G, Harbourside III (*©* **843/785-4558**). Another outfitter, **Drifter & Gypsy Excursions,** South Sea

Pines Dr., South Beach Marina (© **843/363-2900**), takes its 65-foot *Gypsy,* holding 89 passengers, on dolphin watches, sightseeing cruises, and nature cruises. Call for more information to see what's happening (or not) at the time of your visit.

Outings include a 1½-hour dolphin-watch cruise, which costs adults $19 and children $9. A 3-hour sunset cruise aboard the vessel *Adventure* costs adults $20 and children $10.

FISHING

No license is needed for saltwater fishing, although freshwater licenses are required for the island's lakes and ponds. The season for fishing offshore is April through October. Inland fishing is good between September and December. Crabbing is also popular; crabs are easy to catch in low water from docks, boats, or right off a bank.

Off **Hilton Head** ✿, you can go deep-sea fishing for amberjack, barracuda, shark, and king mackerel. Many rentals are available; we've recommended only those with the best track records. The previously recommended **Drifter & Gypsy Excursions,** South Sea Pines Dr., South Beach Marina (© **843/363-2900**), features a 50-passenger, 50-foot drifter vessel that offers 5-hour offshore and inshore fishing excursions. The 32-foot *Boomerang* fishing boat is available for private offshore and inshore custom fishing charters lasting up to 8 hours.

Harbour Town Yacht Basin, Harbour Town Marina (© **843/ 671-2704**), has four boats of various sizes and prices. *The Manatee,* a 40-foot vessel, can carry a group of six and costs $400 for 4 hours, $600 for 6 hours, and $800 for 8 hours. A charge of $13 per hour is added for each additional passenger.

The Hero and *The Echo* are 32-foot ships. Their rates for a group of six are $375 for 4 hours, $570 for 6 hours, and $750 for 8 hours. A smaller, three-passenger inshore boat is priced at $295 for 4 hours, $445 for 6 hours, and $590 for 8 hours.

A cheaper way to go deep-sea fishing—only $47 per person—is aboard *The Drifter* (© **843/363-2900**), a party boat that departs from the South Beach Marina Village. Ocean-bottom fishing is possible at an artificial reef 12 miles offshore.

GOLF

With 24 challenging **golf courses** ✿✿✿ on the island and an additional 16 within a 30-minute drive, this is heaven for both professional and novice golfers. Some of golf's most celebrated architects—including George and Tom Fazio; Robert Trent Jones, Sr.;

Pete Dye; and Jack Nicklaus—have designed championship courses on the island. Wide, scenic fairways and rolling greens have earned Hilton Head the reputation of being the resort with the most courses on the "World's Best" list.

Many of Hilton Head's championship courses are open to the public, including the **George Fazio Course** ✿ at Palmetto Dunes Resort (✆ **843/785-1130**), an 18-hole, 6,534-yard, par-70 course that *Golf Digest* ranked in the top 50 of its "75 Best American Resort Courses." The course has been cited for its combined length and keen accuracy. The cost is $90 for 18 holes, and hours are daily from 6:30am to 6pm.

Old South Golf Links ✿✿✿, 50 Buckingham Plantation Dr., Bluffton (✆ **800/257-8997** or 843/785-5353), is an 18-hole, 6,772-yard, par-72 course, open daily from 7:30am to 7pm. It's recognized as one of the "Top 10 New Public Courses" by *Golf Digest,* which cites its panoramic views and setting ranging from an oak forest to tidal salt marshes. Greens fees range from $65 to $92. The course lies on Highway 278, 1 mile before the bridge leading to Hilton Head.

Hilton Head National, Highway 278 (✆ **843/842-5900**), is a Gary Player Signature Golf Course, including a full-service pro shop and a grill and driving range. It's a 27-hole, 6,779-yard, par-72 course with gorgeous scenery that evokes Scotland. Greens fees range from $50 to $95, and hours are daily 7am to 6pm.

Island West Golf Club, Highway 278 (✆ **843/689-6660**), was nominated in 1992 by *Golf Digest* as the best new course of the year. With its backdrop of oaks, elevated tees, and rolling fairways, it's a challenging but playable 18-hole, 6,803-yard, par-72 course. Greens fees range from $29 to $59, and hours are from 7am to 6pm daily.

Robert Trent Jones Course at the Palmetto Dunes Resort (✆ **843/785-1138**) is an 18-hole, 6,710-yard, par-72 oceanfront course. The greens fees are $90 to $130 for 18 holes, and hours are daily from 7am to 6pm.

HORSEBACK RIDING

Riding through beautiful maritime forests and nature preserves is reason enough to visit Hilton Head. We like **Lawton Stables,** 190 Greenwood Dr., Sea Pines (✆ **843/671-2586**), offering rides for both adults and kids (ages 7 and under ride ponies) through the Sea Pines Forest Preserve. The cost is $50 per person for a ride somewhat longer than an hour. Riders must weigh under 240 pounds. Hours are Monday to Saturday 8:30am to 5:30pm. Reservations are necessary.

KAYAK TOURS

Eco-Kayak Tours, Palmetto Bay Marina (② 843/785-7131), operates guided tours in Broad Creek. About four to five trips are offered
each day; the cost is $30 to $50 per person, and anyone age 7 to 82
is welcome to participate.

South Beach Marina Village (② 843/671-2643) allows you to
tour Low Country waterways by kayak. A 2-hour Dolphin Nature
Tour costs $46 (half-price for children under 12). The tour takes
you through the salt-marsh creeks of the Calibogue Sound or Pinckney Island Wildlife Refuge. The trip begins with instructions on
how to control your boat.

NATURE PRESERVES

Audubon-Newhall Preserve, Palmetto Bay Road (② 843/689-
2989), is a 50-acre preserve on the south end of the island. Here,
you can walk along marked trails to observe wildlife in its native
habitat. Guided tours are available when plants are blooming.
Except for public toilets, there are no amenities. The preserve is
open from sunrise to sunset; admission is free.

The second-leading preserve is also on the south end of the island.
Sea Pines Forest Preserve ⭐⭐, Sea Pines Plantation (② 843/363-
4530), is a 605-acre public wilderness with marked walking trails.
Nearly all the birds and animals known to live on Hilton Head can
be seen here, including alligators, egrets, herons, osprey, and white-
tailed deer. All trails lead to public picnic areas in the center of the
forest. The preserve is open from sunrise to sunset year-round. Maps
and toilets are available.

The **Coastal Discovery Museum,** 100 William Hilton Parkway
(② 843/689-6767), hosts several guided nature tours and cruises
on weekdays; the cost is generally $10 for adults and $5 for children. Check the museum's online Events Calendar at www.coastal
discovery.org for specific dates and times; you can even reserve your
tour online in advance.

PARASAILING

H₂O Water Sports, Harbour Town (② 843/671-4386), takes you
in a Sea Rocket powerboat for parasailing daily from 8am to
6:15pm. The cost is $49 per person for 400 feet of line or $59 for
700 feet of line, and reservations are necessary. Catamaran rides for
up to six passengers are also featured, and sailing lessons are offered.
The business operates from mid-March to mid-October.

SAILING

Pav Hana and *Flying Circus,* Palmetto Bay Marina (© 843/686-2582), are two charter sailboats on Hilton Head piloted by Capt. Jeanne Zailckas. You can pack a picnic lunch and bring your cooler aboard for a 2-hour trip—in the morning or afternoon, or at sunset. The cost is $25 for adults and $15 for children 11 and under. *Flying Circus* offers private 2-hour trips for up to six people costing $150, and a sunset cruise for $180.

H2 Sports, Harbour Town Marina (© 843/671-4386), offers a 27-foot catamaran with captain that goes on scenic sails costing $29 for a 1½-hour trip or $39 for a 2-hour jaunt We especially recommend their eco-tours (or "enviro" as they are called). Passengers head out on Zodiac inflatable boats for close encounters with wildlife, including dolphin sightings and bird-watching. Rates are $24 for adults, $20 for kids 12 and under.

TENNIS

Tennis magazine ranked Hilton Head among its "50 Greatest U.S. Tennis Resorts." No other domestic destination can boast such a concentration of **tennis facilities** 🎾🎾🎾: more than 300 courts that are ideal for beginners, intermediate, and advanced players. The island has 19 tennis clubs, seven of which are open to the public. A wide variety of tennis clinics and daily lessons are available.

Sea Pines Racquet Club 🎾🎾🎾, Sea Pines Plantation (© 843/363-4495), has been ranked by *Tennis* magazine as a top-50 resort and was selected by the *Robb Report* as the best tennis resort in the United States. The club has been the site of more nationally televised tennis events than any other location. Two hours of tennis is complimentary for guests of the hotel; otherwise, there's a $22-per-hour charge. The club has 23 clay courts (two are lit for night play).

Port Royal Racquet Club, Port Royal Plantation (© 843/686-8803), offers 10 clay and four hard courts, plus two natural-grass courts, all of which are lit. Charges range from $20 to $32 per hour, and reservations should be made a day in advance. Clinics are $20 per hour for adults and $12 to $14 for children.

Hilton Head Island Beach and Tennis Resort, 40 Folly Field Rd. (© 843/842-4402), features 10 lighted hard courts, costing only $15 per hour (free to guests).

Palmetto Dunes Tennis Center, Palmetto Dunes Resort (© 843/785-1152), has 23 clay and two hard courts (some lit for night play). The charge is $25 per hour (hotel guests pay $20 per hour).

WINDSURFING

Hilton Head is not recommended as a windsurfing destination. Finding a place to windsurf is quite difficult, and one windsurfer warns that catching a tailwind at the public beaches at the airport and the Holiday Inn could land you at the bombing range on Parris Island, the Marine Corps' basic-training facility.

SHOPPING

Hilton Head has more than 30 shopping centers spread around the island. Chief shopping sites include **Pinelawn Station** (Matthews Dr. and U.S. 278), with more than 30 shops and half a dozen restaurants; and **Coligny Plaza** (Coligny Circle), with more than 60 shops, food stands, and good restaurants. We've found some of the best bargains in the South at **Factory Outlet Stores I and II** (© **843/837-4339**), on Highway 278 at the gateway to Hilton Head. The outlet has more than 45 factory stores, including Ralph Lauren, Brooks Brothers, and J. Crew. The hours of most shops are Monday to Saturday 10am to 9pm, and Sunday 11am to 6pm.

WHERE TO STAY ON HILTON HEAD

Hilton Head has some of the finest hotel properties in the Deep South, and prices are high—unless you book into one of the motels run by national chains. Most facilities offer discount rates from November to March, and golf and tennis packages are available.

The most comprehensive central reservations service on the island, **The Vacation Company,** P.O. Box 5312, Hilton Head Island, SC 29938 (© **800/845-7018** in the United States and Canada; www.hiltonheadcentral.com), can book you into private homes or villas on the island. It's open Monday to Saturday 9am to 5pm.

An option is to rent a private home, villa, or condo yourself. For up-to-date availability, rates, and bookings, contact **Island Rentals and Real Estate,** P.O. Box 5915, Hilton Head Island, SC 29938 (© **800/845-6134** or 843/785-3813). The toll-free number is in operation 24 hours, but office hours are Monday to Saturday 8:30am to 5:30pm.

VERY EXPENSIVE

Hilton Head Marriott Beach & Golf Resort 𝕲𝕲 After a much-needed $23-million renovation, this aging property has emerged in its latest incarnation as a Marriott. Set on 2 acres of landscaped grounds and bordering the oceanfront, the hotel is surrounded by the much more massive acreage of Palmetto Dunes

Plantation and is just 10 minutes from the Hilton Head airport. But the hotel's 10-story tower of rooms dominates everything around it.

Rooms open onto either ocean or island views. Some are smaller and less opulent than you might expect of such a well-rated hotel, but all are comfortably furnished, each with a tiled, midsize bathroom with tub and shower. Most rooms have small balconies. The hotel's program of sports and recreation is among the best on the island.

In Palmetto Dunes Plantation, Hilton Head Island, SC 29938. © **800/228-9290** or 843/686-8400. Fax 843/686-8450. www.marriott.com. 512 units. $205–$249 double; $500–$700 suite. AE, DC, DISC, MC, V. Valet parking $15. **Amenities:** Restaurant; 2 bars; coffee shop; 1 indoor and 2 outdoor pools; 3 18-hole golf courses; 25 tennis courts nearby; health club; full spa; sauna; gift shop; hair salon; limited room service; babysitting; laundry service/dry cleaning; nonsmoking rooms; rooms for those w/limited mobility. *In room:* A/C, TV, dataport, minibar, coffeemaker, hair dryer, iron/ironing board, safe, bathrobe.

Main Street Inn ★★★ *Finds*   Don't expect cozy Americana from this small, luxurious inn, as it's grander and more European in its motifs than its name would imply. Designed like a small-scale villa that you might expect to see in the south of France, it was built in 1996 combining design elements from both New Orleans and Charleston, including cast-iron balustrades and a formal semi-tropical garden where guests are encouraged to indulge in afternoon tea. Inside, you'll find topiaries, French provincial furnishings, and accommodations more luxurious than those of any other hotel in Hilton Head. Floors are crafted from slabs of either stone or heart pine; fabrics are richly textured; and plumbing and bathroom fixtures are aggressively upscale. Bathrooms have tub/shower combinations. Overall, despite a location that requires a drive to the nearest beach, the hotel provides a luxe alternative to the less personalized megahotels that lie nearby. AAA, incidentally, awarded it a much-coveted four-diamond rating.

2200 Main St., Hilton Head Island, SC 29926. © **800/471-3001** or 843/681-3001. Fax 843/681-5541. www.mainstreetinn.com. 33 units. $185–$250 double. $35 surcharge for 3rd occupant of double room. Rates include breakfast. AE, DISC, MC, V. Free parking. **Amenities:** Breakfast room; outdoor pool; spa; massage; laundry service/dry cleaning; nonsmoking rooms; rooms for those w/limited mobility. *In room:* A/C, TV, dataport, minibar, coffeemaker, hair dryer, iron/ironing board.

The Westin Resort ★★   Set near the isolated northern end of Hilton Head Island on 24 landscaped acres, this is the most opulent European-style hotel in town. Its Disneyesque design, including cupolas and postmodern ornamentation that looks vaguely Moorish, evokes fanciful Palm Beach hotels. If there's a drawback, it's the

Hilton Head

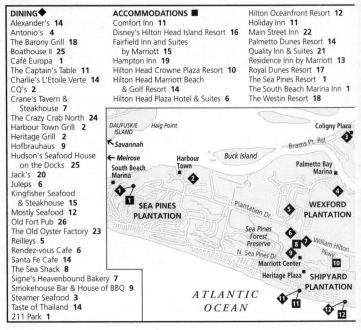

DINING◆
Alexander's **14**
Antonio's **4**
The Barony Grill **18**
Boathouse II **25**
Café Europa **1**
The Captain's Table **11**
Charlie's L'Etoile Verte **14**
CQ's **2**
Crane's Tavern & Steakhouse **7**
The Crazy Crab North **2**
Harbour Town Grill **2**
Heritage Grill **2**
Hofbrauhaus **9**
Hudson's Seafood House on the Docks **25**
Jack's **20**
Juleps **6**
Kingfisher Seafood & Steakhouse **15**
Mostly Seafood **12**
Old Fort Pub **26**
The Old Oyster Factory **23**
Reilleys **5**
Rendez-vous Cafe **6**
Santa Fe Cafe **14**
The Sea Shack **8**
Signe's Heavenbound Bakery **7**
Smokehouse Bar & House of BBQ **9**
Steamer Seafood **3**
Taste of Thailand **14**
211 Park **1**

ACCOMMODATIONS ■
Comfort Inn **11**
Disney's Hilton Head Island Resort **16**
Fairfield Inn and Suites by Marriott **15**
Hampton Inn **19**
Hilton Head Crowne Plaza Resort **10**
Hilton Head Marriott Beach & Golf Resort **14**
Hilton Head Plaza Hotel & Suites **6**

Hilton Oceanfront Resort **12**
Holiday Inn **11**
Main Street Inn **22**
Palmetto Dunes Resort **14**
Quality Inn & Suites **21**
Residence Inn by Marriott **13**
Royal Dunes Resort **17**
The Sea Pines Resort **1**
The South Beach Marina Inn **1**
The Westin Resort **18**

stiff formality. Adults accompanied by a gaggle of children and bathers in swimsuits will not necessarily feel comfortable in the reverently hushed corridors. The rooms, most of which have ocean views, are outfitted in Low Country plantation style, with touches of Asian art for additional glamour. Each unit has a well-kept bathroom with a tub/shower combination. The **Carolina Café** or the **Barony Grill** are the best places for food. Poolside dining is available, and there's also a seafood buffet restaurant.

Two Grasslawn Ave., Hilton Head Island, SC 29928. ℂ 800/WWESTIN-1 or 843/681-4000. Fax 843/681-1087. www.westin.com. 412 units. $209–$459 double; $450–$1,900 suite. Children 17 and under stay free in parent's room; children 4 and under eat free. Special promotions offered. AE, DC, DISC, MC, V. **Amenities:** 3 restaurants; bar; 3 pools; 3 18-hole golf courses; 16 tennis courts; health spa; Jacuzzi; room service; laundry service/dry cleaning; nonsmoking rooms; rooms for those w/limited mobility. *In room:* A/C, TV, minibar, dataport, coffeemaker, hair dryer, iron/ironing board, safe.

EXPENSIVE

Disney's Hilton Head Island Resort ⋆⋆ *Kids*   This family-conscious resort is on a 15-acre island that rises above Hilton Head's

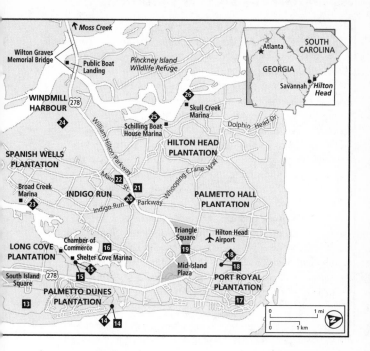

widest estuary, Broad Creek. When it opened in 1996, it was the only U.S.-based Disney resort outside Florida and California. About 20 woodsy-looking buildings are arranged into a compound. Expect lots of pine trees and fallen pine needles, garlands of Spanish moss, plenty of families with children, and an ambience that's several notches less intense than that of hotels in Disney theme parks. Part of the fun are the many summer-camp-style activities. Public areas have outdoorsy colors (forest green and cranberry), stuffed game fish, and varnished pine. All accommodations contain mini-kitchens, suitable for feeding sandwiches and macaroni to the kids; wooden furniture consistent with the resort's vacation-home-in-the-forest theme; and well-kept bathrooms equipped with tub/shower combinations. For elaborate restaurants and bars, make the short trek to the dozen or so eateries and bars at the nearby Shelter Cove Harbour.

22 Harbourside Lane, Hilton Head Island, SC 29928. ℰ **407/DISNEY** or 843/341-4100. Fax 843/341-4130. www.dvcresorts.com. 123 units. $105–$275 studio; $150–$710 villa. AE, DC, DISC, MC, V. **Amenities:** 3 restaurants; bar; 3 outdoor pools; fitness center; health spa; babysitting; laundry service. *In room:* A/C, TV, dataport, kitchenette, coffeemaker, hair dryer, iron/ironing board, safe.

Hilton Head Crowne Plaza Resort ⚐ Tucked away within the Shipyard Plantation, and designed as the centerpiece of that plantation's 800 acres, this five-story inn gives its major competitor, Westin Resort, stiff competition. It underwent a $10-million renovation in 1993 and today has the island's most dignified lobby: a mahogany-sheathed postmodern interpretation of Chippendale decor. The golf course associated with the place has been praised by the National Audubon Society for its respect for local wildlife. Guest rooms are nothing out of the ordinary, with simple furnishings and bathrooms with tub/shower combinations, yet the sheer beauty of the landscaping, the attentive service, the omnipresent nautical theme, and the well-trained staff (dressed in nautically inspired uniforms) can go a long way toward making your stay memorable. On the premises are three restaurants. The most glamorous is Portz, off the establishment's main lobby. A good middle-bracket choice is Brella's, serving both lunch and dinner. The premier bar, Signals Lounge, is the site of live music.

130 Shipyard Dr., Shipyard Plantation, Hilton Head Island, SC 29928. ⓒ 800/465-4329 or 843/842-2400. Fax 843/785-8463. www.cphilton.com. 340 units. $199–$325 double; $375–$615 suite. AE, DC, DISC, MC, V. Free parking. **Amenities:** 2 restaurants; bar; 2 pools (1 indoor); fitness center; bikes; Jacuzzi; room service; laundry service/dry cleaning; nonsmoking rooms; rooms for those w/limited mobility. *In room:* A/C, TV, dataport, minibar, coffeemaker, hair dryer, iron/ironing board, safe.

Hilton Oceanfront Resort ⚐ This award-winning property isn't the most imposing on the island. Many visitors, however, prefer the Hilton because of its hideaway position: tucked at the end of the main road through Palmetto Dunes. The low-rise design features hallways that open to sea breezes at either end. The guest rooms are some of the largest on the island, and balconies angling out toward the beach allow sea views from every unit. Each unit comes with a well-equipped bathroom containing a tub/shower combination. Mostly Seafood is the resort's premier restaurant, although cafes and bars—even a Pizza Hut on the grounds—serve less-expensive fare.

23 Ocean Lane (P.O. Box 6165), Hilton Head Island, SC 29938. ⓒ 800/845-8001 or 843/842-8000. Fax 843/341-8037. www.hilton.com. 324 units (with kitchenette). $99–$159 double; $299–$499 suite. AE, DC, DISC, MC, V. Parking $6. **Amenities:** 3 restaurants; bar; 2 outdoor pools; fitness center; limited room service; laundry service/dry cleaning; coin-operated laundry; nonsmoking rooms; rooms for those w/ limited mobility. *In room:* A/C, TV, dataport, coffeemaker, hair dryer, iron/ironing board, safe.

Royal Dunes Resort ⚐ Comfortable and clean, but blandly standardized and somewhat anonymous, this is a compound of three-bedroom, three-bathroom apartments, occupancy of which has been aggressively marketed to independent investors as a time-share investment. Whenever the investors aren't in residence, the apartments become available for rentals. They occupy a quartet of four-story buildings located within the Port Royal Plantation. Each has a pale gray exterior; a washer and dryer; a conservative and durable collection of wicker, rattan, and southern Colonial furniture; and a bathroom with tub/shower combination. On the premises are two adult swimming pools, a children's pool, a hot tub, a sauna, and landscaping that includes bougainvillea and all the palms, palmettos, and flowering shrubs you'd expect. The compound's location is at the edge of a forested greenbelt, a 10-minute walk from the beach.

8 Wimbledon Court, Hilton Head, SC 29928. ℂ **843/681-9718.** Fax 843/681-2003. www.royaldunes.com. 56 units. $175–$235 villa. AE, MC, V. **Amenities:** 2 outdoor pools; children's wading pool; gym; hot tub; sauna; bike rentals; barbecue area. *In room:* A/C, TV, full kitchen, iron, washer/dryer.

MODERATE

Holiday Inn ⚝ The island's leading motor hotel, across from Coligny Plaza, this five-story high-rise opens onto a quiet stretch of beach on the southern side of the island, near Shipyard Plantation. The rooms are spacious and well furnished, decorated in tropical pastels, but the balconies are generally too small for use. The upper floors have the views, so you should try for accommodations there. All units have well-kept bathrooms with tub/shower combinations. In summer, planned children's activities are offered.

1 S. Forest Beach Dr. (P.O. Box 5728), Hilton Head Island, SC 29938. ℂ **800/ HOLIDAY** or 843/785-5126. Fax 843/785-6678. www.holiday-inn.com. 201 units. $169–$239 double. AE, DC, DISC, MC, V. Free parking. **Amenities:** Restaurant; bar; outdoor pool; exercise room; limited room service; laundry service; nonsmoking rooms; rooms for those w/limited mobility. *In room:* A/C, TV, dataport, coffeemaker, hair dryer, iron/ironing board, safe.

Residence Inn by Marriott Set on the eastern edge of Hilton Head's main traffic artery, midway between the Palmetto Dunes and Shipyard plantations, this is a three-story complex of functionally furnished but comfortable one-bedroom suites. The setting is wooded and parklike, and both cost-conscious families and business travelers on extended stays appreciate the simple cooking facilities in each unit. Each also has a well-kept bathroom with a tub/shower combination as well as an icemaker, microwave, and coffeemaker.

12 Park Lane (in Central Park), Hilton Head Island, SC 29938. ℂ **800/331-3131** or 843/686-5700. Fax 843/686-3952. www.marriott.com. 156 units. Apr–Sept

$109–$149 suite; Oct–Mar $109–$119 suite. Rates include continental breakfast. AE, DC, DISC, MC, V. **Amenities:** Breakfast room; outdoor pool; 2 tennis courts; basketball court; fitness center; Jacuzzi; laundry service/dry cleaning, coin-operated laundry; nonsmoking rooms; rooms for those w/ limited mobility. *In room:* A/C, TV, dataport, kitchenette, coffeemaker, hair dryer, iron/ironing board.

The South Beach Marina Inn 🐾 *Finds*   Of the dozens of available accommodations in Sea Pines Plantation, this 1986 clapboard-sided complex of marinafront buildings is the only place offering traditional hotel-style rooms by the night. With lots of charm, the inn meanders over a labyrinth of catwalks and stairways above a complex of shops, souvenir kiosks, and restaurants. Each unit is cozily outfitted with country-style braided rugs, pinewood floors, and homespun-charm decor celebrating rural 19th-century America. All units include kitchenettes and well-kept bathrooms containing tub/shower combinations.

232 S. Sea Pines Dr. (in Sea Pines Plantation), Hilton Head Island, SC 29920. 📞 800/367-3909 or 843/671-6498. www.southbeachvillage.com. 17 units. $69–$200 suite. AE, DISC, MC, V. Free parking. **Amenities:** Courtyard; outdoor pool; nonsmoking rooms. *In room:* A/C, TV, kitchenette, coffeemaker, hair dryer, iron/ironing board.

INEXPENSIVE

Comfort Inn *Kids*   Solid, conservative, reliable, and patterned on the formula of the national chain, this five-story, cement-sided hotel was built in 1988 in a wooded area that's a 5-minute walk from the island's public beach. It's the official lodging of Hilton Head's largest tennis school and "clinic," the Van Der Meer Tennis University and, as such, rents a goodly percentage of its rooms to tennis enthusiasts enrolled at the clinic nearby. Despite its setting in a scrub-and-pinewood forest, there's a shopping area (65 shops and four restaurants) within a short walk, and a vivid sense of connection to other resort-industry businesses nearby. This is a good choice for families with children, thanks to its self-image as a reliable, albeit not terribly imaginative, middle-bracket resort, and thanks to the on-site pair of swimming pools with water slides, a toddler pool, and a video arcade. Rooms are cheerfully decorated in a chain-hotel format, with tiled bathrooms and combination tub/showers. About 85% of the rooms have private balconies.

2 Tanglewood Dr., Hilton Head, SC 29928. 📞 843/842-6662. Fax 843/842-6664. www.comfortinnhiltonhead.com. 153 units. $89–$169 double. Off-season discounts apply. Rates include continental breakfast. AE, DC, DISC, MC, V. **Amenities:** 2 outdoor pools; bike rentals; water park; coin-operated laundry; snack bar; arcade. *In room:* A/C, TV, fridge, coffeemaker, microwave, hair dryer, iron, safe.

Fairfield Inn and Suites by Marriott   This three-story motel in Shelter Cove has all the features of Marriott's budget chain, including complimentary coffee in the lobby, nonsmoking rooms, and same-day dry cleaning. The inn provides easy access to the beach, golf, tennis, marinas, and shopping. The rooms are wheelchair-accessible and, although they're unremarkable, they are a good value for expensive Hilton Head. Each unit comes with a well-maintained bathroom with a tub/shower combination. Families can save money by using the grills outside for home-style barbecues, to be enjoyed at the picnic tables. In addition, a heated pool is provided.

9 Marina Side Dr., Hilton Head Island, SC 29938. ℂ **800/228-2800** or 843/842-4800. Fax 843/842-5388. www.marriott.com. 119 units. $59–$129 double; $159 suite. Rates include continental breakfast. Senior discounts available. AE, DISC, MC, V. Free parking. **Amenities:** Breakfast room; lounge; outdoor pool; coin-operated laundry; nonsmoking rooms; rooms for those w/limited mobility. *In room:* A/C, TV, dataport, hair dryer, iron/ironing board, safe.

Hampton Inn   Although edged out by its major competitor, the Fairfield Inn by Marriott, this is the second most sought-after motel on Hilton Head, especially by families and business travelers. It's 5 miles from the bridge and the closest motel to the airport. Rooms in pastel pinks and greens are quite comfortable and well maintained. Some units have refrigerators. All units have well-kept bathrooms with tub/shower combinations. Local calls are free.

1 Dillon Rd., Hilton Head Island, SC 29926. ℂ **800/HAMPTON** or 843/681-7900. Fax 843/681-4330. www.hamptoninn.hilton.com. 125 units (11 with kitchens). $79–$119 double. Children under 18 stay free in parent's room. Rates include continental breakfast. AE, DC, DISC, MC, V. **Amenities:** Breakfast room; outdoor pool; putting green; fitness center; coin-operated laundry; nonsmoking rooms; rooms for those w/limited mobility. *In room:* A/C, TV, dataport, coffeemaker, hair dryer, iron/ironing board, safe.

Hilton Head Plaza Hotel & Suites *(Kids)*   Affordable, and favored by families with children, this 1970s-era hotel is a five-story, white concrete hotel set directly across from the island's premier beach. Much about the place seems generic to the hotel industry as a whole: Rooms are outfitted with conventional contemporary-looking furniture, each has the kind of amenities that can make a stay here comfortable and convenient, and each is configured in a bland, universal style duplicated in other Best Westerns throughout the world. Tile-sheathed bathrooms come with tub/shower combinations. The rooms were renovated in the early 21st century. The hotel lies across the street from Hilton Head Island's busiest beach, and virtually everything on Hilton Head is within a 15-minute drive.

Expect lots of families with children, especially during the peak holiday months of midsummer.

36 S. Forest Dr., Hilton Head, SC 29928. ℂ **800/535-3248** or 843/842-3100. $60–$99 low season double; $99–$129 high season double. Rates include continental breakfast. AE, DC, DISC, MC, V. **Amenities:** Outdoor pool; gym; game room; all nonsmoking rooms; rooms for those w/limited mobility. *In room:* A/C, TV, dataport, kitchenette (in some), coffeemaker, hair dryer, iron.

Quality Inn & Suites Neck and neck with the Red Roof Inn, this motel attracts families watching their budgets. It's acceptable and clean in every way. Part of the Shoney empire, it offers basic guest rooms with streamlined modern furnishings. Some units are reserved for nonsmokers and people with disabilities. Rooms have king-size or double beds and well-kept bathrooms with tub/shower combinations. A large outdoor pool is on-site, and a Chinese restaurant is right next door. The motel's own restaurant serves breakfast, lunch, and dinner, and meals can be charged to your room. Golf and tennis can be arranged nearby.

Hwy. 278, 200 Museum St., Hilton Head Island, SC 29926. ℂ **843/681-3655.** Fax 843/681-5698. www.qualityinn.com. 127 units. $100–$160 double. AE, DC, DISC, MC, V. **Amenities:** Restaurant; lounge; outdoor pool; putting green; bike rentals; business center; laundry service/dry cleaning; nonsmoking rooms; rooms for those w/limited mobility. *In room:* A/C, TV, dataport, fridge, microwave, hair dryer, safe.

VILLA RENTALS

Palmetto Dunes Resort 🏊 *Kids* This relaxed and informal enclave of privately owned villas is set within the sprawling 1,800-acre complex of Palmetto Dunes Plantation, 7 miles south of the bridge. Accommodations range from one-bedroom condos, booked mostly by groups, to four-bedroom villas, each furnished in the owner's personal taste. This is the place for longer stays, ideal for families that want a home away from home while traveling. In 2003 it was ranked as the "Number 1 Family Resort" in the continental U.S. and Canada by *Travel & Leisure Family.* Villas are fully equipped and receive housekeeping service; they're located on the ocean, fairways, or lagoons. Each villa comes with a full kitchen, washer and dryer, living room and dining area, and balcony or patio. All units have well-kept bathrooms with tub/shower combinations.

P.O. Box 5606, Palmetto Dunes, Hilton Head Island, SC 29938. ℂ **800/845-6130** or 843/785-1161. Fax 843/686-2877. www.palmettodunesresort.com. 500 units. $700–$3,500 per week condo or villa. Golf and honeymoon packages available. 2-night minimum stay. 50% deposit for reservations. AE, DC, DISC, MC, V. Free parking. **Amenities:** 20 restaurants; 12 bars; 28 pools; 3 18-hole golf courses; 25 tennis courts; 200 slip marina; nonsmoking rooms; rooms for those w/limited mobility. *In room:* A/C, TV, dataport, safe (in some).

The Sea Pines Resort ✦✦✦ This condo development sprawls across 5,500 acres at the southernmost tip of the island. Don't come to Sea Pines looking for quick overnight accommodations. The entire place encourages stays of at least a week. Lodgings vary— everything from one- to four-bedroom villas to opulent private homes available when the owners are away. Units have well-kept bathrooms with either showers or tub/shower combinations. The clientele here includes hordes of golfers, because Sea Pines is the home of the WorldCom Classic, a major stop on the PGA Tour. If you're not a Sea Pines guest, you can eat, shop, or enjoy some aspects of its nightlife. For full details on this varied resort/residential complex, write for a free "Sea Pines Vacation" brochure.

Sea Pines (P.O. Box 7000), Hilton Head Island, SC 29938. ℂ **888/807-6873** or 843/785-3333. Fax 843/842-1475. www.seapines.com. 400–500 units. $150–$230 1-bedroom villa; $225–$320 2-bedroom villa; $250–$375 3-bedroom villa. Rates are daily, based on 3-night stay. AE, DC, DISC, MC, V. **Amenities:** 12 restaurants; 12 bars; 2 outdoor pools; 3 18-hole golf courses; 28 tennis courts; fitness center; health spa; watersports; horseback riding; massage; babysitting; nonsmoking rooms; rooms for those w/limited mobility. *In room:* A/C, TV, kitchen, washer/dryer.

WHERE TO DINE ON HILTON HEAD
EXPENSIVE

The Barony Grill ✦✦✦ INTERNATIONAL The Barony, quick to promote itself as one of only two AAA four-diamond restaurants on Hilton Head Island, has a decor that blends a stage set in Old Vienna with a brick-lined, two-fisted steakhouse. The lighting is suitably dim; the drinks are appropriately stiff. As you dine in your plush, upholstered alcove, you can stare at what might be the largest wrought-iron chandelier in the state. The place caters to a resort-going crowd of casual diners. Everything is well prepared and in copious portions, although the chef doesn't stray far from a limited selection of tried-and-true steak-and-lobster fare. Your meal might include New York strip steak, tenderloin of pork with purée of mangos, lobster Thermidor, or fresh Atlantic swordfish with pistachios.

In the Westin Resort, 2 Grass Lawn Ave. ℂ **843/681-4000.** Reservations recommended. Main courses $26–$35. AE, DC, DISC, MC, V. Wed–Sun 6–10pm.

MODERATE

All of these so-called moderately priced restaurants have expensive shellfish dishes. However, if you order from the lower end of the price scale, enjoying mainly meat and poultry dishes, platters can cost $20 or less. Portions are, for the most part, generous, so you'll rarely need to order appetizers, which will keep your overall cost in the more affordable price range.

Alexander's ✍ SEAFOOD/INTERNATIONAL   One of the most visible independent restaurants (in other words, not associated with a hotel) on Hilton Head lies in a gray-stained, wood-sided building just inside the main entrance to Palmetto Dunes. The decor includes Oriental carpets, big-windowed views over the salt marshes, wicker furniture, and an incongruous—some say startling—collection of vintage Harley Davidson motorcycles, none with more than 1,000 miles on them, dating from 1946, 1948, 1966, and 1993, respectively. Powerful flavors and a forthright approach to food are the rules of the kitchen. The chefs don't allow a lot of innovation on their menu—you've had all these dishes before—but fine ingredients are used, and each dish is prepared with discretion and restraint. Try the oysters Savannah or the bacon-wrapped shrimp, and most definitely try a bowl of Low Country seafood chowder. Guaranteed to get you salivating are the seafood pasta and the grilled Chilean sea bass in an herb vinaigrette. Steak, duck, rack of lamb, and pork—all in familiar versions—round out the menu.

76 Queen's Folly, Palmetto Dunes. ✆ **843/785-4999.** Reservations recommended. Main courses $19–$29. AE, DC, DISC, MC, V. Daily 5–10pm.

Antonio's ✍ ITALIAN   Located at the Village at Wexford, this island favorite with its elegant decor and fine Italian cuisine continues its bold quest to duplicate the flavors of sunny Italy, and more or less succeeds admirably. Chef Simone is a whiz at using recipes from all the provinces of Italy, although classic preparations of Italian seafood are clearly his favorite. After a drink at the intimate bar, you can absorb the setting, including a mural of the Tuscan hills and a brick fireplace. Piano music adds to the ambience, as does a visit to the Wine Room, where you can see Hilton Head's most comprehensive assemblage of bottles of *vino* from Italy.

The antipasti selection is the island's best, including many classics such as mussels sautéed in olive oil with garlic, herbs, and white wine; and roasted red pepper stuffed with an herbed goat cheese. The chef prepares succulent pastas, including one based on such fruits of the sea as sautéed shrimp, scallops, and mussels flavored with garlic and diced tomato. Calf's liver appears delectably flamed in brandy and served with an applewood smoked bacon and an herbed four-cheese polenta. The *zuppa di pesca,* based on a recipe from Puglia, is a great kettle of fish loaded with Mediterranean flavor.

Village at Wexford, G-2. ✆ **843/842-5505.** Reservations recommended. Main courses $15–$30. AE, DC, DISC, MC, V. Daily 5:30–10pm. Closed Christmas Eve.

Boathouse II *Kids* SEAFOOD   The nautical lodge decor and the view over salt marshes and Skull Creek form an appropriate venue for the serving of fine seafood at affordable prices. From some tables you can see the Pinckney Island Wildlife Preserve and the adjacent marina. You can dine indoors or on an enclosed veranda decorated with hand-painted murals depicting local marine life. On cool nights, the tavern room is a cozy retreat with its large fireplace. Walk under a canopy of giant oaks to enjoy a drink at the Market 13 outdoor bar. Live entertainment is offered, and the family-friendly place has a children's menu. Plenty of fresh seafood is prepared with that old Charleston flavor, including shrimp and stone-ground grits, Southern catfish with Carolina fixin's, and the chef's own Boathouse bouillabaisse. Excellent crab cakes are another specialty. For meat fanciers, slow-roasted baby back ribs in a sour mash sauce are served with buttermilk "smashed" potatoes and collards. Filet mignon and prime rib are also on the menu.

397 Squire Pope Rd. (£) **843/681-3663.** Brunch $9.95–$15; lunch $8–$12; main courses $16–$25. AE, DC, DISC, MC, V. Daily 11:30am–3pm and 5–9pm. Closed Christmas Day.

Café Europa *&* CONTINENTAL/SEAFOOD   This fine European restaurant is at the base of the much-photographed Harbour Town Lighthouse, opening onto a panoramic view of Calibogue Sound and Daufuskie Island. In an informal, cheerful atmosphere, you can order fish that's poached, grilled, baked, or even fried. Baked Shrimp Daufuskie was inspired by local catches; it's stuffed with crab, green peppers, and onions. Grilled grouper is offered with a sauté of tomato, cucumber, dill, and white wine. Specialty dishes include country-style chicken from Charleston, made with honey, fresh cream, and pecans. *Tournedos au poivre* are flambéed with brandy and simmered in a robust green-peppercorn sauce. The omelets, 14 in all, are perfectly prepared at breakfast (beginning at 9am) and are the island's finest. The bartender's Bloody Mary won an award as the island's best in a *Hilton Head News* contest.

Harbour Town, Sea Pines Plantation. (£) **843/671-3399.** Reservations recommended for dinner. Breakfast $6–$12; lunch $8–$13; main courses $18–$28. AE, DC, MC, V. Daily 9am–2:30pm and 5:30–10pm.

The Captain's Table *&* SEAFOOD/AMERICAN/LOW COUNTRY   Located in Old Sea Crest, this two-level restaurant opens onto panoramic views through its floor-to-ceiling windows. A bright, contemporary restaurant, it hardly depends on its view and lovely setting. The chef procures the best seafood from local catches and prepares an array of sophisticated and well-prepared dishes. For down-home flavor, start with the cornmeal fried oysters with bacon-chive sour cream or else jumbo lump-crab cocktail seasoned with lemon zest. The chef concocts a Louisiana-inspired shrimp-and-scallop jambalaya with smoked sausage and Tasso ham, and wins our approval with his potato-crusted Carolina trout filet with a lemon parsley butter sauce and almond wild rice. Blackened scallops are excellent, served with a saffron lobster broth and roasted garlic polenta. Sunday brunch is a good time to visit if you wish to sample local Low Country classics such as rock shrimp over garlic cheddar grits with a charred tomato coulis, or else a fish plate holding the catch of the day.

10 N. Forest Beach Rd. ℂ **843/686-4300.** Reservations recommended. Main courses $15–$25. MC, V. Daily 5–10pm. Closed Christmas.

Charlie's L'Etoile Verte 𝓡𝓡 INTERNATIONAL   Outfitted like a tongue-in-cheek version of a Parisian bistro, our favorite restaurant on Hilton Head Island was also a favorite with former president Bill Clinton during one of his island conferences. The atmosphere is unpretentious but elegant. The service is attentive, polite, and infused with an appealingly hip mixture of old- and new-world courtesy. Begin with shrimp-stuffed ravioli, and move on to grilled tuna with a jalapeño *beurre blanc* (white butter) sauce, grilled quail with shiitake mushrooms and a Merlot sauce, or veal chops in a peppercorn sauce. End this rare dining experience with biscotti or a "sailor's trifle." The wine list is impressive.

8 New Orleans Rd. ℂ **843/785-9277.** Reservations required. Lunch $10–$15; main courses $23–$30. AE, DISC, MC, V. Tues–Sat 11:30am–2pm; Mon–Sat 6–9pm.

CQ's 𝓡𝓡 AMERICAN/LOW COUNTRY   With a design based on a 19th-century rice barn, this Harbour Town restaurant is a successful conversion of an already existing property. You dine on hardwood floors against a backdrop of stained glass, photographs, and memorabilia. The extensive wine list, some 400 vintages, is one of the best on the island. A tradition on Hilton Head since 1973, the restaurant will allow you to craft your own menu at *La Table du Vin*, with the assistance of a creative culinary team.

The well-thought-out menu of Low Country and American classics reflects the rich bounty of South Carolina—fresh seafood, beef, and game—and also shows a French influence. For a sampling of harmonious appetizers, try such delights as Brie *en croûte* with a raspberry purée and crisp apples, or a Maine lobster and Boursin cheesecake with a sherry butter cream, the latter one of our favorites.

Count yourself lucky if you arrive when game is on the menu. Our party recently took delight in the seared medallions of venison with roasted onions, shallots, leeks, and asparagus, with a Madeira wine reduction adding that extra-special flavor.

140-A Lighthouse Lane. ℂ 843/671-2779. Reservations recommended. Main courses $19–$34. AE, DC, DISC, MC, V. Daily 5–10pm (winter hours daily 5:30–9:30pm).

Crane's Tavern & Steakhouse ℱ STEAK/SEAFOOD   The original Crane's Steakhouse was launched in Philadelphia at the dawn of the 20th century and was one of the most popular taverns there until Prohibition. Always a family business, it was established by Hank Crane, originally from Ireland, and handed down through generations of Crane sons. Crane's is now a tradition on Hilton Head.

As Hilton Head restaurants rush to claim the best seafood, Crane's bases its simple, classic fare on prime beef. Each of the choicest cuts is prepared to your taste—can any trencherman cope with the whopper, 20 ounces? A 12-ounce prime rib was the best we could manage, and it was tender, well flavored, and quite succulent. Steaks get the focus, but the other offerings are good as well, including jumbo lump-crab cakes or the duck egg roll. The pumpkin ravioli was a delightful surprise in a sage and pine-nut butter sauce. One of our party opted for the "Low Country Trio," which featured a boneless chicken breast and andouille sausage atop a cheddar grit cake, smothered in gumbo gravy and topped with plum-fried oysters. Personally, we found all that a bit much. The owners are justifiably proud of their bar, the handmade English type.

26 New Orleans Rd. ℂ 843/341-2333. Reservations recommended. Main courses $16–$36. AE, DC, DISC, MC, V. Daily 5–10pm. Closed Thanksgiving and Christmas.

The Crazy Crab North SEAFOOD   This is a branch of the chain that's most likely to be patronized by locals. In a modern, low-slung building near the bridge that connects the island with the South Carolina mainland, it serves baked, broiled, or fried versions of stuffed flounder; seafood kabobs; oysters; the catch of the day; and any combination thereof. She-crab soup and New England–style clam chowder are prepared fresh daily; children's menus are available; and desserts are a high point for chocoholics.

U.S. 278 at Jarvis Creek. ℂ 843/681-5021. Reservations not accepted. Lunch $6–$12; main courses $13–$22. AE, DC, DISC, MC, V. Daily 11:30am–4pm and 5–10pm.

Harbour Town Grill ℱ 𝘍𝘪𝘯𝘥𝘴 AMERICAN   For ages, this woodsy-looking refuge was open only to members of the nearby golf club and their guests. Several years ago, however, it opened to the public at large, a fact that's still not widely publicized in Hilton Head, and which sometimes seems to catch some local residents by surprise. Looking something like a postmodern version of a French château, this small-scale affair has views over the 9th hole and room for only about 50 diners at a time. Inside, it's sporty-looking and relatively informal during the day, when most of the menu is devoted to thick-stuffed deli-style sandwiches and salads named in honor of golf stars. Dinners are more formal and elaborate, with good-tasting dishes such as local shrimp sautéed with ginger, Vidalia onions, and collard greens; roasted rack of American lamb with white beans, spinach, and rosemary; and an array of thick-cut slabs of meat that include beef, lamb, veal, and chicken.

In the Harbour Town Golf Links Clubhouse, Sea Pines. ℭ 843/363-4080. Reservations recommended for dinner only. Breakfast $6–$11; lunch sandwiches and platters $9–$13; dinner main courses $20–$35. AE, DC, DISC, MC, V. Daily 7am–3pm; Wed–Sun 6–10pm.

Hudson's Seafood House on the Docks SEAFOOD   Built as a seafood-processing factory in 1912, this restaurant still processes fish, clams, and oysters for local distribution, so you know that everything is fresh. If you're seated in the north dining room, you'll be eating in the original oyster factory. We strongly recommend the crab cakes, steamed shrimp, and the especially appealing blackened catch of the day. Local oysters (seasonal) are also a specialty, breaded and deep-fried. Before and after dinner, stroll on the docks past shrimp boats, and enjoy the view of the mainland and nearby Parris Island. Sunsets here are panoramic. Lunch is served in the Oyster Bar.

1 Hudson Rd. (Go to Skull Creek just off Square Pope Rd. signposted from U.S. 278.) ℭ 843/681-2772. Reservations not accepted. Main courses $8–$15 lunch, $15–$35 dinner. AE, DC, MC, V. Daily 11am–2:30pm and 5–10pm.

Jack's ℛ ITALIAN   One of the best restaurants on Hilton Head is tucked behind the big windows of what was originally conceived as a shop, inside a busy shopping mall near a Wal-Mart store. Behind the white translucent curtains you'll find the airy, breezy kind of Italian restaurant you might expect on southern Italy's Costa Smeralda. Amid mahogany and granite trim and a mostly cream-colored decor, you can enjoy a rich inventory of summery dishes, with a menu that's enhanced by at least a dozen daily specials every day. Examples include thin-sliced veal served either with smoked prosciutto or with brandy, sausages, and mushrooms; charbroiled tuna on a bed of baked onions and herbs; and savory portobello mushrooms with goat cheese. Extensively promoted by *The Food Network*, this is the kind of place where well-heeled local residents come with friends and family to dine.

105 Festival Center, Rte. 278. ⓒ **843/342-2400.** Reservations recommended. Main courses $16–$29. AE, MC, V. Mon–Sat 5–10pm.

Juleps ⓡⓡ AMERICAN/SOUTHERN   This is the Hilton Head restaurant where we'd take Jefferson Davis, former president of the Confederacy, should he miraculously appear and want dinner. It has that nostalgic atmosphere, with its beveled glass, French doors, glass-framed windows, cream and taupe colors—a walk into a time capsule. This is the friendly oasis maintained by Sam and Melissa Cochran—he a longtime islander and she a first-rate chef. Served in three dining areas, with a lively bar, are their original concoctions. Excellent ingredients go into such starters as barbecued duck breast over a corn pancake, or savory Cajun-blackened oysters. Here's your chance to try that Southern favorite, fried green tomatoes over creamy grits in a red pepper sauce seasoned with fresh scallions. Nothing is more typical of the Carolinas than a dish of quail with andouille sausage. Desserts are worth making room for, especially the berry shortcake full of strawberries, blackberries, and blueberries.

14 Greenwood Dr. ⓒ **843/842-5857.** Reservations recommended. Main courses $20–$26. AE, DC, DISC, MC, V. Mon–Sat 5:30–10pm. Closed July 4th and Christmas Day.

Kingfisher Seafood & Steakhouse ⓡ SEAFOOD/STEAK "Fresh fish—never frozen" is the motto of this popular restaurant at Shelter Cove, with a panoramic view of the harbor through large picture windows in every dining room. A full menu is offered, but the focus is on fresh fish and steak. The fish catch of the day is prepared several ways, including grilled, blackened, herb encrusted, or Greek style with tomatoes, onions, mushrooms, spinach, artichokes, and feta cheese. Served crisp and cold, oysters come on the half shell. Each day there are different varieties. For pasta lovers, the chef makes a creative lasagna every day. Seafood selections range from a very respectable Scottish fish and chips to a more typical Charleston-style shrimp and grits in white gravy. Our recently sampled ahi tuna came seared medium rare with a ponzu sauce, wasabi mashed potatoes, and Asian slaw. The filet mignons offered here are tender and full of flavor and served with a creamy béarnaise sauce. For something more Southern, however, opt for the 12-ounce bone-in pork chop topped with applewood pepper gravy and served with collards. Live music nightly.

8 Harbour Lane. ⓒ **843/785-4442.** Reservations recommended. Main courses $15–$28. AE, DISC, MC, V. Daily 5–10pm. Closed Christmas Eve and Christmas Day.

Mostly Seafood 🐟🐟 SEAFOOD/AMERICAN   The most ele-gant and innovative restaurant in the Hilton resort, Mostly Seafood is noted for its chefs' imaginative dishes made with fresh seafood. Something about the decor—backlighting and glass-backed murals in designs of sea-green and blue—creates the illusion that you're floating in a boat. Menu items include fresh grouper, snapper, swordfish, flounder, salmon, trout, halibut, and pompano, prepared in any of seven ways. Dishes that consistently draw applause are corn-crusted filet of salmon with essence of hickory-smoked veal bacon and peach relish; and "fish in the bag," prepared with fresh grouper, scallops, and shrimp, laced with a dill-flavored cream sauce, and baked in a brown paper bag.

In the Hilton Oceanfront Resort, Palmetto Dunes Plantation. ⓒ **843/842-8000.** Reservations recommended. Main courses $18–$35. AE, DC, DISC, MC, V. Daily 5:30–10pm.

Old Fort Pub 🐟🐟 SOUTHERN   The setting doesn't get more romantic on Hilton Head. Surrounded by moss-draped live oak trees, the restaurant overlooks the Intracoastal Waterway on the banks of Skull Creek. We particularly enjoy views of the setting sun from the panoramic windows or the alfresco dining porch. The restaurant occupies a historic setting and is named for the adjacent Civil War shore battery of Fort Mitchell, which was occupied by Union troops during the Civil War, much to the horror of Charleston.

Recently named one of only two AAA four-diamond restaurants on Hilton Head, here you experience a combination of Southern hospitality and award-winning chef Heath's menus. He's a master at artful blending that results in dishes such as pork porterhouse with smoked gouda polenta and—adding the right punch—a Calvados sauce. Harmony and balance are also achieved by such starters as a quail spring roll with Thai red curry and coconut sauce, or the grilled sea scallops in a champagne and caviar *beurre blanc*. At last, here is a chef who pays careful attention to his salads, including our favorite: fresh field greens with caramelized pecans, scallions, and a cracked black pepper vinaigrette.

Sunday brunch here is among the best on island, waking up your palate with such delights as buckwheat crepes with sausage and apple stuffing covered with a rum and maple syrup, or banana brioche French toast with macadamia nuts and mango preserves.

65 Skull Dr. © **843/681-2386.** Reservations recommended. Brunch $12–$16; main courses $19–$30. AE, DC, DISC, MC, V. Daily 5–10pm; Sun 11am–2pm.

The Old Oyster Factory ♣ SEAFOOD/STEAK   Built on the site of one of Hilton Head's original oyster canneries, this land-mark offers waterfront dining overlooking Broad Creek. The restaurant's post-and-beam decor has garnered several architectural awards. At sunset, every table enjoys a panoramic view as diners sip their "sundowners."

All the dishes here can be found on seafood menus from Maine to Hawaii. But that doesn't mean they're not good. The cuisine is truly palate-friendly, beginning with such appetizers as a tangy ket-tle of clams steamed in a lemon butter sauce, or a delectable crab cake sautéed and served in a chile-garlic tartar sauce. Will it be oys-ters Rockefeller (baked with spinach and a béarnaise sauce) or oys-ters Savannah (cooked with shrimp, crabmeat, and smoked bacon)? Almond-crusted mahimahi is among the more tantalizing main courses, as are seafood pasta and broiled sea scallops. Nonseafood eaters can go for a chargrilled chicken breast.

101 Marsh Rd. © **843/681-6040.** Reservations not accepted. Main courses $18–$23. AE, DC, DISC, MC, V. Daily 5–10pm (closing times can vary).

Reilleys IRISH/AMERICAN   A favorite with golfers, this is a good ol' boy place with an Irish pub atmosphere and Boston sports memorabilia on the walls. It offers a spacious dining area and a wel-coming bar where you can order Harp, Bass and, of course, Guin-ness on tap. Your hosts are Tom Reilley and Gary Duren, who very quickly get to know you. The location is Sea Pines Circle, and the pub draws its faithful clients along with constantly arriving drinkers "from anywhere." The menu's predictable Blarney burgers include a hot one made with jalapeño peppers. Pastas are served, some with shrimp, and deli sandwiches range from a Dagwood to your own creation—choose either ham, turkey, corned beef, Genoa salami, or pastrami. Some of the biggest and best stuffed sandwiches are a daily feature, everything from plump fried oysters in a hoagie to a meat-loaf-and-cheddar concoction. The pub is also a place for children, and a special corner of the menu is reserved just for kids.

7-D Greenwood Dr. © **843/842-4414.** Main courses $6–$17. AE, MC, V. Daily 11:30–11pm; bar until 2am. Closed Christmas Day.

Rendez-Vous Café ♣ *Finds* FRENCH/PROVENÇAL   Some of the best French dining in eastern South Carolina is served here in this bistro, which offers a piano player on Wednesday and Thursday nights. The Provençal decor and inventive cookery characterize this popular dining spot. The list of hors d'oeuvres is the island's finest, ranging from classics such as French onion soup gratinée or escargots bourguignonne to such delights as a French country pâté with duck mousse combo. The main courses are prepared with finesse, including crab cakes Mediterranean with ratatouille and polenta, or else frogs' legs Provençal on a bed of couscous. Grouper is prepared Riviera-style—that is, sautéed in olive oil with sweet red bell peppers. The chefs are diligent and maintain high standards, relying on market-fresh products. The reliable cuisine is nowhere as heavy or as laden with sauces as you might expect from classic French cuisine in the Escoffier tradition.

14 Greenwood Dr., Seapines Circle. ℂ 843/785-5070. Reservations recommended. Main courses $8.95–$15 lunch, $15–$27 dinner. MC, V. Mon–Fri 11:30am–2pm; Mon–Sat 5:30–9pm.

Santa Fe Cafe 𝒢 MEXICAN   The best, most stylish Mexican restaurant on Hilton Head, the Santa Fe has rustic, Southwestern-inspired decor and cuisine that infuses traditional recipes with nouvelle flair. Menu items are often presented in colors as bright as the Painted Desert. Dishes might include tequila shrimp; herb-roasted chicken with jalapeño corn-bread stuffing and mashed potatoes laced with red chiles; grilled tenderloin of pork with smoked habanero sauce and sweet-potato fries; and worthy burritos and chimichangas. The chiles rellenos are exceptional, stuffed with California goat cheese and sun-dried tomatoes. The quesadilla is one of the most beautifully presented dishes of any restaurant in town.

700 Plantation Center. ℂ 843/785-3838. Reservations recommended. Main courses $6–$8 lunch; $20–$30 dinner. AE, DISC, MC, V. Mon–Fri noon–2pm; daily 6–10pm.

211 Park AMERICAN/SOUTHERN/ITALIAN   In the Park Plaza Shopping Center, this combined wine bar and bistro with a contemporary decor is a popular gathering place at night. Actual islanders posed for the mural used as a backdrop. Bill Cubbage, who long ago tired of hearing his name pronounced like a vegetable, opened this place in 1996, and has enjoyed a loyal following since.

Many of his dishes are adaptations of international recipes—for example, Bill's takeoff on traditional paella. Here it includes some of the same ingredients as in Spain, but it's served over grits. Shellfish is served in a black Thai sauce, and you might also watch for the specials announced nightly. Pizza comes with smoked salmon, feta cheese, dill, capers, and onions; or you might opt for one of the pasta dishes, the most popular being a Jamaican-inspired "rasta pasta" with chicken, shrimp, andouille sausage, peppers, and a jerk cream sauce. The chef won our esteem with his cedar-planked salmon topped with whole-grain mustard and broiled to give the fish a slightly smoky flavor. The dish emerged with a sweet-potato waffle and collards (how Southern can you get?).

211 Park Plaza. ✆ 843/686-5212. Reservations recommended. Main courses $17–$26. AE, DC, DISC, MC, V. Mon–Sat 5:30–10pm. Closed New Year's, Thanksgiving, Christmas.

INEXPENSIVE

Hofbrauhaus *Kids* GERMAN   A sanitized German beer hall, this family favorite serves locals and visitors such national specialties as grilled bratwurst and smoked Westphalian ham, along with Wiener schnitzel and sauerbraten. One specialty that we like to order is roast duckling with spaetzle, red cabbage, and orange sauce. Helpings are so big here that most diners will settle for one plate, which is more than adequate for every appetite. For example, our recent serving of a house specialty, prime strip of sirloin, turned out to be 14 ounces of aged beef, charbroiled and served with a red wine mushroom sauce, buttered whipped potatoes, and fresh crisp garden vegetables. Note the stein and mug collection as you're deciding which of the German beers to order from the large variety. A children's menu is available. Live music plays on Tuesday, Wednesday, Thursday, and Friday nights.

In the Pope Ave. Mall. ✆ 843/785-3663. Reservations recommended. Early-bird dinner (5–6:30pm only) $14; main courses $16–$24. AE, MC, V. Daily 5–10pm.

The Sea Shack *Value* SEAFOOD   Mostly known to locals, this little discovery evokes a seafood shack somewhere on Cape Cod. Completely unpretentious, it serves the freshest catch of the day in town, which you can order grilled, fried, or blackened. Stand at the counter and make your selection, and then find a seat at one of the old tables. Your platter of fresh seafood will be brought to you. We always like to begin with the fish soup as an appetizer. At lunch the fried oyster sandwich is a local favorite. At night we prefer the grilled grouper dinner. One of the chef's signature dishes is Caribbean jerk grouper, a rare dish in these parts, that has been featured on *The Food Network.* Prices are affordable, and the portions are most generous.

6 Pope Ave. ✆ 843/785-2464. Main courses $5–$10 lunch; $10–$12 dinner. AE, MC, V. Mon–Sat 11am–3pm and 5–9pm.

Signe's Heavenbound Bakery *Value* BAKED GOODS   No one in this resort area turns out an array of delectable pastries and breads like Signe's. Featured on *The Food Network,* it has a menu that immediately starts your mouth watering: Hilton Head sourdough bread, along with specialty cakes such as pink lemonade cake, Key lime almond cake, pecan praline cream cake, carrot hazelnut cake, and forever Valentine (chocolate ganache over almond and chocolate layers with a raspberry filling). The bakery's butter pecan praline pound cake may be the best in South Carolina, and their old-fashioned cream cheesecake with a graham cracker crust is the stuff of dreams. Signe's fruited breads come in such flavors as French oat apricot, Swiss pear, and cranberry raisin. You can visit for breakfast or lunch. In the cheery dining room, with its garden-inspired decor, you can enjoy breakfast, perhaps the signature blueberry French toast, or else a fluffy frittata. Lunches consist of hot and cold sandwiches made with bread freshly baked in the oven. "Hob nobs" are their latest version of the sub. Cold sandwiches feature the likes of beef and Swiss, or else tuna salad "our way."

93 Arrow Rd. ℭ **843/785-9118.** Breakfast $7–$8.50; sandwiches $5–$7. Cake slices from $2.50. AE, DC, DISC, MC, V. Mon–Fri 8am–4pm; Sat 9am–2pm.

Smokehouse Bar & House of BBQ *(Kids* BARBECUE This is Hilton Head's only authentic barbecue restaurant, serving fine, hickory-smoked meats in a casual Western atmosphere with a large outdoor deck attached to the restaurant. There is also takeout. It's an ideal family place with affordable prices. Both native islanders and visitors come here nightly, raving about the "pulled" pork, the sliced or pulled brisket, and the barbecued chicken. The joint has won awards for its barbecue and for its chili, and the portions are man-sized. Beachgoers are welcome; management only asks that you wear shoes. The menu is corny—salads are called rabbit food, appetizers "orderves." But once you get beyond that, the food is rather tasty. Their specialties are those smokehouse ribs, either a half or a full rack. Other down-home favorites include a pork barbecue plate, barbecued chicken breast, and fried catfish.

102 Pope Ave. ℭ **843/842-4227.** Reservations recommended. Main courses $6–$21. AE, MC, V. Daily 11:30am–10pm.

Steamer Seafood ✿ SEAFOOD/LOW COUNTRY In Coligny Plaza, next to the Piggy Wiggly grocery store, this is a fun, affordably priced joint suitable for the whole family. It's a place where men eat while wearing baseball caps, and many of the diners look as if they've made too many trips to the barbecue pit. Nonetheless, it's a very convivial and welcoming tavern with Low Country specialties on the menu such as Charleston she-crab soup or shrimp gumbo to get you going. The fare is very familiar, and the portions are generous. Many old-time Southern coastal classics are offered, including Frogmore stew (large shrimp, smoked sausage, yellow onion, and red potatoes). You can ask the server to name the catch of the day, which is served grilled or blackened. The "rebel yell" rib-eye is a juicy, well-trimmed, 14-ounce slab of beef blackened or chargrilled, as you desire it. The biggest seafood platters on the island are dished up here. After all that, dare you try the rich, creamy, chocolate peanut-butter pie or the fruit cobbler of the day?

29 Coligny Plaza. ℂ 843/785-2070. Lunch $4.50–$7.95; main courses $6.95–$27. AE, MC, V. Daily 11:30am–10pm.

Taste of Thailand 🌟 *Finds* THAI   Offering exotic flavors, this eatery does a bustling business with cost-conscious diners who appreciate the emphasis on exotic curries, lemon grass, and coconut. Among scattered examples of Thai woodcarvings and handicrafts, you can enjoy a choice but limited menu offering beef, pork, chicken, shrimp, mussels, or tofu in many flavors. One of our favorites is chicken with stir-fried vegetables, Thai basil, and oyster sauce. The hottest dish is the green curry, but equally delectable is the curry with roasted peanuts and red chiles flavored with cumin seeds. Cold Thai spring rolls appear as an appetizer. A hot and sour soup is always on the menu, as is a spicy squid salad. Most dishes are at inexpensive.

Plantation Center, 807 William Hilton Pkwy., Suite 1200. ℂ **843/341-6500.** Reservations recommended. Main courses $12–$25. AE, DC, MC, V. Mon–Sat 5–11pm.

HILTON HEAD AFTER DARK

Hilton Head doesn't have Myrtle Beach's nightlife, but it has enough, centered mainly in hotels and resorts. Casual dress (but not swimming attire) is acceptable in most clubs.

Cultural interest focuses on the **Arts Center of Coastal Carolina,** in the Self Family Arts Center, 14 Shelter Cove Lane (ℂ 843/842-ARTS; www.artscenter-hhi.org), which enjoys one of the best theatrical reputations in the Southeast. The Elizabeth Wallace Theater, a 350-seat, state-of-the-art theater, was added to the multiplex in 1996. The older Dunnagan's Alley Theater is located in a renovated warehouse. A wide range of musicals, contemporary comedies, and classic dramas is presented. Show times are 8pm Tuesday to Saturday, with a Sunday matinee at 2pm. Adult ticket prices range from $45 for a musical to $35 for a play. Children 16 and under are charged $18 to $23. The box office is open 10am to 5pm Monday to Friday.

The island abounds in sports bars, far too many to document here. The two best ones are **Callahan Sports Bar & Grill,** 38 New Orleans Rd. (*C* **843/686-7665**); and **Casey's Sports Bar & Grill,** 37 New Orleans Rd. (*C* **843/785-2255**).

Quarterdeck   Our favorite waterfront lounge is the best place on the island to watch sunsets, but you can visit at any time during the afternoon and in the evening until 2am. Try to go early and grab one of the outdoor rocking chairs to prepare yourself for nature's light show. There's dancing every night to beach music and top-40 hits. Daily 11am to 2am. Harbour Town, Sea Pines Plantation. *C* **843/671-2222.**

Remy's   Got the munchies? At Remy's, you can devour buckets of oysters or shrimp, served with the inevitable fries. The setting is rustic and raffish, and live music is provided. Daily 11am to 4am. 28 Arrow Rd. *C* **843/842-3800.**

The Salty Dog Cafe   Locals used to keep this laid-back place near the beach to themselves, but now more and more visitors are showing up. Soft guitar music or Jimmy Buffett is often played. Dress is casual. Sit under one of the sycamores, enjoying your choice of food from an outdoor grill or buffet. Daily until 2am. South Beach Marina. *C* **843/671-2233.**

Signals   In this upscale resort, you can enjoy live bands (often performing 1940s golden oldies), along with R & B, blues, and jazz. The dance floor is generally crowded. Live bands perform Tuesday to Sunday 9pm to 1am, and live jazz is presented on Monday 6 to 9:30pm. A Sunday jazz brunch is held from 11am to 1:30pm. 130 Shipyard Dr., in the Crowne Plaza Resort. *C* **843/842-2400.**

3 Daufuskie Island (*★*)

1 nautical mile W of Hilton Head

Rich in legend, lore, and history, Daufuskie Island is relatively cut off from the world. Its heyday came in the mid–19th century when Southern plantations here produced the famous Sea Island cotton, until the boll weevil put an end to that industry. The island is also known to readers as the setting for Pat Conroy's book, *The Water Is Wide.* The movie, *Conrack,* was filmed on Daufuskie.

Lying between Hilton Head and Savannah, and accessible only by boat, half the island has remained an undeveloped wilderness of forest, marshland, and wildlife. In 1980, the other half was purchased for the development of golf courses and elegant "plantations" where people live in condos.

The 5,200-acre island is home to about 300 permanent residents, mostly Gullahs, descendants of slaves freed after the Civil War. The island was originally inhabited by the Cusabo and later the Yemassee Indians. Indian pottery, some of the oldest in America, has been found on Daufuskie, going back 9,000 years.

The English eventually took over the island and converted it into a plantation culture, focusing on indigo as its main export. Indigo eventually yielded to cotton plantations. After the boll weevil, an oyster-canning industry took over until it was forced out of business by the pollution of the Savannah River.

The island is a nature retreat, with thick, ancient live oaks and angel oaks along with ospreys, egrets, and other waterfowl living among the reeds and rushes.

GETTING THERE

There is only one way to Daufuskie Island, and that's by boat. If you aren't coming here on one of the organized ferries/tours, then contact the **Daufuskie Resort** (© 843/842-2000) to arrange a ride. The ride is free for guests, but everyone else is charged $37 round-trip. To find the Embarkation Center on Hilton Head, turn left on Squire Pope Road. The Embarkation Center is 2 miles on the left just before the Cypress Gate to Hilton Head Plantation.

CRUISES & TOURS

Several tempting tours are offered to Daufuskie, which has beaches, "whispering" marshes, ancient forests of moss-draped oaks, and two of the best golf courses in America. What it doesn't have are stoplights, crowds, and shopping centers.

Adventure Cruises, Inc., Shelter Cove Harbour, Suite G, Harbourside III (© 843/785-4558), offers a nature cruise to Daufuskie Island with a guided safari on a jungle bus. The round-trip cost is adults $18 and children $9. Departures are Monday to Friday at 12:15pm, with a return to Hilton Head at 4:45pm.

The **Calibogue Cruises** ferry (© 843/342-8687) leaves from Broad Creek Marina off Marshland Road on Hilton Head. The ferry ride is $40 per person, and the tour is $45 per person. The tour visits the Mount Carmel and First Union African Baptist churches, the Lighthouse, the Old Winery, and cemeteries dating back hundreds of years. You'll sample the delicious Daufuskie Island Deviled Crab. You also have the option of renting a Club Cart (golf cart) for $40 to explore the island on your own. Tours depart once a day Monday to Saturday (call ahead for times).

Daufuskie Island Adventure Cruise's *Vagabond* (© 843/842-4155) departs from Harbour Town. The cruise is narrated by naturalist/historian captains. Once you're on the island, this tour is the only one that goes inside the 125-year-old Baptist Church and the school where Pat Conroy taught. Tours depart on Tuesday, Wednesday, and Saturday (call ahead for times), and last 3 hours. The cost is $45 per adult, $25 per child.

Outside Hilton Head, **Daufuskie Island Tour** offers two tours to Daufuskie, departing from South Beach Marina at Sea Pines Resort (© 800/686-6996 or 843/686-6996). The 4-hour tour is $85 per person (includes boat shuttle, golf carts, and guide). Once on the island, you will board golf carts and tour historic sites. The 8-hour day tour is $145 per person (includes boat shuttle, golf carts, lunch, and guide). You will be transported to Page Island, where you will kayak to Daufuskie Island. By golf cart, you will tour Indian sites, the old Baptist church, Pat Conroy's school, and other locations. Lunch at a "funky" island restaurant is included in the price.

GOLF COURSES **Melrose & Bloody Point Golf Courses** are both at the Daufuskie Island Resort, Daufuskie Island (© 888/909-4653 or 843/341-4810 for both courses). Melrose Golf Course is an 18-hole, Jack Nicklaus–designed, 7,081-yard, par-72 course that sweeps along the Atlantic Ocean. Greens fees range from $60 to $114 (depending on the season) for resort guests; $71 to $129 for day golf visitors (which includes ferry, greens fees, and cart). Hours are daily 7:30am to 6pm (earlier closing time in winter). The Bloody Point Golf course is an 18-hole, Tom Weiskop/Jay Morrish–designed, 6,900-yard, 72-par course on the Mungen River; it winds through coastal marshes and dark water lagoons. Greens fees range from $69 to $125 (depending on the season) for resort guests; $71 to $129 for day golf visitors (which includes ferry, greens fees, and cart). Hours are 7:30am to 6pm (earlier closing time in winter).

WHERE TO STAY ON DAUFUSKIE ISLAND

Daufuskie Island Resort & Breathe Spa *Finds* Lying 1 mile off the coast of Hilton Head, this is an exclusive island retreat operated like a private club for escapists. With two championship golf courses, 3 miles of pristine white-sand beach, and a trio of swimming pools, this resort is devoted to *la dolce vita*. Most guests here are club members who enjoy use of the facilities, although the resort does set aside some accommodations for the general public.

The spacious guest rooms are furnished for upscale comfort, with heavy wood furniture and bright, colorful bedspreads. Beautiful bathrooms come with tub and shower. The resort competes with those on Hilton Head in terms of its recreational activities—not just golf, but tennis, boating, and even an equestrian center nearby. Most of the accommodations rented out to transient residents, as opposed to club members, are in two-story cottages.

421 Squire Pope Rd., Hilton Head Island, SC 29926-1399. (*C*) **800/648-6778** or 843/842-2000. Fax 843/686-3755. www.daufuskieresort.com. 190 units. $129–$259 double; $300–$480 2-bedroom cottage. AE, DC, DISC, MC, V. **Amenities:** 4 restaurants; 2 bars; 3 outdoor pools; 2 golf courses; gym; sauna; children's activities; limited room service; babysitting; nonsmoking rooms. *In room:* A/C, TV, kitchen, washer/dryer.

4 Beaufort ★★

46 miles NE of Savannah

The town of Beaufort was the inspiration for the setting of Pat Conroy's novel *The Prince of Tides* (among other bestsellers). The town is full of old-fashioned inns, rustic pubs, and tiny stores along a tailored waterfront park.

Beaufort (Low Country pronunciation: *Bew*-fort) is an old seaport with narrow streets shaded by huge live oaks and lined with 18th-century homes. The oldest house (at Port Republic and New sts.) was built in 1717. This was the second area in North America discovered by the Spanish (1520), the site of the first fort on the continent (1525), and the first attempted settlement (1562). Several forts have been excavated, dating from 1566 and 1577.

Beaufort has been used as a setting for several films, including *The Big Chill.* Scenes from the Paramount blockbuster *Forrest Gump,* starring Tom Hanks, and from *The Prince of Tides,* were also shot here.

GETTING THERE

If you're traveling from the north, take I-95 to exit 33; then follow the signs to the center of Beaufort. If you're leaving from Charleston, take U.S. 17 South, then head left on U.S. 21, and follow signs to Beaufort. From Hilton Head, go on U.S. 278 West; after it turns into 278 Alt you will exit onto S.C. 170. Follow S.C. 170 into Beaufort.

VISITOR INFORMATION

Beaufort Chamber of Commerce, 1106 Carteret St. (P.O. Box 910), Beaufort, SC 29901 (*C*) **843/524-3163;** www.beaufortsc.org), has information and self-guided tours of this historic town. It's open daily 9am to 5:30pm.

ORGANIZED TOURS

If your plans are for early to mid-October, contact the **Historic Beaufort Foundation,** P.O. Box 11, Beaufort, SC 29901 (© **843/ 379-3331;** www.historic-beaufort.org), for dates and details regarding its 3 days of antebellum house and garden tours.

A tour called **The Spirit of Old Beaufort,** 103 West St. extension (© **843/525-0459;** www.spiritofoldbeaufort.com), takes you on a journey through the old town, exploring local history, architecture, horticulture, and Low Country life. You'll see houses that are not accessible on other tours. Your host, clad in period costume, will guide you for 2-hour tours held from Monday to Saturday at 10:30am and 2:30pm. The cost is $13 for adults, $7.50 for children 6 to 12. Tours depart from just behind the John Market Verdier House Museum.

SEEING THE SIGHTS

John Mark Verdier House Museum, 801 Bay St. (© **843/379- 6335**), is a restored 1802 house partially furnished to depict the life of a merchant planter from 1800–25. It's one of the best examples of the Federal period and was once known as the Lafayette Building, because the Marquis de Lafayette reportedly spoke here in 1825. It's open Monday to Saturday from 11:30am to 3:30pm, charging $6 for adults and $3 for children; children under 6 enter free.

St. Helena's Episcopal Church, 507 New Castle St. (© **843/ 522-1712**), traces its origin back to 1712. Visitors, admitted free Monday to Saturday from 10am to 4pm, can see its classic interior and visit the graveyard, where tombstones served as operating tables during the Civil War.

Beaufort is the home of the **U.S. Marine Corps Recruit Depot.** The visitor center (go to Building 283) is open daily from 6am to 6pm. You can take a driving tour or a bus tour (free) around the grounds, where you'll see an Iwo Jima monument; a monument to the Spanish settlement of Santa Elena (1521); and a memorial to Jean Ribaut, the Huguenot who founded Beaufort in 1562. Vehicle operators must possess a valid driver's license, vehicle registration, and proof of automobile insurance. In a country at war with terrorists, you can expect tightened security.

WHERE TO STAY IN BEAUFORT
EXPENSIVE

Beaufort Inn ✸✸   Built in 1897, this is the most appealing hotel in Beaufort and the place where whatever movie star happens to be

ACCOMMODATIONS ■
Best Inn 1
Beaufort Inn 9
Craven Street Inn 4
Cuthbert House Inn 11
The Rhett House Inn 5
Sea Island Inn 7
Two Suns Inn 3

DINING ◆
The Bank Waterfront Grill
  & Bar 7
The Beaufort Inn Restaurant
  & Wine Bar 9
Broad River Seafood 2
Emily's 6
Kathleen's Grille 10
Ollie's Seafood Restaurant 11

shooting a film in town is likely to stay. The woodwork and mold-ings inside are among the finest in Beaufort, and the circular, four-story staircase has been the subject of numerous photographs and architectural awards. The guest rooms, each decorated in brightly colored individual style, are conversation pieces. Each unit has a well-kept bathroom with a tub/shower combination. A wine bar, grill room, and rose garden are more recent additions.

809 Port Republic St., Beaufort, SC 29902. ℂ **843/521-9000.** Fax 843/521-9500. www.beaufortinn.com. 21 units. $145–$350 double; $215-$350 suite. Rates include full gourmet breakfast. AE, DISC, MC, V. No children under 8. **Amenities:** Restaurant; bar; limited room service; nonsmoking rooms. *In room:* A/C, TV, data-port, coffeemaker, hair dryer, iron/ironing board.

The Rhett House Inn ✿✿✿   This inn is certainly very popular, at least with Hollywood film crews. Because it was a site for *Forrest Gump, The Prince of Tides,* and *The Big Chill,* chances are that you've seen it before. It's a Mobil and AAA four-diamond inn in a restored 1820 Greek Revival plantation-type home. Rooms are furnished with English and American antiques, and ornamented with Oriental rugs; eight contain whirlpools. All units contain well-kept bathrooms with tub/shower combinations. The veranda makes an ideal place to sit and view the gardens. The inn is open year-round.

1009 Craven St., Beaufort, SC 29902. © **888/480-9530** or 843/524-9030. Fax 843/524-1310. www.rhetthouseinn.com. 17 units. $195–$325 double. Rates include full breakfast, afternoon tea, and evening hors d'oeuvres. AE, DISC, MC, V. Free parking. No children under 5. **Amenities:** Breakfast room; lounge; nonsmoking rooms. *In room:* A/C, TV, dataport, minibar (in some), hair dryer, iron/ironing board.

MODERATE

Craven Street Inn Charging rates that are about 40% less than those at its more expensive sibling, the Beaufort Inn, this is a gracefully proportioned clapboard-sided house (ca. 1870) whose double tier of wide verandas invite sitting on stifling days. It was originally built by the Lipton family, whose fortunes derived from selling shoes to new recruits at the nearby Marine base at Parris Island. Today, it sports four rooms in its central core, an additional four units in what was built in the 1920s as a carriage house, and two suites in a once-unrelated house across the street. Regardless of their location, guest rooms have soaring ceilings, heart pine floors, fireplaces, and a Victorian-inspired decor that includes a mixture of antique and reproduction furniture. Bathrooms have either single showers or tub/shower combinations. The location is a block from the waterfront in the town's historic core. Access to the double tier of verandas, site of several rocking chairs, is available to all guests, regardless of their room assignments, through the common hallways.

1103 Craven St., Beaufort, SC 29920. © **888/522-0250** or 843/522-1668. www.thecravenstreetinn.com. 10 units. $138–$170 double; $215 suite. Rates include full breakfast. AE, DISC, MC, V. No children under 8. **Amenities:** Breakfast room; laundry service/dry cleaning. *In room:* A/C, TV, dataport, coffeemaker, hair dryer, iron/ironing board, fireplace.

Cuthbert House Inn 🏛🏛 One of the grand old B&Bs of South Carolina, this showcase Southern home was built in 1790 in classic style. The inn was remodeled after the Civil War to take on a more Victorian air, but its present owner, Sharon Groves, has worked to modernize it without sacrificing its grace or antiquity. Graffiti carved by Union soldiers can still be seen on the mantel in the Eastlake Room. The inn is filled with large parlors and sitting rooms, and has the spacious hallways and 12-foot ceilings characteristic of Greek Revival homes. Modern amenities and conveniences have been tastefully tucked in. Guest rooms are elegantly furnished in Southern plantation style, some with four-poster beds. All units come equipped with bathrooms containing tub/shower combinations. Some bathrooms have the old cast-iron soaking tubs. At breakfast in the conservatory, you can order such delights as Georgia ice cream (cheese grits) and freshly made breads.

1203 Bay St., Beaufort, SC 29901. © **800/327-9275** or 843/521-1315. Fax 843/521-1314. www.cuthberthouseinn.com. 7 units. $145–$215 double; $195–$265 suite year-round. Rates include full breakfast and afternoon tea or refreshments. AE, DISC, MC, V. Free parking. **Amenities:** Breakfast room; lounge; bikes; nonsmoking rooms. *In room:* A/C, TV, dataport, fridge, hair dryer, iron/ironing board.

INEXPENSIVE

Best Inn *Value* You'll be happiest at this simple member of a local hotel chain if you know what it doesn't contain: There's no restaurant, no bar, and no pool since the ground they originally occupied was bought by a neighboring business in 2001. What you do get is a cost-effective hotel room outfitted in a bland contemporary style, with solid, well-maintained, and somewhat unimaginative furnishings. Set 2 miles north of Beaufort's commercial core, it's a slightly dowdy but friendly and carefully maintained place to stay. There are lots of restaurants and bars within a short drive, the staff is conscientious and stable, and overall, it's a worthy choice for families with children or for business travelers who simply need a no-frills place to spend the night.

2448 Boundary St., Beaufort, SC 29903. © **843/524-3322.** Fax 843/524-7264. 51 units. $59–$85 double. Rates include continental breakfast. AE, DC, DISC, MC, V. *In room:* A/C, TV, iron.

Sea Island Inn This is a basic two-story motel with reasonable rates for what you get. Few of the rooms have sea views; all contain well-kept bathrooms with tub/shower combinations. Although the rooms are nothing special, they're comfortable and clean.

1015 Bay St., Beaufort, SC 29902. © **800/528-1234** or 843/522-2090. Fax 843/521-4858. www.bestwestern.com. 43 units. $109–$165 double. Rates include continental breakfast. AE, DC, DISC, MC, V. **Amenities:** Breakfast room; lounge; pool; fitness center. *In room:* A/C, TV, hair dryer.

Two Suns Inn When this place was built in 1917, it was one of the grandest homes in its prosperous neighborhood, offering views of the coastal road and the tidal flatlands beyond. Every imaginable modern (at the time) convenience was added, including a baseboard vacuum-cleaning system, an electric call box, and steam heat. Later, when the inn became housing for unmarried teachers in the public schools, the place became run-down. Now it's a cozy B&B. Part of the inn's appeal stems from its lack of pretension, as a glance at the homey bedrooms with simple furnishings and neatly kept bathrooms with showers shows you.

1705 Bay St., Beaufort, SC 29902. ✆ **800/532-4244** or 843/522-1122. Fax 843/522-1122. www.twosunsinn.com. 5 units. $135–$200 double. Rates include full breakfast and afternoon cordials. AE, DISC, MC, V. Free parking. No children under 12. **Amenities:** Breakfast room; lounge; nonsmoking rooms; rooms for those w/limited mobility. *In room:* A/C, TV, dataport, hair dryer.

WHERE TO DINE IN BEAUFORT
EXPENSIVE
The Beaufort Inn Restaurant & Wine Bar ✿ INTERNATIONAL   Stylish, urbane, and awash with Colonial lowland references, this is the local choice for celebratory or business dinners, amid candlelit surrounds. Meat courses include chicken piccata with artichokes and sun-dried tomatoes, and an excellent grilled filet mignon with herbal Gorgonzola butter and shiitake mushrooms; vegetarian main courses include roasted-pepper-and-eggplant torte. On the menu is a variation on a dish whose invention has been claimed by many restaurants in the Low Country: crispy whole flounder with strawberry-watermelon chutney.

In the Beaufort Inn, 809 Port Republic St. ✆ **843/521-9000.** Reservations recommended. Main courses $17–$30. AE, DISC, MC, V. Mon–Sat 6–10pm; Sun 11:30am–2pm and 6–10pm.

Emily's INTERNATIONAL   This is our favorite restaurant in Beaufort, a spot whose ambience and attitude put us in mind of Scandinavia. That's hardly surprising, because the bearded owner is an emigré from Sweden who feels comfortable in the South Carolina lowlands after years of life at sea. Some folks go to the bar to sample tapas: miniature portions of tempura shrimp, fried scallops, stuffed peppers, and at least 50 other items. Menu items might include rich cream of mussel and shrimp soup; filet "black and white" (filets of beef and pork served with béarnaise sauce); duck with orange sauce; and a meltingly tender Wiener schnitzel. Everything is served in stomach-stretching portions.

906 Port Republic St. ✆ **843/522-1866.** Reservations recommended. Tapas $8; main courses $20–$27. AE, DISC, MC, V. Drinks and tapas Mon–Sat 4–10pm; main courses Mon–Sat 6–10pm.

MODERATE
Fans of the former Ollie's by the Bay in downtown Beaufort should know that the restaurant has moved to Lady's Island and changed its name to **Ollie's Seafood Restaurant** (71 Sea Island Parkway; ✆ **843/525-6333**). It still serves some of the best steaks in the area,

and shrimp burgers are a house specialty. The catch of the day can be broiled, blackened, or sautéed.

The Bank Waterfront Grill & Bar AMERICAN   This restaurant, known for its good food, lies on Bay Street with a waterfront view from its terrace. Before it was successfully converted into a restaurant, the building was once a bank and later a movie theater. Today's premises have won several awards for the restoration to its former grandeur. In such a setting, you get locally produced food, with about 70 menu items featured daily, ranging from fresh local seafood to burgers and steaks, along with the usual assortment of pastas and freshly made salads.

A wide range of appetizers include local favorites such as oysters on the half shell, "loaded potato skins," and stuffed jalapeño peppers. At lunch the sandwiches are the best stuffed in town, or you can order fried seafood lunch baskets with french fries and hush puppies for a real calorie fix. At night the chef shines brightly with his catch of the day—grilled, broiled, or blackened. A tasty specialty is his Frogmore stew: real Low Country dining with shrimp, smoked sausages, new potatoes, onions, and corn on the cob. The bartender makes the best margaritas in Beaufort.

926 Bay St. ℂ 843/522-8831. Reservations recommended. Lunch $6.95–$9.95; main courses $9.95–$19. AE, DC, DISC, MC, V. Daily 11am–10pm. Closed Thanksgiving and Christmas.

Claude's 🐾 (Kids) LOW COUNTRY   At the entrance to Parris Island, this is a brightly lit, nautically themed restaurant, which the local newspaper twice voted as Beaufort's best all-around dining room. It's the place to go for steaks, prime rib, and fresh seafood. Many dishes are for kids 12 and under. Adults devour a wide range of well-prepared appetizers—all the usual favorites like fried mushrooms or shrimp cocktail, but with some down-home Low Country offerings as well, such as fried green tomatoes and shrimp flavored with garlic and basil. Locals rave about the shrimp and grits, but we always gravitate to the fresh local seafood, especially the catch of the day. You can also order special treats such as teriyaki sirloin, blackened-chicken pasta, or slow-roasted prime rib.

19 Marina Village Lane, Beaufort, SC. ℂ 843/522-3235. Reservations recommended. Main courses $12–$23. AE, MC, V. Mon–Thurs 5–9:30pm; Fri–Sat 5–10pm.

Kathleen's Grille (Finds) SEAFOOD/SOUTHERN   In the space formerly occupied by Ollie's by the Bay, this local eatery has plenty of Low Country atmosphere and is known for its fresh fish dinners.

We'd go here for its "Southern starters" alone, including fried green tomatoes topped with a shrimp salsa or its "classy" crab chowder. For lunch you can partake of offerings from the "sandwich showcase," including a soft-shell crab or fresh grouper. Salads, including a seafood pasta version, are made fresh daily. At night the stove heats up to sauté some of the best fish platters in the area, including grilled shrimp or boiled oysters. For the meat lover, there is the inevitable rib eye or pork chops, the latter coming with a sweet and spicy berry glaze. One section of the menu is ridiculously simple, reserved for "Kathleen's kids," but with such meager offerings as fresh boxed cereals or a hot dog, they may be nutritionally deprived.

822 Bay St. ⓒ **843/524-2500.** Reservations not required. Lunch $6.99–$8.99; main courses $14.95–$17.95. AE, DISC, MC, V. Mon–Fri 11am–10pm; Sat-Sun 7am-9pm.

INEXPENSIVE

Broad River Seafood *(Value* SEAFOOD   This restaurant on Highway 21 opens onto a lovely marsh view at high tide. Nautically themed, it features some of the best seafood in the area, and nightly specialty buffets are part of its extensive menu. For example, on our most recent visit, the Admiral's Buffet (the "granddaddy" of all their seafood buffets) was the feature, with the largest selection of fish, including crab legs. One of the most unusual offerings under "The Captain's Catch" is flounder filets bathed in buttermilk for a tasty breading. Coleslaw, hush puppies, and the regular fixin's accompany most platters. For that rare meat eater who shows up here, the chef will grill a skinless chicken breast or throw a rib-eye steak on the grill.

2601 Boundary St., Hwy. 21. ⓒ **843/524-2001.** Lunch $4.95–$6.95; main courses $10–$18; seafood buffets $13–$30. AE, DISC, MC, V. Mon–Thurs 11:30am–9pm; Fri–Sat 11:30am–9:30pm; Sun 11:30am–7pm. Closed Christmas Eve, Christmas Day, and New Year's Day.

5 St. Simons Island (★(★

80 miles S of Savannah

A drive of some 1½ hours (depending on traffic) will bring you to the southern periphery of Savannah, where you'll find one of the great vacation playgrounds of the South. Georgia's barrier islands extend along the Atlantic Coast from Ossabaw Island near Savannah all the way down to Cumberland Island near Florida.

The largest of the Golden Isles, St. Simons, is the most popular for its beaches, golf courses, scenery, and many tennis courts.

ESSENTIALS

GETTING THERE   Take I-95 to Ga. 25 (the Island Pkwy.) or U.S. 17 to Brunswick, where signs direct visitors across the F. J. Torras Causeway to St. Simons Island.

VISITOR INFORMATION   The **St. Simons Island Visitors Center & Chamber of Commerce,** 530 Beachview Dr. W. (© **912/638-9014**), offers maps and information, particularly on beaches. It's open daily 9am to 5pm.

SEEING THE ISLAND

The best way to introduce yourself to the island is via **St. Simons Trolley Island Tours** (© **912/638-8954**), which acquaint you with 400 years of history and folklore. A 1½-hour tour costs $18 for adults and $10 for children 10 and under. Tours depart March 15 to Labor Day, daily at 11am and 1pm; off season, daily at 11am.

The island's chief attraction is **Fort Frederica National Monument** (© **912/638-3639**; www.nps.gov/fofr), on the northwest end of the island (signposted). Go first to the National Park Service Visitor Center, where a film and displays explain the role of the fort. There isn't much left; about all you'll see of the original construction is a small portion of the king's magazine and the barracks tower, but archaeological excavations have unearthed many foundations. The fort was constructed in 1736 by Gen. James Oglethorpe. On the grounds is a gift shop, and walking tours can be arranged. Admission is $5 per car. Hours are 9am to 5pm daily.

The **Museum of Coastal History,** 101 12th St. (© **912/638-4666**), is in a restored lighthouse keeper's house next to St. Simons Light. A gallery dispenses information about the coastal region on the ground floor. Climb the lighthouse's 129 steps for a panoramic view of the Golden Isles, which is far more intriguing than any of the museum's exhibits. Adults pay $5 and children 6 to 12 are charged $2.50 (children 5 and under enter free). It's open Monday to Saturday from 10am to 5pm and on Sunday from 1:30 to 5pm.

Christ Church, 6329 Frederica Rd., at the north end of the island, was built in 1820. It was virtually destroyed when Union troops camped here during the Civil War, burning the pews for firewood and butchering cattle in the chapel. In 1886, Anson Greene Phelps Dodge, Jr., restored the church as a memorial to his first wife, who had died on their honeymoon. The serene white building nestled under huge old oaks is open every day from 2 to 5pm during daylight saving time, 1 to 4pm at other times. There's no admission charge.

Scattered from end to end on St. Simons are ruins of the plantation era: **Hampton Plantation** (where Aaron Burr spent a month after his duel with Alexander Hamilton) and **Cannon's Point** on the north side; **West Point, Pines Bluff,** and **Hamilton Plantations** on the west side along the Frederica River; **Harrington Hall** and **Mulberry Grove** in the interior; **Lawrence, St. Clair, Black Banks, The Village,** and **Kelvyn Grove** on the east side; and **Retreat Plantation** on the south side. There's a restored chapel on West Point Plantation made of tabby, with mortar turned pink from an unusual lichen. Locals say it reflects blood on the hands of Dr. Thomas Hazzard, who killed a neighbor in a land dispute and built the chapel after being so ostracized that he would not attend Christ Church.

BEACHES, GOLF & OTHER OUTDOOR PURSUITS

St. Simons not only attracts families looking for a beach—it's also heaven for golfers, with 99 holes. One golfer who's played every hole said that each one presents a worthy challenge. Other sports are boating, inshore and offshore fishing, and water-skiing. Jet-skiing, parasailing, charter fishing, scuba diving, and cruising can also be arranged at **Golden Isles Marina Docks,** 206 Marina Dr. (© **912/ 634-1128**), on the F. J. Torras Causeway.

Neptune Park, at the island's south end, has miniature golf, a kids' playground, picnics under the oaks, and pier fishing. There's beach access from the park.

BEACHES   You'll find two white-sand public beaches here, foremost of which is **Massingale Park Beach,** Ocean Boulevard. The county-maintained beach has a picnic area and a bathhouse. It's open with a lifeguard on duty June 1 to Labor Day, daily from 8am to 4pm. Parking is free in designated areas. Drinking is allowed on the beach, but only from plastic containers (no glasses). Fishing is free from the beach but allowed only from 4 to 11pm.

Another public beach is the **Coast Guard Station Beach,** East Beach Causeway, again family-oriented, with a bathhouse and showers. Lifeguards are on duty from June 1 to Labor Day weekend, daily from 10am to 4pm. Parking is free in designated areas, and fishing is permitted during nonswimming hours from 4:30 to 11pm. Drinking is allowed on the beach from plastic containers only.

Further information about beaches can be obtained from the **Glynn County Recreation Department** (© **912/554-7780**).

BIKE RENTALS   **Ocean Motion,** 1300 Ocean Blvd. (© **800/669- 5215** or 912/638-5225), suggests that you explore St. Simons by bike, and will provide details for the best routes. The island is relatively flat, so biking is easy. Beach cruisers are available for men, women, and kids, with infant seats and helmets. Bike rentals cost $9 for 4 hours or $14 for a full day.

FISHING   Your best bet is **Golden Isles Charter Fishing,** 104 Marina Dr., Golden Isles Marina Village (© **912/638-7673**), which offers deep-sea fishing and both offshore and inshore fishing. Captain Mark Noble is your guide.

GOLF   It's golf—not tennis—that makes St. Simons Island a star attraction. Foremost among the courses is **Sea Island Golf Club** 🏌🏌🏌, 100 Retreat Ave. (© **912/638-5118**), owned by The Cloister of Sea Island. At the end of the "Avenue of Oaks" at historic Retreat Plantation, the club consists of a number of courses: the Retreat Course (9 holes, 3,260 yd., par 36), the Plantation Course (18 holes, 6,549 yd., par 72), the Seaside Course (9 holes, 3,185 yd., par 36), and the Ocean Forest (18 holes, 7,011 yd., par 72).

The club opened in 1927, and offers dramatic ocean views. The state-of-the-art Golf Learning Center on the grounds can help improve even an experienced golfer's game. Its greatest fans mention it with the same reverence as St. Andrews, Pebble Beach, or Ballybunion. Former president George H. W. Bush liked the courses so much that he played 36 holes a day. Seaside and Retreat are the most requested nines, with Seaside definitely the most famous of all— known for the 414-yard no. 7. *Golf Digest* has called this hole one of the best in golf and among the toughest in Georgia. A drive has to clear a marsh-lined stream and avoid a gaping fairway bunker.

Greens fees for hotel guests only are $135 to $230, with cart included. Clubs rent for $40, and professional instruction is available for $100 to $230 per half-hour. Caddies cost $29 plus tip. On the grounds are a pro shop, clubhouse, and restaurant. The course is open daily from 7am to 7pm.

St. Simons Island Club, 100 Kings Way (© **912/638-3611**), is an 18-hole, par-72 course of 6,200 yards. Known for its Low Country architecture, it hosts several popular tournaments every year. The demanding course, designed by Joe Lee, features narrow fairways lined by lagoons and towering pines. Greens fees for Cloister guests are $105 to $135; cottage guests at Sea Island pay the same amount. Professional instruction is available at $95 to $250 per hour through arrangements made at the clubhouse and pro shop. There's a restaurant on the premises. Play is available daily from 7am to 7pm.

Sea Palms Golf & Tennis Resort, 5445 Frederica Rd. (© **912/ 638-3351**), offers outstanding golf on its Tall Pines/Great Oaks (18 holes, 6,500 yd., par 72), Great Oaks/Sea Palms West (18 holes, 6,200 yd., par 72), and Sea Palms West/Tall Pines (9 holes, 2,500 yd., par 72) courses. Some holes nestle alongside scenic marshes and meandering tidal creeks. Reserved tee times are recommended, and cart use is required. The courses are open daily from 7am to 7pm, charging greens fees of $69 for hotel guests and $84 for nonguests, with cart rentals included. Professional instruction costs $30 for a 30-minute session, $50 for an hour.

NATURE TOURS   Ocean Motion Surf Co., 1300 Ocean Blvd. (© **912/638-5225**), offers nature tours by kayak of the island's marsh creeks and secluded beaches. Choose either a 2-hour dolphin nature tour at $39, or a 4-hour wildlife tour only by request at $75.

SAILBOAT RENTALS   Barry's Beach Service, Inc., at the King and Prince Beach Hotel, 420 Arnold Rd. (© **912/638-8053**), arranges hourly, half-day, or full-day sailboat rentals, along with sailing lessons (by experienced instructors) and sailboat rides. Kayak rentals, tours, and instruction are available.

TENNIS   There are two public tennis courts on the island. **Mallory Park Courts,** Mallory Street, has two lighted courts open year-round, and admission is free. The two courts at **Epworth Park,** on Lady Huntington Drive, are open 24 hours but are not equipped with lights; admission is free.

WHERE TO STAY ON ST. SIMONS ISLAND

In addition to the accommodations listed below, private cottages are available for weekly or monthly rental on St. Simons. You can get an illustrated brochure with rates and availability information from **Parker-Kaufman Realtors,** 1699 Frederica Rd., St. Simons Island, GA 31522 (© **912/638-3368**). The office is open Monday to Friday 9am to 5pm and on Saturday 9am to 1pm. Vacation rental cottages can range from one to four bedrooms. Rentals begin at $550 per week in summer, lowered to as little as $450 per week off season.

Best Western Island Inn   This unassuming, brick-sided motel was built in the late 1980s, about 2½ miles from the nearest beach. The efficiencies have kitchenettes, and the guest rooms are no-nonsense, unfrilly, and economical. All units have well-kept bathrooms with tub/shower combinations. About a dozen of them can be connected with adjoining rooms to allow families to create their own living arrangements.

301 Main St., St. Simons Island, GA 31522. ⓒ 800/937-8376 or 912/638-7805. Fax 912/694-4720. www.bestwestern.com. 61 units. $75–$96 double; $108–$135 suite. Rates include continental breakfast. AE, DC, DISC, MC, V. **Amenities:** Breakfast room; lounge; outdoor pool; Jacuzzi; health club privileges; playground; business services; nonsmoking rooms; rooms for those w/limited mobility. *In room:* A/C, TV, dataport, hair dryer.

King and Prince Beach Resort   This is a midsize oceanfront resort founded in 1932 by partners who were evicted from the Jekyll Island Club. Today's reincarnation of five Spanish-style buildings is a venue for frequent corporate conventions. Frankly, it seems devoid of any real pizzazz, and during high tide, the beach completely disappears. The condo apartments have kitchenettes. All units have neatly kept bathrooms with tub/shower combinations.

201 Arnold Rd., St. Simons Island, GA 31522. ⓒ 800/342-0212 or 912/638-3631. Fax 912/634-1720. www.kingandprince.com. 187 units. $119–$269 double; $249–$469 villa. AE, DC, MC, V. **Amenities:** Restaurant; bar; 5 pools (1 indoor); 4 tennis courts; exercise room; Jacuzzi; limited room service; massage; babysitting; laundry service/dry cleaning; nonsmoking rooms; rooms for those w/limited mobility. *In room:* A/C, TV, kitchenette (in some), hair dryer, safe.

The Lodge at Sea Island Golf Club ⓡⓡ   Golfers who have stayed at some of the greatest resorts in California and the Carolinas justifiably rave about this resort. A great golfing experience and first-rate accommodations are combined into this smoothly operating lodge. It doesn't pretend to have the grandeur of its sibling, The Cloister on Sea Island (see below), but for a luxurious, casual retreat, it's hard to beat. Attached to one of America's premier golf clubs, the lodge has been created in the spirit of a private club in Newport or the Hamptons. An English manor house decor prevails throughout. The guest rooms are spacious and beautifully furnished; deluxe bathrooms have a tub/shower combo. The inn's premier restaurant, Colt & Alison's, specializes in steaks, chops, and live Maine lobster. Guests of the lodge have full access to all of the amenities of The Cloister (see below).

100 Retreat Ave., St. Simons Island, GA 31522. ⓒ 866/GOLF-LODGE or 912/634-4300. Fax 912/634-3909. www.golflodge.com. $300–$700 double; $450–$900 suite. AE, DISC, DC, MC, V. **Amenities:** 4 restaurants; 2 bars; 3 18-hole golf courses; exercise room; spa; Jacuzzi; sauna; game room, 24-hr. room service; babysitting; laundry service/dry cleaning; nonsmoking rooms; rooms for those w/limited mobility. *In room:* A/C, TV, dataport, minibar, hair dryer, safe, 24-hr. butler service (lodge only).

Sea Gate Inn   Its charms and advantages are often underestimated because of its low-rise format, unpretentious entrance, and position near other, much larger hotels. Despite that, this is a clean, respectable hotel whose accommodations are divided into two buildings separated from one another by a quiet road that runs parallel to the sea. The more desirable (and expensive) of the two is the Ocean House. The less expensive lodgings are clustered around a swimming pool, roadside-motel style. All units contain well-kept bathrooms with tub/shower combinations. Some units contain modest kitchenettes.

1014 Ocean Blvd., St. Simons Island, GA 31522. © **800/562-8812** or 912/ 638-8661. Fax 912/638-4932. www.seagateinn.com. 48 units. $75–$110 double; $93–$155 suite. DISC, MC, V. **Amenities:** Lounge; outdoor pool. *In room:* A/C, TV, kitchenette (in some).

Sea Palms Golf & Tennis Resort 🏵🏵   This place imitates the older and more upscale resorts nearby. Sprawled over 800 landscaped acres, it combines aspects of a retirement community with a family-friendly resort. Most people stay 3 to 5 days.

After registering in a woodsy bungalow near the entrance, you'll be waved off to carry your own bags to your accommodations. If you're looking for maximum isolation, this place might be appropriate; otherwise, you may feel it's too anonymous. All units are simply decorated and contain well-maintained bathrooms with tub/shower combinations. Each suite contains a kitchenette. There's a golf course on the premises, but the nearest good beach is about 4 miles away.

5445 Frederica Rd., St. Simons Island, GA 31522. © **800/841-6268** or 912/638-3351. Fax 912/634-8029. www.seapalms.com. 154 units. $119–$169 double; $169–$289 1- or 2-bedroom suite. Children 17 and under stay free in parent's room. Golf, tennis, and honeymoon packages available. AE, DC, MC, V. **Amenities:** Restaurant; bar; 2 outdoor pools; 27-hole golf course; 12 tennis courts; fitness center; sauna; babysitting; laundry service/dry cleaning; nonsmoking rooms; rooms for those w/limited mobility. *In room:* A/C, TV, dataport, hair dryer.

WHERE TO DINE ON ST. SIMONS ISLAND
EXPENSIVE
The Restaurant at the Sea Island Golf Club 🏵 INTERNATIONAL   Despite the name, this place stands firmly on St. Simons Island. It was built on the ruins of a cow barn at a plantation great house that long ago burned to the ground. The restaurant occupies a simple square dining room in back of the golf course's clubhouse, and has big windows extending over the landscape of trees and lawns. Uniformed staff members give the impression of being longtime family retainers as they serve a luncheon menu of burgers, salads, club sandwiches, and fresh fish. Dinner is more formal, offering worthy but not particularly experimental dishes,

including boned and browned Blue Ridge salmon trout, seafood fettuccine, seafood crepes, and grilled steaks.

100 Retreat Ave. ✆ **912/638-5154.** Reservations not necessary at lunch, recommended for dinner. Main courses $27–$40. AE, DC, MC, V. Tues–Sun noon–3:30pm and 6:30–9pm.

MODERATE

Chelsea's INTERNATIONAL   Set close to the road, a few steps from the larger and more visible King and Prince Hotel, this well-known restaurant combines aspects of a singles bar with a relaxed, unpretentious dining room. It's in a long, low-rise building trimmed with ferns, lattices, and wine racks. You never know who you might meet at the bar. The menu includes steaks, salads, pastas, lobster-tail fingers, chicken breasts crusted in Romano cheese, and roast lamb. A menu like that offers few surprises—but few disappointments, either.

1226 Ocean Blvd. ✆ **912/638-2047.** Reservations recommended. Main courses $12–$32. AE, DISC, MC, V. Daily 5:30–10pm.

INEXPENSIVE

Bennie's Red Barn *Value* STEAKS/SEAFOOD   Established in 1954, the place has a Southern folksiness, almost a hillbilly kind of charm. Menu items include an uncomplicated medley of food to please everyone's Southern grandmother, including fried or broiled fish, chicken, and shrimp. Steaks are sizable slabs, woodfire-grilled and appropriately seasoned. Dinners include house salad, potato, rolls, and tea or coffee. If you're a biscuit-and-gravy kind of diner, you've arrived.

5514 Frederica Rd. ✆ **912/638-2844.** Reservations recommended Sat–Sun. Main courses $11–$23. AE, DISC, MC, V. Daily 6–10pm.

Blue Water Bistro AMERICAN   Set in the island's most congested neighborhood a few steps from the waterfront, this place is New South all the way. It also knows how to throw a good party. Look for the bronze bank-deposit vault piercing its facade, a hint of the building's original role as a commercial landmark. Inside you'll find cozy nautical decor, an antique Wurlitzer jukebox, and an Atlanta brand of hip. Dishes range from Mardi Gras pasta (with shellfish and andouille sausage) to more urban dishes such as Mediterranean chicken, *pescado veracruzano,* and a stew of deep-sea scallops with green-lip mussels. For dessert there's Southern-style bread pudding like Mother used to make.

115 Mallory St. ✆ **912/638-7007.** Reservations recommended. Main courses $6.95–$15. AE, DISC, MC, V. Mon–Sat 11am–10pm.

The Crab Trap *(Kids* SEAFOOD   For the family trade in pursuit of coleslaw, hush puppies, and fried shrimp, the Crab Trap is the island's most popular seafood restaurant and a good buy. Forget fancy trappings—the place is downright plain. Fresh seafood is offered daily, and you can order it fried, broiled, blackened, or grilled. Appetizers include oysters on the half shell and crab soup. Boiled crab is the chef's specialty. The seafood platter is big enough for three. Steaks in various cuts are also available. That hole in the middle of your table is for depositing shrimp shells and corncobs. Dress as if you're going on a summer fishing trip.

1209 Ocean Blvd. *(℃* **912/638-3552.** Main courses $8.95–$19. AE, MC, V. Mon–Thurs 5–10pm; Fri–Sat 5–10:30pm; Sun 5–10pm. Closed Thanksgiving and Christmas.

Frannie's Place on St. Simons *(℟* *(Finds* SOUTHERN   Chef-owners Lisa Cook (an appropriate last name) and Fran Kelly win many awards for making the "Best Brunswick Stew" in the Golden Isles. They are the "Stewbilee" champs. Cook makes 20 gallons of the stew every day, and Kelly estimates that some 95% of the diners order the signature soup either as a main dish or as an appetizer. Most customers request a big steaming bowl with homemade corn bread and "sweet tea" on the side. It's topped off with a generous slice of pecan or Key lime pie. Of course, you can order other items here, including sandwiches, salads, and even vegetarian dishes. We like the crab cakes and shrimp salad.

318 Mallory St. *(℃* **912/638-1001.** Breakfast specials $4.95–$5.95. Lunch $4.95–$8.95; bowl of Brunswick stew $3.95. No credit cards. Wed–Sun 11am–2:30pm.

6 Sea Island *(★(★*

11 miles E of Brunswick

Since 1928 this has been the domain of The Cloister hotel (see below). Today, in addition to the hotel, it's home to some of the most elegant villas and mansions in the Southeast. Most of Sea Island's homes—many in the Spanish-Mediterranean style—are second homes to CEOs and other rich folk. Some can be rented at **Sea Island Cottage Rentals** *(℃* **912/638-5112;** www.seaisland cottages.com), but be prepared for higher mathematics.

The island was acquired by Ohio-based Howard Earle Coffin, an automobile executive, in 1925. Still owned by Coffin's descendants, The Cloister encompasses 10,000 acres of forest, lawn, and marsh-land, plus 5 miles of beachfront. The island has impressed everybody from Margaret Thatcher to Queen Juliana of the Netherlands, plus four U.S. presidents, including George H. W. Bush, who honeymooned here with Barbara in the 1940s. Many day visitors who can't afford the high prices of The Cloister come for a scenic drive along Sea Island Drive, called "Millionaire's Row"—there's no tollgate.

ESSENTIALS

GETTING THERE   From Brunswick, take the F. J. Torras Causeway to St. Simons Island and follow Sea Island Road to Sea Island.

VISITOR INFORMATION   There is no welcome center. Information is provided by The Cloister, but the staff prefers to cater to registered guests.

WHERE TO STAY & DINE ON SEA ISLAND

The Cloister 🏨🏨🏨   Georgia's poshest hotel retreat, set amid the most elaborate landscaping on the coast, is a vast compound between the Atlantic Ocean and the Black Banks River. It takes in about 50 carefully maintained buildings, most of which replicate the Iberian–Moorish Revival style of the resort's original architect, Addison Mizner.

Everyone from honeymooners to golfers checks in here, with the family trade predominating in July and August. Traditionalists prefer a room in the main building, with twin, double, or king-size beds, often with a private balcony or patio. These rooms tend to be smaller than the newer units. The secluded cottages and beach houses also contain accommodations. The oceanfront rooms are in contemporary buildings with sumptuous modern furnishings, lacking tradition but offering greater comfort and more room to breathe. All units have well-kept bathrooms with tub/shower combinations.

Full American Plan (lodging with three meals included) is required of all guests at The Cloister. The Main Dining Room is the most lavish restaurant in the region, with sumptuous buffets and vestiges of the 1940s apparent in the uniformed service and the hushed, very polite tones of both staff and guests.

Sea Island, GA 31561. © **800/732-4752** or 912/638-3611. Fax 912/638-5159. www.seaisland.com. $250–$700 double; $1,200 suite. Meals $35 per day. Children 18 and under stay free in parent's room. Golf, tennis, or honeymoon packages available. AE, DC, DISC, MC, V. **Amenities:** 4 restaurants; 2 bars; 3 outdoor pools; 3 18-hole golf courses; 10 tennis courts; beach club; fitness center; spa; salon; boutiques; limited room service; massage; babysitting; laundry service/dry cleaning; nonsmoking rooms; rooms for those w/limited mobility. *In room:* A/C, TV, dataport., minibar (in some), hair dryer.

Index

See also Accommodations and Restaurant indexes below.

GENERAL INDEX

A
AARP, 32
Abercorn Antique Village, 107
Accommodations, 40–59
    Beaufort, 158–162
    best bets, 4–6
    Daufuskie Island, 156–157
    family-friendly, 45
    Hilton Head, 132–141
    St. Simons Island, 168–170
    Tybee Island, 122–123
Active vacations, 28–29
Adler, Lee, House, 98
African-Americans, 39
    Juneteenth, 26
    sights and attractions, 85–89
Aiken, Conrad, 87, 89
Airlines, 34
Alex Raskin Antiques, 99, 108
American Foundation for the Blind
    (AFB), 31
American Revolution, 11–12
Amicks Deep Sea Fishing, 94
Amtrak, 32
Andrew Low House, 78
Annual Holiday Tour of Homes, 27
Antiques, 107–108
Architecture, 17–20
Armstrong House, 100
Art, 20–21
Art galleries, 108–109
Arts Center of Coastal Carolina
    (Hilton Head), 153
Audubon-Newhall Preserve
    (Hilton Head), 130
Avis Rent a Car, 30, 38

B
Bacon Park, 94, 95
Baker's Pride Bakery, 109
Bars and pubs, 3–4, 115
    gay and lesbian, 118–119

Beaches, 28
    Hilton Head, 126–127
    St. Simons Island, 166
Beaufort, 157–164
Bellaire Woods Campground, 92
Bernies, 115
Biking, 92
    Hilton Head, 127
    St. Simons Island, 166–167
Boat tours and cruises, 91
    Daufuskie Island, 155–156
    dinner cruises, 119
    Hilton Head, 127–128
Bonaventure Cemetery, 3, 86–87
The Book Gift Shop, 110
Bookstores, 109–110
Book Warehouse, 109
Bus travel, 33, 38
Byrd Cookie Company, 110

C
calendar of events, 26–27
Camping, 28–29, 92
Candy, 110
Carriage House Shop, 89
Carriage Tours of Savannah, 90
Car travel, 32–34, 38
Cathedral of St. John the Baptist, 81
Cemeteries, 85–87
Charlotte's Corner, 111
Chippewa Square, 106
Christ Church (St. Simons Island), 165
Christ Episcopal Church, 81–82
Christmas 1864, 27
The Christmas Shop, 111
Chuck's Bar, 118–119
Churches and synagogues
    Beaufort, 158
    St. Simons Island, 165
    Savannah, 81–84
        African-American, 86–89
Churchill's Pub, 115–116
City Hall, 104

City Market, 36, 104, 107
   restaurants in and around, 71–73
City Market Art Center, 104–105
Civil War, 13–14
Climate, 25
Clipper Trading Company, 108
Club One, 4, 119
Cluskey, Charles B., 19
Coastal Discovery Museum (Hilton Head), 126, 130
Coast Guard Station Beach (St. Simons Island), 166
Colonial Park Cemetery, 85, 106
Compass Prints, Inc./Ray Ellis Gallery, 108
Congregation Mickve Israel, 82, 99–100
Cotton, 12–13
Crafts Festival & Cane Grinding, 27
Crystal Beer Parlor, 116
Cuisine, 21–24

D affin Park, 95
Daufuskie Island, 154–157
Davenport House Museum, 78
Dawes, Serena, House, 98–99
Dejá Groove, 114
Dentists, 38
Dinner cruises, 119
Disabilities, travelers with, 30–31
Diving, 93–94
Diving Locker-Ski Chalet, 93–94
Drugstores, 38
Duncan, Virginia and John, House, 101

E. Jones St., 101
Elderhostel, 32
Emergencies, 33, 38
Enchantments, 111
E. Shaver, Bookseller, 110

F aces, 119
Factors Walk, 104
Factors Walk and Factors Row, 83
Families with children, 32
   sights and attractions, 90
   Restaurants, 70
Festivals and special events, 26–27
A Fine Choice, 111
First African Baptist Church, 86

First Bryan Baptist Church, 88–89
Fishing, 29, 94
   Hilton Head, 128
   St. Simons Island, 167
Flannery O'Connor Childhood Home, 89
The Folk Traditions Store, 112
Folly Field Beach, 127
Food stores, 110
Forrest Gump, 3, 5, 47, 106
Forsyth Parkside Apartments, 100
Fort Frederica National Monument (St. Simons Island), 165
Fort McAllister, 84
Fort Pulaski, 84–85
Fort Screven (Tybee Island), 121

G allery 209, 108
Gay and lesbian travelers
   bars, 118–119
   information and resources, 31
George Fazio Course (Hilton Head), 129
Ghost Talk Ghost Walk, 91
Gifts and collectibles, 110–111
Golf, 29, 94
   Daufuskie Island, 156
   Hilton Head, 126, 128–129
   St. Simons Island, 167
Gray Line Savannah Tours, 90
Green-Meldrim Home, 78, 80
Greyhound/Trailways, 33

H amilton-Turner Inn, 102
Hampton Plantation (St. Simons Island), 166
Hannah's East, 114
Hartsfield International Airport (Atlanta), 32
Haunted History tour, 90
Henderson Golf Club, 94
Hiking, 29
Hilton Head, 125–154
   accommodations, 132–141
   nightlife, 153–154
   outdoor activities, 126–132
   restaurants, 141–153
   shopping, 132
   special events, 126
   taxis, 126
   traveling to, 125
   visitor information, 125–126

Hilton Head Island Beach and Tennis Resort, 131
Hilton Head National, 129
Historic District, 35
  accommodations, 44–57
  restaurants, 65–71
Historic homes, 78–80
Historic Savannah Foundation Tours, 90
History of Savannah, 9–17
Horseback riding, Hilton Head, 129
Hospitals, 39
Hunting, 29

I Can, 31
In-line skating, 94
Island West Golf Club (Hilton Head), 129
Isle of Hope, 2, 124

J. D. Weed & Co., 108
Joe Odom's First House, 101
Jogging, 94
John Mark Verdier House Museum (Beaufort), 158
Johnny Mercer Theater, 113
John P. Rousakis Plaza, 103
Johnson Square, 113
John Tucker Fine Arts, 108
Juliette Gordon Low's Birthplace, 78
Juneteenth, 26–27

K ayak tours
  Hilton Head, 130
  St. Simons Island, 168
Kevin Barry's Irish Pub, 116

L ake Mayer Park, 95
Lakes, 29
Laurel Grove-South Cemetery, 85
Le Belle Maison, 111
Lee Adler's House, 98
Levy Jewelers, 112
Liquor laws, 33
Literary landmarks, 89
Live music clubs, 114–115
Low, Andrew, House, 78
Low, Juliette Gordon, Birthplace, 78
Low Country River Excursions, 91–92

Lucas Theatre, 113
Lutheran Church of the Ascension, 82

M ary Calder golf course, 94
Massie Heritage Interpretation Center, 90
Massingale Park Beach, 166
Mellow Mushroom, 116
Melrose & Bloody Point Golf Courses (Daufuskie Island), 156
Memorial Day at Old Fort Jackson, 26
Memory Lane, 108
Mercer House, 89, 96–98
Mercer House Carriage Shop, 98
Mercer House Williams Museum, 89
Mercury Lounge, 116–117
Midnight in the Garden of Good and Evil, 1, 3–5, 8, 16, 46, 48, 72–73, 76, 81, 86, 89, 114
  guided tour, 90
  memorabilia, 110
  self-guided walking tour, 96–102
MONEYGRAM, 27
Money matters, 27–28
Monkey Bar, 114
Monterey Square, 98
Morning Star Gallery, 109
MossRehab, 30–31
Museum of Coastal History (St. Simons Island), 165

N ature preserves, Hilton Head, 130
Nature watches, 94–95
Neighborhoods, 35–37
Neptune Park (St. Simons Island), 166
Newspapers, 39
Nicholsonboro Baptist Church, 87
Nightlife, 113–119
  Hilton Head, 153–154
Norris, John, 19
North Forest Beach, 127

O 'Connor, Flannery, 89
Odom, Joe, First House, 101
Oglethorpe, James Edward, 9–10
Oglethorpe Club, 100
Oglethorpe Mall, 107
Oglethorpe Square, 106
Old Customs House, 91

Old Fort Jackson, 84
Old South Golf Links (Hilton Head), 129
Old Town Trolley Tours, 90
Organized tours, 90–92. *See also* Boat tours and cruises
    Beaufort, 158
    St. Simons Island, 165
Outdoor activities, 92–95
Owens-Thomas House and Museum, 80

P almetto Coast Charters, 94–95
Palmetto Dunes Tennis Center (Hilton Head), 131
Parasailing, 130
Performing arts, 113–114
Plantations, 124, 166
Plantation Sweets Vidalia Onions, 110
Planters Tavern, 114–115
Port Royal Racquet Club (Hilton Head), 131
Post offices, 39

Q uarterdeck (Hilton Head), 154

R ail, The, 117
Rainfall, average, 25
Ralph Mark Gilbert Civil Rights Museum, 88
Reconstruction, 14–16
Regency style, 19, 81
Remy's (Hilton Head), 154
Reservations, hotel, 40
Restaurants, 2–3
    Beaufort, 162–164
    best bets, 6–8
    family-friendly, 70
    Hilton Head, 141–153
    St. Simons Island, 170–172
    Tybee Island, 123–124
Riverfront, 35
    accommodations along the, 40, 42–57
    restaurants along or near the, 59–65
River's End Campground and RV Park, 92–93
River Street, 103, 107
River Street Sweets, 110
Robert Trent Jones Course (Hilton Head), 129
Rose of Sharon, 102

S afety, 39
Sailboat rentals, St. Simons Island, 168
Sail Harbor, 95
Sailing, 95
    Hilton Head, 131
St. Helena's Episcopal Church (Beaufort), 158
St. Patrick's Day Celebration on the River, 26
St. Phillip Monumental A.M.E. Church, 88
St. Simons Island, 164–172
St. Simons Island Club, 167
The Salty Dog Cafe (Hilton Head), 154
SATH (Society for Accessible Travel & Hospitality), 31
Savannah Blues, 115
Savannah Cotton Exchange, 104
Savannah Festival Factory Stores, 107
Savannah Hilton Head International Airport, 34
Savannah History Museum, 80
Savannah Irish Festival, 26
Savannah Jazz Festival, 27, 113
Savannah Mall, 107
Savannah Music Festival, 26
Savannah National Wildlife Refuge, 93
Savannah Riverboat Cruises, 91
Savannah's Candy Kitchen, 110
Savannah Smiles, 117
Savannah Theater, 113–114
Savannah Tour of Homes, 26
Scuba diving, 93–94
Sea Island, 172–173
Sea Island Golf Club (St. Simons Island), 167
Sea Palms Golf & Tennis Resort (St. Simons Island), 168
Sea Pines Forest Preserve (Hilton Head), 130
Sea Pines Racquet Club (Hilton Head), 131
Seasons, 25
Second African Baptist Church, 88
Seniors, 31–32
Serena Dawes's House, 98–99
17 Hundred 90 Lounge, 117

Ships of the Sea Maritime
Museum, 80
Shopping, 107–112
Hilton Head, 132
Sightseeing suggestions, 76–77
Signals (Hilton Head), 154
Simply Silver, 112
Six Pence Pub, 117–118
Skidaway Island State Park, 92
South Forest Beach, 127
Special events and festivals, 26–27
Springfest (Hilton Head), 126

T axes, 33, 39
Taxis, 38
Telfair Mansion and Art Museum, 81,
105
Telfair Square, 105
Temperatures, average, 25
Temple Mickve Israel, 82, 99–100
Tennis
Hilton Head, 131
St. Simons Island, 168
Time zone, 33
Tours, organized, 90–92. *See also*
Boat tours and cruises
Beaufort, 158
St. Simons Island, 165
Train travel, 32, 34
Transit information, 39
Transportation, 38
Travel agencies
for disabled travelers, 30
for gay and lesbian travelers, 31
Traveling to Savannah, 32–33
Trinity United Methodist Church, 83
True Grits, 111
Tybee Island, 4, 120–124
Tybee Lighthouse, 121–122
Tybee Marine Center, 122
Tybee Museum, 121–122

U .S. Marine Corps Recruit Depot
(Beaufort), 158

V &J Duncan Antique Maps, Prints,
and Books, 101
Velvet Lounge, 115
Victorian District, 37
restaurant, 74
Village Craftsmen, 109

Villa rentals, Hilton Head, 140–141
Virginia & John Duncan's House, 101
Visitor information, 25, 34–35

W alking tours, self-guided, 96–106
historic Savannah, 103–106
*Midnight in the Garden of Good and
Evil,* 96–102
Walsh Mountain Ironworks, 109
Waving Girl Statue, 103
Weather updates, 39
Wesley Monumental Methodist
Church, 83–84
West Point Plantation (St. Simons
Island), 166
Wet Willie's, 118
Whitefield Square, 102
Windsurfing, 132
Wonderful Things, 112
Wormsloe Colonial Faire and
Muster, 26
Wormsloe Plantation, 124
Wormsloe State Historic Site, 2
Wright Square, 105–106

Y amacraws, 10, 105

Z oo, The, 118

ACCOMMODATIONS
Azalea Inn, 48
Ballastone Inn, 5, 44–45
Baymont Inn & Suites, 57
Beaufort Inn, 158–159
Bed & Breakfast Inn, 6, 56
Best Inn (Beaufort), 161
Best Western Island Inn (St. Simons
Island), 168–169
Catherine Ward House Inn, 48–49
The Cloister (Sea Island), 173
Clubhouse Inn & Suites, 5, 58
Comfort Inn (Hilton Head), 138
Courtyard Savannah Historic District,
56–57
Craven Street Inn (Beaufort), 160
Cuthbert House Inn (Beaufort),
160–161
Daufuskie Island Resort & Breathe
Spa, 156–157

Days Inn & Suites Historic District, 52
Disney's Hilton Head Island Resort, 134–135
East Bay Inn, 49
Eliza Thompson House, 49–50
Fairfield Inn and Suites by Marriott (Hilton Head), 139
Fairfield Inn by Marriott, 57
Foley House Inn, 50
The Forsyth Park Inn, 52–53
Gaston Gallery Bed & Breakfast, 53
The Gastonian, 5, 45–46
Hamilton-Turner Inn, 5, 46–47
Hampton Inn (Hilton Head), 139
Hampton Inn Historic District, 6, 45, 53–54
Hilton Head Crowne Plaza Resort, 136
Hilton Head Marriott Beach & Golf Resort, 132–133
Hilton Head Plaza Hotel & Suites, 139–140
Hilton Oceanfront Resort (Hilton Head), 136
Hilton Savannah DeSoto, 6, 50–51
Holiday Inn (Hilton Head), 137
Homewood Suites by Hilton, 58
Howard Johnson's Admiral Inn (Tybee Island), 122
Hyatt Regency Savannah, 40, 42
Kehoe House, 5, 47
King and Prince Beach Resort (St. Simons Island), 169
The Lodge at Sea Island Golf Club (St. Simons Island), 169
Magnolia Place Inn, 47–48
Main Street Inn (Hilton Head), 133
Marriott Riverfront Hotel, 42
The Marshall House, 54
Master's Inn Suites, Savannah Midtown, 58–59
The Mulberry Inn, 45, 51
Ocean Plaza Beach Resort (Tybee Island), 122–123
Olde Georgian Inn, 6, 51
Olde Harbour Inn, 43–44
Palmetto Dunes Resort (Hilton Head), 140
Park Avenue Manor, 54–55
Planters Inn, 55
The President's Quarters Inn, 55
Quality Inn & Suites (Hilton Head), 140
Residence Inn by Marriott (Hilton Head), 137–138

The Rhett House Inn (Beaufort), 159–160
River Street Inn, 4–5, 44, 45
Royal Dunes Resort (Hilton Head), 136–137
Sea Gate Inn (St. Simons Island), 169–170
Sea Island Cottage Rentals, 172
Sea Island Inn (Beaufort), 161
Sea Palms Golf & Tennis Resort (St. Simons Island), 170
The Sea Pines Resort (Hilton Head), 141
17 Hundred 90, 55–56
The South Beach Marina Inn (Hilton Head), 138
Two Suns Inn (Beaufort), 161–162
The Westin Resort (Hilton Head), 133–134
Westin Savannah Harbor Golf Resort & Spa, 42–43
Whitaker-Huntington Inn, 52
Wingate Inn, 59

RESTAURANTS

Alexander's (Hilton Head), 142
Antonio's (Hilton Head), 142
The Bank Waterfront Grill & Bar (Beaufort), 163
Barnes Restaurant, 69, 70
The Barony Grill (Hilton Head), 141
The Beaufort Inn Restaurant & Wine Bar, 162
Belford's, 71, 72
Bennie's Red Barn (St. Simons Island), 171
Bistro Savannah, 8, 62
Blue Water Bistro (St. Simons Island), 171
Boathouse II (Hilton Head), 143
The Breakfast Club (Tybee Island), 123–124
Broad River Seafood (Beaufort), 164
Café at City Market, 70, 72–73
Café Europa (Hilton Head), 143
The Captain's Table (Hilton Head), 143–144
Casbah, 68
Charlie's L'Etoile Verte (Hilton Head), 144
The Chart House, 59
Chelsea's (St. Simons Island), 171

Clary's Café, 8, 69–70, 102
Claude's (Beaufort), 163
CQ's (Hilton Head), 144–145
The Crab Shack (Tybee Island), 123
The Crab Trap (St. Simons Island), 172
Crane's Tavern & Steakhouse
  (Hilton Head), 145
The Crazy Crab North (Hilton
  Head), 145
Dockside Seafood Restaurant &
  Steakhouse, 63, 70
Elizabeth on 37th, 6, 74
Emily's (Beaufort), 162
45 South, 7, 67
Frannie's Place on St. Simons, 172
Garibaldi's, 72
Gottlieb's Restaurant & Dessert
  Bar, 66
Harbour Town Grill (Hilton Head),
  145–146
Hofbrauhaus (Hilton Head), 151
Hudson's Seafood House on the
  Docks (Hilton Head), 146
Huey's, 7, 62–63
Il Pasticcio, 68
Jack's (Hilton Head), 146–147
Johnny Harris Restaurant, 74
Juleps (Hilton Head), 147
Kathleen's Grille (Beaufort), 163–164
Kingfisher Seafood & Steakhouse
  (Hilton Head), 147–148
The Lady & Sons, 6, 63–64
MacElwees (Tybee Island), 123
Mostly Seafood (Hilton Head), 148
Moon River Bewing Company, 73

Mrs. Wilkes' Dining Room, 8, 70, 71
Musashi, 8, 74–75
The Olde Pink House Restaurant,
  7, 67
Old Fort Pub (Hilton Head), 148–149
The Old Oyster Factory (Hilton
  Head), 149
Ollie's Seafood Restaurant (Beaufort),
  162–163
Pearl's Saltwater Grille, 68–69
Reilleys (Hilton Head), 149
Rendez-Vous Café (Hilton Head),
  149–150
The Restaurant at the Sea Island Golf
  Club (St. Simons Island), 170–171
The River Grill, 64
River House Seafood, 59, 62
Santa Fe Cafe (Hilton Head), 150
Sapphire Grill, 7, 66–67
The Sea Shack (Hilton Head), 151
17 Hundred 90, 67
Shrimp Factory, 64–65
Signe's Heavenbound Bakery
  (Hilton Head), 151–152
Smokehouse Bar & House of BBQ
  (Hilton Head), 152
Steamer Seafood (Hilton Head),
  152–153
Taste of Thailand (Hilton Head), 153
Toucan Café, 75
Tubby's Tank House, 65
211 Park, 150–151
Wall's, 7–8, 70, 71
Wet Willie's, 104

FROMMER'S® NATIONAL PARK GUIDES

Algonquin Provincial Park
Banff & Jasper
Family Vacations in the National
  Parks

Grand Canyon
National Parks of the American
  West
Rocky Mountain

Yellowstone & Grand Teton
Yosemite & Sequoia/Kings
  Canyon
Zion & Bryce Canyon

FROMMER'S® MEMORABLE WALKS

Chicago
London

New York
Paris

San Francisco

FROMMER'S® WITH KIDS GUIDES

Chicago
Las Vegas
New York City

Ottawa
San Francisco
Toronto

Vancouver
Walt Disney World® & Orlando
Washington, D.C.

SUZY GERSHMAN'S BORN TO SHOP GUIDES

Born to Shop: France
Born to Shop: Hong Kong,
  Shanghai & Beijing

Born to Shop: Italy
Born to Shop: London

Born to Shop: New York
Born to Shop: Paris

FROMMER'S® IRREVERENT GUIDES

Amsterdam
Boston
Chicago
Las Vegas
London

Los Angeles
Manhattan
New Orleans
Paris
Rome

San Francisco
Seattle & Portland
Vancouver
Walt Disney World®
Washington, D.C.

FROMMER'S® BEST-LOVED DRIVING TOURS

Austria
Britain
California
France

Germany
Ireland
Italy
New England

Northern Italy
Scotland
Spain
Tuscany & Umbria

THE UNOFFICIAL GUIDES®

Beyond Disney
California with Kids
Central Italy
Chicago
Cruises
Disneyland®
England
Florida
Florida with Kids
Inside Disney

Hawaii
Las Vegas
London
Maui
Mexico's Best Beach Resorts
Mini Las Vegas
Mini Mickey
New Orleans
New York City
Paris

San Francisco
Skiing & Snowboarding in the
  West
South Florida including Miami &
  the Keys
Walt Disney World®
Walt Disney World® for
  Grown-ups
Walt Disney World® with Kids
Washington, D.C.

SPECIAL-INTEREST TITLES

Athens Past & Present
Cities Ranked & Rated
Frommer's Best Day Trips from London
Frommer's Best RV & Tent Campgrounds
  in the U.S.A.
Frommer's Caribbean Hideaways
Frommer's China: The 50 Most Memorable Trips
Frommer's Exploring America by RV
Frommer's Gay & Lesbian Europe
Frommer's NYC Free & Dirt Cheap

Frommer's Road Atlas Europe
Frommer's Road Atlas France
Frommer's Road Atlas Ireland
Frommer's Wonderful Weekends from
  New York City
The New York Times' Guide to Unforgettable
  Weekends
Retirement Places Rated
Rome Past & Present

Travel Tip: He who finds the best hotel deal has more to spend on facials involving knobbly vegetables.

Hello, the Roaming Gnome here. I've been nabbed from the garden and taken round the world. The people who took me are so terribly clever. They find the best offerings on Travelocity. For very little cha-ching. And that means I get to be pampered and exfoliated till I'm pink as a bunny's doodah.

travelocity®

1-888-TRAVELOCITY / travelocity.com / America Online Keyword: Travel

Travel Tip: Make sure there's customer service for any change of plans — involving friendly natives, for example.

One can plan and plan, but if you don't book with the right people you can't seize le moment and canoodle with the poodle named Pansy. I, for one, am all for fraternizing with the locals. Better yet, if I need to extend my stay and my gnome nappers are willing, it can all be arranged through the 800 number at, oh look, how convenient, the lovely company coat of arms.

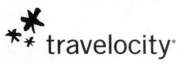

travelocity®

1-888-TRAVELOCITY / travelocity.com / America Online Keyword: Travel